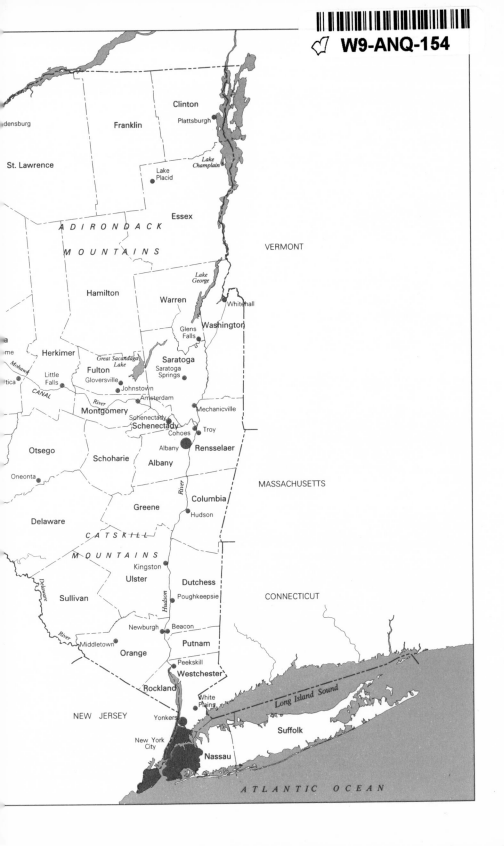

W9-ANQ-154

densburg

Clinton

Franklin

Plattsburgh

St. Lawrence

Lake Champlain

Lake Placid

Essex

A D I R O N D A C K

M O U N T A I N S

VERMONT

Lake George

Hamilton

Warren

Whitehall

Glens Falls

Washington

Herkimer

Great Sacandaga Lake

Saratoga

me

Mohawk

Fulton

Saratoga Springs

Little Falls

Gloversville

tica

CANAL

Johnstown

River

Amsterdam

Montgomery

Mechanicville

Schenectady

Schenectady

Cohoes

Troy

Otsego

Albany

Rensselaer

Schoharie

Albany

Oneonta

River

Columbia

Greene

Hudson

Delaware

C A T S K I L L

M O U N T A I N S

MASSACHUSETTS

Kingston

Ulster

Dutchess

Delaware

Sullivan

Hudson

Poughkeepsie

CONNECTICUT

Newburgh

Beacon

River

Middletown

Putnam

Orange

Peekskill

Westchester

Rockland

White Plains

Long Island Sound

NEW JERSEY

Yonkers

Suffolk

New York City

Nassau

A T L A N T I C   O C E A N

THE
NEW
YORK
IDEA

Also by Mario Cuomo

More than Words
Diaries of Mario M. Cuomo
Forest Hills Diary
Lincoln on Democracy (editor, with Harold Holzer)

The Cuomo Commission Report (1988) and *America's Agenda:*
Rebuilding Economic Strength (1992), both produced by the
Cuomo Commission on Trade and Competitiveness,
include introductions by Governor Cuomo.

MARIO CUOMO

THE
NEW
YORK
IDEA

AN
EXPERIMENT
IN DEMOCRACY

Crown Publishers, Inc.

New York

Published by Crown Publishers, Inc., a division of Crown Publishers, Inc., 201 East 50th Street, New York, New York 10022. Member of the Crown Publishing Group.

Random House, Inc. New York, Toronto, London, Sydney, Auckland

CROWN is a trademark of Crown Publishers, Inc.
Manufactured in the United States of America

Design by Leonard Henderson

Library of Congress Cataloging-in-Publication Data
Cuomo, Mario Matthew.
    The New York idea : an experiment in democracy / by Mario Cuomo.—1st ed.
    p. cm.
    Includes index.
    1. New York (State)—Economic policy. 2. New York (State)—Social policy.
    3. New York (State)—Politics and government—1982–
    I. Title.
    HC107.N7C86 1994
    338.9747—dc20
    93-39537
    CIP

ISBN 0-517-59644-X

10 9 8 7 6 5 4 3 2 1

First Edition

To all those who love this place,
want to know it better,
and want to share it with others
who do not know it as well.

CONTENTS

Preface	ix
Acknowledgments	xv
Introduction	1
Freedom	13
The Idea That Gave Birth to America	15
The Lessons of Immigration	17
The Politics of Inclusion	26
Work	39
Cultivating the Ingredients for Economic Growth	41
Capital—Forging a Public-Private Bond Through Investment	43
Infrastructure—How New York Helped Build Its Economy	48
Energy—Fueling a Half-Trillion-Dollar Economy	54
Industry, Ideas, and High Technology	62
Preparing New York's Changing Workforce for the Twenty-first Century	75
Other Strengths to Build On	89
A Vibrant Culture That Is Good for Business	90
Strengthening the Economy Through Sports and Recreation	94
Agriculture—One of Our Oldest and Most Valued Industries	98
Creating a Leaner, More Responsive Government	103
Wealth, Taxes, and Fiscal Responsibility	108
The Bitter Fruit of the New Federalism	116
Justice	119
A Century of Social Justice	123
New York's Progressive Legacy	130

Providing Protection to the Defenseless   133

Creating Affordable Housing   141

Health Care   144

The Current Toll of Social Pain   158

Decade of the Child   162

Welfare Reform: The Path to Independence   170

Toward a More Responsive Criminal Justice System   176

Political Reform   188

Beauty   199

Keeping New York Clean and Green   201

The National and International Environmental Challenge   217

Hope   223

Toward an Investment-Led Recovery   225

Reforming Our Approach to Borrowing   225

Building a New, New York   227

Laying the Tracks for High Technology   233

The International State in the Twenty-first Century   236

Global New York   238

Attracting Foreign Investment   239

Renewing the Partnership for National Economic Growth   243

Conclusion   245

APPENDIX A: Regions of New York   251

APPENDIX B: National Firsts, 1983–July 1993   259

APPENDIX C: New York All-Time Firsts   263

Bibliography   269

Index   275

PREFACE

Growing up in this great Empire State, I would never in my wildest imaginings have dreamed I could become its governor. But if only to prove what a place of miracles it really is, the state gave me the privilege of serving three terms. They have been marvelously exciting and satisfying years and have left me believing that New York is a unique part of the American experience, which ought to be better known and understood.

The Empire State is an exciting and instructive story, but it's not a story that has been read or heard by most people. When Americans descend on the crowded island of Manhattan, as they did in the summer of 1992 for the Democratic National Convention, the reviews are almost always favorable. This is sometimes a surprise to visitors—but not to me. Our tourist industry always thrives. Millions have been drawn to the skyline of the city that never sleeps, to Niagara Falls, the treelines and shorelines of the Adirondacks, the Catskills, the Finger Lakes, the Thousand Islands, and the beaches of Long Island.

If they stay long enough and move about, they discover there are at least two New Yorks. First, there is the vast expanse of land stretched between Canada and Massachusetts and Pennsylvania, known loosely as "upstate New York." There's an old joke that for natives of New York City, which sits at the southern end of the state, "upstate" is anything north of Times Square. Although the quiet charm and Yankee traditions of the dozens of upstate counties seem far removed from the moods and rhythms of the city's five boroughs, the regions north of New York City and Long Island represent nearly 45 percent of the state's population and by far the larger part of our land.

Then there is the other New York—New York City: one of the world's most spectacular urban centers.

New York City itself is misperceived on the most basic level. Just as there's more to New York State than the nation's largest metropolis, there is more to New York City than just Manhattan. Indeed, Manhattan Island is the center of the Big Apple, one of the most frequently visited and talked-about places in the world, but most residents of the big city live in its four outer boroughs. One of them, Brooklyn, would by itself constitute one of the most populated cities in the nation, with some 2.3 million residents. Another, Queens, is home to more people than the entire state of Nebraska, about two million. The Bronx, which is much greater in landmass than Manhattan, is not the ravaged ghetto that has been portrayed, although a portion of it has been devastated by the urban failures of the last half century. It has solid middle-class neighborhoods and some elegant communities and is home to the New York Botanical Garden, the great Bronx Zoo, City Island, and Yankee Stadium. Then there is Richmond County, better known as Staten Island, a typical ex-urban landscape of a type found all over America. It has its own rich history. The Sandy Ground settlement, for example, is home to the descendants of freed slaves who settled there in the nineteenth century to make their living as merchants and shellfishermen.

The descriptions in this book offer an attempt to describe our state honestly and clearly, but you ought to know that it has been put together by a group of people who love the whole place profoundly. I was born here, walking distance from where I still live in Queens County. I did not get into public life until after I had done a lot of other things as a lawyer, part-time professor, and community activist . . . all of it in New York. For nearly twenty years I helped people who might not otherwise have had a voice to oppose what I thought was overbearing government, including dozens of lawsuits—an experience that left me with a healthy distaste for politicians and politics. At one point I decided that I had done all I could from the outside and that if I really meant to change things, I ought to try it from the inside.

That experience, though humbling, has given me a unique vantage point for learning about New York and New Yorkers. The more I have traveled New York's sixty-two counties, its smaller cities, towns, and villages, the more I have learned.

I have been a New Yorker all my life—from the depths of the Great Depression through the end of the Cold War to the coming dawn of the twenty-first century. I know the Empire State about as well as anyone. New York gave me an education, careers, an endless adventure. I have traveled its length and breadth countless times. I've marveled at all its sites—the mountains, the wilderness, the inland oceans we call the Great Lakes, the rolling plains of the Southern Tier, the startling gorges of central New York, the quiet beauty of the Hudson valley, the quaint towns and beaches of Long Island, and the cacophony of the Big Apple. The topography is as diverse as that found anywhere else on earth—a marvelous amalgam of mountains and forests, valleys and pastures, skyscrapers, highways, apartments, and homes. More than places, though, New York is its people.

Immigrants landed in New York City, moved up the Hudson, through the Erie Canal that the world said couldn't be built, and on to what is now the nation's Midwest. Eventually they settled across the state and seeded the rest of the country. For generations, the oppressed, the impoverished, and the discontented from all over the globe have come here with little more than a desire to realize themselves. They carved a refuge out of the wilderness and then, in just two hundred years, built it into the most dynamic state in the most powerful nation on earth.

Most came here believing that through their own strength, applied to the chore of building the greatest nation in the world, they could earn security, comfort, maybe even affluence. Many did it all. They fled dictators and despots, wars and famine, seeking the chance for a new life. Some came highly skilled, educated, and wealthy; most came with little more than the children in their arms and the hope in their hearts. They invented the American Dream—lived it—and passed it on.

My father and mother were among those people. They came to America from southern Italy. Neither could speak English. They never received a day's education in the United States. My father dug ditches in Jersey City, New Jersey, making trenches for sewer pipes until he could save enough money to give his family a better life. A cousin of his who worked in Queens County introduced him to a man named Kessler who owned a small grocery store, abandoned a few years earlier at the start of the Depression, with stock still on the shelves. Mr. Kessler gave my mother and father the chance to build a small business and make it on their own.

At first they struggled in a poor, working-class neighborhood, saving pennies, barely scratching out enough to pay the bills. Later on during the war years, they kept the store open twenty-four hours a day to capture a few dollars from the factory workers in the neighborhood who labored around the clock. Only a city ordinance requiring them to close the store on Sunday mornings and afternoons eventually forced them to take any time off. They took turns sleeping a few hours at night. It was harder for my mother; she had to raise the children. They had four, but one died an infant, before I was born and I was given his name.

Together, my parents nearly worked themselves to death. My father remained illiterate, and my mother had difficulty counting, but with a little help—and a lot of heart—they got by. At the end of every month, my father put away a few dollars, in each of his three savings accounts: "Andrea Cuomo in trust for Franc Cuomo, for Maria Cuomo, for Mario Cuomo"—dollars saved in a little bankbook to buy a college education or a business for his boys and a sit-down wedding for his daughter.

They were passionate, creative, and loving in their approach to the world, blessed with a spirit that refused to be denied by hard circumstances. Eventually they saved enough so that we could afford to move from behind the grocery store to a house a few miles away in Holliswood, Queens—a good neighborhood where you couldn't smell the cooking next door or hear the neighbors arguing behind adjacent walls. In less than a generation they went from Jersey City and South Jamaica to a comfortable middle-class life . . . they had lived the American Dream.

I learned a lot from the experience and one lesson has remained a vital part of all my thinking about life and government, the importance of the concept of family, the idea of what we can achieve when people of diverse strengths and interests join together for the common good. From my limited view behind the counter of my father's grocery store in Queens, I saw how Italians and Irish and Jews and Blacks and people of all colors could live and work together, helping each other, making a better life together. More recently, Hispanics, Jamaicans, Haitians, Koreans, and other seekers have come to New York, hoping to make their way as my parents did.

So, New York is still a place for immigrants, a place where people come to fulfill their dreams, a place that still accepts hopeful newcomers to America's shores. From the beginning, people of every color, race, and condition have come here speaking every imaginable dialect, clothed in the styles and traditions of every culture, and most of them have done well.

But with all the cultural richness and all the stories of those who have come here and succeeded, there are others who have not thrived. There is suffering everywhere in the world, and New York surely has its share.

I know New York's problems probably as well as anybody: the second most populous state, home to the world's greatest city, with too many needs and too few resources; the terrible homelessness; the violence and tragedy created by drugs; the tensions and violence caused by economic frustration and over-crowding. As I write, seventeen million Americans cannot find enough work: more than one million of them are New Yorkers.

Two decades ago when I first entered public life as secretary of state, I could not have envisioned how much more difficult governing would become as the immensity of the human needs in this state outpaced our ability to meet them. Nor could I have foreseen how we seem, as an entire society, to be taking a step backward as discord grows between races and religions. It saddens me to know that despite all we have been blessed with in this wonderful state, we should be recording more crimes motivated by racial hatred now than at any other time in our modern history. Nor is it consoling to know these economic and social challenges belong not just to New York City, not just to the rest of the state, but to the entire nation.

In a real sense, New York is America and every day I can see New York's—and America's—distress in our rural towns upstate where people struggle without enough services, hoping simply to get through the day; and in the burned-out ghettos of our cities where children come to recognize the sound of gunfire before they ever hear the sound of an orchestra. Often the problems seem so daunting that some suggest giving up searching for solutions. But New York cannot accept despair, any more than the rest of America can. This book will make that clear.

In the end, like much of America, New York is a place where people have overcome great odds to pursue the American Dream by earning their own bread, and more, in a free enterprise economy. There has been more success here than in most places because we have been specially blessed in many ways. We have a good climate, abundant water, staggering natural beauty. We sit in the center of one of the world's greatest markets. The hundreds of years of immigrants coming here to work have left us with a diverse and richly talented workforce. We have added a vast infrastructure of roads, bridges, and transportation systems, one of the nation's most prestigious university systems, thirteen Centers for Advanced Technology, each on the cutting edge. We are still the world's financial and banking center, as well as the nation's advertising, publishing, and broadcasting capital. The reason we were so badly hurt by the last great national recession is that we have a disproportionately large number of the largest American international corporations, all of which were devastated by the nation's decline in global competitiveness—companies like General Motors, IBM, and Kodak.

We also have more than our share of the nation's social ills because of the great concentration of populations, resident and transitory.

Altogether it is a fantastic place, our New York, a vital part of America's history. Nearly twenty years of service at the state level has helped me see in the New York experience something central and relevant for Americans everywhere. It has also given me a deeper appreciation for the delicate, umbilical relationship between the states and the federal government created two centuries ago by our Federalist system.

Because we believe our future will contribute in a significant way to the nation's, we wanted to share New York with you: the grand history, the dynamic present, our strengths, our weaknesses, our failures, our successes . . . and our hopes.

Putting together this book gave us a chance to review what we have done, an exercise that will surely help prepare us and the rest of the state for the next part of the journey. In writing about that experience, we have been careful to remember what this book is not meant to be. We did not attempt to write a history of New York or a polemic. Neither is this a journalistic account or a memoir. Rather, it is an honest attempt to describe, in an integrated way, how the major functions of state government affect the life and culture of New York, written from the perspective of people who understand New York's vast power, have been touched by its pain, and believe they see clearly its tremendous potential.

Mario Cuomo
Albany, New York
November 1993

ACKNOWLEDGMENTS

This book would have been difficult to write without two people. Luciano Siracusano, my former Special Assistant for Communications, was instrumental in getting the project in motion. No one knows better than Luciano how much work goes into our struggling effort to communicate and to do. I am grateful to him for helping me tell the story of the "Real New York."

Doug Garr, another aide who worked side by side with Luciano, was chosen for his editorial expertise and his experience in writing books. Doug and Luciano outlined, researched, and helped me shape the book. Over the many months it took to produce *The New York Idea*, they tirelessly refined numerous drafts. Any author fortunate enough to have either of them as literary collaborators would be pleased. I was doubly lucky.

Martha Eddison and Kim Gold, two of my aides in the Executive Chamber, played critical roles in the preparation of the manuscript; Martha's editorial suggestions were invaluable, and Kim made us aware of the state's mass of facts, accomplishments, and misdeeds. Throughout the entire process, their comments and recommendations were extremely useful. David Weinraub, Jason Halperin, John Charlson, and David Wright also gave me thoughtful advice.

Frank Mauro from the Nelson Rockefeller Institute and Mitchell Moss at NYU's Urban Research Center gave us guidance during the early going, suggesting a reading list and pointing us toward experts in various disciplines.

At the World Trade Center, Bob Sullivan, Jim O'Hanlon, Marty Rosenblatt, and Alex Choe supervised a team of research interns—local graduate students and undergraduates who serve New York State on a pro bono basis. They also played an important role in unearthing innumerable facts.

In Albany, Janet Butlin from the Division of the Budget was indispensable to us; no source, no news clipping seemed to be beyond her immediate grasp.

Don Pollard, who is vested with the responsibility of photographing official state events, put in extra duty as the photo editor on this book. He also contributed several of his own pictures and persuaded other talented photographers to allow us to reproduce their work gratis.

We appreciate the work done by Geri Thoma of the Elaine Markson literary agency, who steered the book to Crown Publishers, Inc. At Crown, Betty Prashker and Jim Wade, who run the shop, exhibited early enthusiasm for the idea. Stephen Topping, our editor, was an indefatigable midwife. His insight and patience in honing the final result are greatly appreciated. State commissioners, division heads, and public information officers commented on various sections of the book. I am grateful to them as well as to several members of my staff who read and commented on it in manuscript form.

Lastly, hundreds of people who have worked with me and served New York State over the past decade made cumulative contributions to this book in ways they will never know. They are too numerous to mention by name, but I thank them all.

THE
NEW
YORK
IDEA

INTRODUCTION

Every national election is described as historic, but the 1992 election was probably historic in a larger sense than most. Not since 1932 had there been such an urgent need for great leadership. In the fall of 1992, the dominant reality in both New York and the country was the failing national economy. We had suddenly become uncertain, anxious, even frightened by our loss of economic dominance and the withering of the American Dream. Lost jobs and sagging incomes brought a deterioration of hope, aspiration, even peacefulness. With a failing economy we become a meaner, more violent, more troubled society.

In 1990 I spoke at the National Press Club in Washington a few weeks before U.S. forces drove Iraqi soldiers out of Kuwait. I said we were facing the worst recession since the Great Depression and a long-term economic crisis that posed a more serious threat to our future well-being than Saddam Hussein. Some said I was overstating the case. The rest of the country didn't see the menace as clearly as we did in New York because we were among the first states to suffer.

New York's huge investment-banking industry was an early target; the junk bond business all but imploded. Not too long ago, the latest Wall Street whiz kids, just out of college, made $100,000 a year and their bosses much more than that. We depended on tax revenues from these large salaries to help poorer parts of the state. Then—almost without warning—the whole industry stumbled, and these high earners were laid off in droves.

Olympia & York, the largest real estate company in the world, bought big chunks of property when real estate investments seemed like an endless source of profits. Counting on the prospect that the real estate market would continue to soar, bankers overextended the company's loans. Then everything collapsed when the bottom fell out of the real estate market in the Northeast and in other oversubscribed parts of the country.

Ironically, the end of the Cold War also had an unhappy effect on the economy. The transition to peacetime production has meant fewer Pentagon contracts for our defense industry, with no better prospects for the future. Military bases in my state and others were suddenly put in jeopardy. Grumman Aircraft, the largest employer on Long Island, was forced to reduce its work force dramatically.

Other large companies were also hit hard. Because General Motors' market share has diminished steadily, the company, once a symbol of American might, laid off 75,000 workers from California to New York. Corporate stalwarts like GM, Kodak, and IBM announced huge personnel cuts, throwing tens of thousands of New Yorkers out of work, causing a sharp decrease in the anticipated tax revenues—and a sharp increase in expenses for unemployment, welfare, Medicaid, and health care.

We have felt the recession as acutely as any other state, except for California, which has been devastated. On my monthly radio show, a fifty-five-year-old caller from Syracuse, confused and frightened, put it simply enough: "Governor, it's getting harder and harder to live here."

The truth is, it has gotten harder for most working Americans to live throughout the United States. Like most states, New York has suffered from larger forces that were exacerbated by the national economic and governmental policies of the 1980s.

Ever since 1973, the peak year for real hourly wages, deep, structural problems within the American economy have led to stagnating living standards for the majority of the American people. The oil shocks of the 1970s, the inflation that followed, the globalization of production, and the federal budget deficit (roughly $73 billion in 1980) prompted policy makers to debate a new course for the 1980s. Out of that debate and confusion emerged a simplistic answer to the nation's economic woes: Cut taxes on the "producers of wealth," build up the military, and let the individual states deal with what were once considered national concerns.

In the early 1980s the states were told that they would be able to build a stronger nation without the aid of the federal government. They would, instead, be delivered to Elysian Fields by a magical force called "supply-side economics." Supply side's magic started with huge income tax cuts, benefitting especially the most successful Americans. The theory was that because the wealthy had so much money already, they would not consume this new bonanza but would instead invest it in the private economy. The private economy would then get so strong, it would create enough new revenues to balance the federal budget in three years, despite these huge tax cuts and an accompanying $1.46 trillion military buildup. There would be loaves and fishes for everyone. Supply side, as described by former White House budget director David Stockman, gave Washington an excuse to reject any national duty to marshal resources and invest in all the ingredients necessary for national economic growth.

So robust would the new economy be that, with the states gathering huge amounts of new revenues at *their* level, the federal government could rationalize cutting back federal support for education, housing, child nutrition, nondefense research, energy, and roads and bridges. As the theory evolved, this "New Federalism" called for the federal government to withdraw from previous commitments to help the states meet national needs. The resulting federal cutbacks over the decade of the 1980s were massive. Housing aid was cut 80 percent; energy conservation, 67 percent; job training, 65 percent; revenue sharing, obliterated; urban development grants, eliminated. Money for education, the environment, mass transit—all were cut.

Washington dumped these federal concerns onto state and local governments, as new state and local costs for education, health care, and law enforcement exploded. By 1992 the cumulative weight of this decade-long shift of the burden, combined with shrinking revenues as a result of the national recession, was crushing the states. Thirty-five states, home to 85 percent of the American people, were driven into a sea of red ink—some of them facing budget deficits larger and more threatening than anything they had ever experienced.[1]

In August of 1991, *The Wall Street Journal*, no bastion of liberalism, documented the consequences of the New Federalism, noting that over the previous decade "Federal grants to state and local governments [had] dropped from 15 percent of all Federal outlays to 11 percent, and from 26 percent of all state and local expenditures to 18 percent. . . . Federal funds, for example, now support less than 10 percent of troubled New York City's budget, about half the rate of a decade ago."[2]

Many states, facing huge budget gaps, were forced to cut their investments and to raise taxes to preserve the programs that remained. California was reduced to issuing promissory notes to pay for its current expenses. At one

---

[1] In New York City, for example, by 1992, the decade-long federal withdrawal had added more than $2 billion to the city's budget gap, forcing higher local taxes, service cuts, and layoffs of city workers.

[2] Alfred L. Malabre, Jr., "States and Localities May Slow Recovery," *The Wall Street Journal*, August 5, 1991, p. 1.

point, in late 1992, California's outlook was so bleak that the Bank of America refused to take these notes. From one coast to the other, a weakened economy was further threatened by the debilitating convulsions from our states and major cities, feeding the recessionary cycle, prolonging the pain and the misery.

As we know now, the supply-side miracle never happened. The supply-siders were off—by over $3 trillion. While investors gobbled up junk bonds and bad real estate, net savings declined compared with those of previous decades, as did overall investment and productivity. Commonsense deregulation turned into a license for reckless savings and loans to gamble away more than $500 billion of the taxpayers' money, leading to the greatest bank robbery in American history.

Together the New Federalism and supply-side economics led to a massive, simultaneous, twin redistribution. They redistributed a large part of the burden of national problems away from the national government and onto the states, separately. And they have simultaneously produced a massive redistribution of the nation's wealth away from the middle class and into the relatively small stratum of our most successful Americans. The progressive nature of our taxes, meaning their relationship to the amount of income and ability to pay, was seriously distorted. At the federal level, the top income tax rate for the wealthiest Americans was cut from 70 percent down to a low of 28 percent in 1988. At the same time, the payroll tax, a blatantly regressive charge, went up for 132 million American workers and their employers—a total of $340 billion by 1992. As the income tax went down, depriving the national treasury of revenues it needed, Social Security taxes increased dramatically and were used to fill the hole.[3]

This regressive taxation also trickled down to the state and local levels. Washington politicians chanted boastful slogans about their income tax cuts, but state and local governments were forced to raise revenues to assume national burdens Washington once carried. As a result, states and localities looked to the taxes they believed would least threaten their competitive posi-

---

[3]These tax increases, which continued throughout the Reagan-Bush years—and which were intended to go into a trust fund to help the baby boomers when they reached retirement age—were not used to build reserves for future retirement benefits. Instead they were used to mask the true size of the federal budget deficit, replacing the trust fund with IOUs that can be repaid only later by massive tax increases.

tion. The answer: sales and real estate taxes—taxes, like the payroll tax, that also bear *no* effective relationship to one's ability to pay. Nationally, sales and real estate taxes doubled in the 1980s. In effect, the middle class and the working poor have been paying for the huge income tax cuts at the federal level. Prosperity never trickled down in the 1980s. Only the tax burden did.

The New Federalism offered up in 1980—and the supply-side miracle that was supposed to make it work—for a while fooled the nation into believing we could overcome our national challenges without a unified national response. They also left us off balance as we struggle to regain our footing for the global economic competition.

We have lost the economic dominance we took for granted for four decades. We used to be the world's greatest maker and seller of things of value—radios, TVs, autos, steel, garments. We once sold these products to other countries for their marks and yen and francs. Now we buy them with our dollars. We used to be the world's greatest seller, lender, creditor nation. Now we are the buyers and borrowers—the world's greatest debtor nation.

No one has ever had a national debt like ours—$4.4 trillion by 1993 plus $6.5 trillion more in contingent liabilities with annual federal deficits running more than $300 billion a year. The federal government spends more paying *interest* on the national debt than it does on all the state and local governments of America combined—more than $200 billion a year for interest that does not build a single building, create a single job, or feed a single person. In concept, it's no different from the gambler who owes money to his local bookmaker. The interest is called "vigorish." You pay it every week, or every month, for as long as you owe the principal. But it doesn't pay down the principal or the debt. All it does is keep the bookie from breaking your knees. Both the debt and the interest payments on that debt prevented the nation from making productive investments.

With each day that the investment is deferred, the need for investment grows greater. We fall farther behind in education. Health care costs spiral out of control. The lag in our commercial research and development gets worse. The deterioration of our vital infrastructure accelerates. And every day—even with their own problems—our competitors for world economic power become more formidable.

One of the worst, unintended consequences of the nation's borrow-and-spend orgy was that it decreased our national savings and drove up the cost of capital by keeping real interest rates higher than they otherwise would have

been. This discouraged new capital investment in plant and equipment in the
United States. Productivity gains in the manufacturing sector, which came
largely through a reduction in personnel and advances in new management
techniques, did not translate into greater real wages for the average American
worker. As a result, average hourly wages, when adjusted for inflation, have
been declining since 1973. In fact, today, more Americans are employed in
government than in manufacturing.

Germany, which was divided into two halves not long ago, has 31 percent
of its work force in manufacturing—one of three workers making things.
Japan, which just a little more than a generation ago made products that
were synonymous with poor quality, has one in four of its workers making
things. The United States now has only 16 percent of its labor force in manufacturing.

While we have an admirable and efficient service sector, we still need to
rebuild our manufacturing base. Historically, American manufacturing jobs
provided a gateway into the economy, offering decent wages for new laborers,
higher pay for skilled workers. The spin-off benefits of the manufacturing
sector generated contracts for suppliers and small businesses, built up the tax
bases of local communities, and helped to create the largest consumer market
and, until recently, the highest standard of living the world has ever known.

The policies of the 1980s did not strengthen the nation's industrial base or
raise real wages for American workers. The United States generated more
millionaires and billionaires than ever before, but, by the beginning of the
1990s, we had produced more poor than ever, more uneducated, more angry.
Today, fourteen million American children grow up in poverty. Twenty-three
million adults can't read a job application. We are humiliated by our illiteracy
as our education system falls behind that of our competitors.

It took a conservative commentator, Kevin Phillips, to document all these
trends in a book, *The Politics of Rich and Poor,* before opinion makers finally
conceded how the middle class and the working poor have been paying for
the policies of the 1980s. Today, millions who managed to keep their heads
above water in the 1980s by working longer hours, taking a second job when
they could find it, sending their kids to work, doubt that this will be enough,
or even possible, in the 1990s. They are struggling to hold on to what they
have in the face of diminishing jobs, escalating health care and education
costs, and a federal debt that appears nearly out of control.

Worst of all, perhaps, has been the effect that a decade of "social Darwinism" has had on our collective psyche and soul.

When I was sworn into office in January of 1983, the national mood had swung toward the political philosophy introduced with the election of Ronald Reagan in 1980. As I understood it, the proponents of the new ethic rejected the idea of collective responsibility and, instead, declared that it was not the business of government to participate in the sharing of benefits and burdens. They told us that government had no business making social policy out of the Bible's insistent command to compassion. Such idealism, they argued, impeded the evolution of society. The way to give everyone a place at the table, they proclaimed, was to make the rich richer and the strong stronger, and as the powerful ascended to this world's successes, the sheer size and force of their ascent would carry the rest of creation with them.

"Never mind," we were told, that there were more poor people, more homeless, half a generation of minority children born to poverty, despite unprecedented wealth generated by the private sector. We were encouraged to dismiss these troubling realities as the hard, unalterable facts of life; and we were prodded to believe that any efforts by government to improve the lot of the needy would only make things worse. Washington advised the country to give up the impossible ideal of making out of all this land's vastness, complexity, and diversity, a family.

I had difficulty accepting this idea. For me, the defining American belief that through hard work and individual initiative one can elevate oneself in this world is more than just a nostalgic notion to be trotted out in election years. Many of us who were helped along the way to achieve individual success are aware that there has always been another part to the American Dream.

The greatness of this state and this nation is attributable to more than just the heroism of rugged individuals and solitary sojourners riding alone toward the horizon, seeking and seizing their own fortunes. The secret of our success has been not just in the cumulative good fortune of individuals, but in the ability of the American people to create a collective generosity that pools our strengths and uses them to widen the circle of opportunity for the next generation of seekers, for the vulnerable, and for all those who—without our help—would never reach the first rung of the ladder of success.

This state, throughout its history, has helped New Yorkers and the rest of the nation see that the only way we can truly succeed—not just as individuals, but as a *people*—is together. That's why for most of this century, New Yorkers, through their *government*, have reached out constantly to include the excluded and underutilized: impoverished immigrants, the victims of slavery and prejudice, women, people born blind or disabled.

The power of our free enterprise system and the support of government have *together* created the belief that each generation can live better than the one before. That belief—the inherited expectation that each generation could earn at least the comfort and security of the one before it and probably more—is now being challenged in a fundamental way, even in New York. If we lose that vision of the American Dream, we will lose the nation as we have known it.

To prevent that, we must do all we can to free ourselves from the recession that has paralyzed our region; at the same time we must work with our leaders in Washington to lay the groundwork for an investment-led recovery. That will require not just a change in style, tone, and temperament, but a change in the nation's long-term economic policies. Certainly, New York cannot create a lasting recovery without the rest of the nation pulling in the same direction. Our role is to lead, as we have for most of our history.

Both New York and the nation have lived through and escaped much worse times than these, and government has often led us out of the darkness. As a rule, Americans have always preferred to do without government wherever possible. After all, the place was founded largely as a refuge from harsh and offensive authority. It is also true, however, that there is a time for government to step in and meet the challenges of the day. Abraham Lincoln taught us that "the legitimate object of government is to do for the people what needs to be done, but which they cannot, by individual effort, do at all, or do so well, for themselves."[4]

Lincoln's notion has been at the core of everything we have tried to do in New York. It has been at the heart of the philosophy I tried to define when I first took office in 1983. At the time, many religious leaders advised that we should aspire to something better than social Darwinism, reminding us that we had a moral imperative to the whole of humankind, which I applauded. As a public servant, as one in the trenches fighting the battles for consensus, I urged New Yorkers to approach our obligations to each other this way: even

---

[4]Mario M. Cuomo and Harold Holzer, eds., *Lincoln on Democracy* (New York: HarperCollins, 1990), 64.

if people don't feel obliged to love, they ought to consider their own self-interest. If we bring children into this world and let them go hungry and uneducated, if we are indifferent to the drugs and squalor that surround them and the despair that overwhelms them, then all of us—even those whose children have been raised in comfort and security—will share the outcome. We will *all* share in paying to maintain the growing number of people living at subsistence levels. We will *all* spend more on jail cells and police. We will *all* live in fear, in enclaves separated from each other's struggles—but never free of them.

For those of us struggling to live out our belief in this world—no matter which argument we use, whether we appeal to compassion or to common sense—we must understand that the important thing is to keep trying, because however we make the case, we know that it is wrong not to try. In fact, not to try would be to reject all New York State has done throughout its history.

New Yorkers have always had the choice of ignoring those who needed help; of letting the hungry starve; of letting the working poor labor and die in sweat shops and tenements; of letting the aged and the helpless suffer in the cold; of allowing higher education to remain the preserve of the wealthy few. In some cases, we did ignore our neediest, for long periods. Ultimately, however, enough New Yorkers concluded that this was neither the generous nor the intelligent approach. We have helped people because we came to understand that the effort to expand and enlarge the middle class was common sense, not charity. We knew that if we simply ignored the enormous potential contributions generations of immigrants might make to our economy, the cost would be staggering. Time and again, New Yorkers, through their government, have chosen to weather the darkest storms so that the state—and nation—could move to higher ground.

There are times when I sense that too many people have been exasperated and worn down by the "system." Government has become too big to comprehend. I share in that frustration. We do not think about government, especially state government, until we need it or until it fails us.

My first year in public service, 1975, was one of those years. After New York City and New York State had flirted with bankruptcy, many of us pledged never again to take our state's good fortune for granted. We recognized that we had ignored some of our traditional strengths while allowing taxes to soar so high that they were bleeding New York dry. We needed to change. We needed to work more aggressively to bring back the businesses we used to take for granted. We needed to invest again in our infrastructure. And after New York City's fiscal vulnerability revealed the state's vulnerability, we needed New Yorkers to understand how, in the future, their own personal prosperity would be inextricably linked to the well-being of the entire state.

Over the last decade a consensus has evolved, shared by New York Republicans and Democrats, upstate and downstate, business and labor leaders alike. In order to accomplish our goals, we need a vigorous economy built on the private payroll, creating good-paying private sector jobs that hold together cities and communities; jobs that spin off a swift and self-sustaining magic cycle of investments and savings, providing the tax revenues government needs to do those things that can only be accomplished collectively.

In New York, I have called this "The New York Idea": government using its resources to help create private sector growth, then requiring those who benefit from that growth to share some part of it so that hope and opportunity are extended to those who have not been as fortunate. We also do this so that we can take care of those who will never be able to care for themselves.

The New York Idea, although it steers away from any ideological imperatives, is predicated on certain basic values—on principles—that define it.

We begin with free enterprise. We believe that the foundation of our entire economy must be a strong private sector payroll, not a public sector payroll. In this complex world, we must also understand and make use of our interdependence, if we wish to survive and certainly if we want to thrive. That means government must enter into *partnership* with the private sector, depending on it for expertise and advice, for help in carrying out its essential functions. It means the private sector can look to government for support in creating capital resources, in leveraging investments, in rebuilding the underpinnings of prosperity. Partnership also means government acting as a catalyst, bringing together industry and our universities to promote economic growth.

To the extent we are succeeding—and success is hard to measure because of the ebb and flow of larger trends and forces, including national recessions—it is because of the level of partnership in New York among our public and private sectors, state and local governments, private foundations and not-for-profit organizations, management and labor, academics and entrepreneurs.

But partnership by itself isn't enough. If our partnerships are to succeed, then we must live by a second principle—balance. Balance requires that government will know when to involve itself in the economy and when not to; that it understands the difference between intelligent regulation and unnecessary meddling; that it pays careful attention to the effects of its policies on the growth of the private sector, investing wisely and taxing prudently. In some cases the principle of balance goes beyond taxes; it translates into less government. In New York, we've deregulated the banking and financial services industries. In other instances, we've regulated vigorously. The environment is an obvious case, and we have implemented programs to protect the quality of life in this state without shortchanging our potential for economic growth.

Finally, there is the principle of family. Some of my aides used to wince when I mentioned the word *family*, but I've continued to use it because I think it is the best—and most accurate—metaphor we have for expressing not only *what* we should be trying to do as a society, but *how*. Everybody understands family. Talk to people about the "social imperative of mutuality" and their eyes glaze over. Talk to them about "family" and they know immediately what it means, they appreciate completely the relationship it suggests. Family is more than intelligent and self-interested cooperation, although it is certainly that. Family also insists on an even more fundamental obligation: an obligation to the old, to the very young, to the distraught and disabled, people without work, without enough to eat; to those who sometimes lack a roof over their heads; to people whom the promise of free enterprise has yet to reach.

None of these concepts is particularly novel. The New York Idea has been around a long time. What is new—and important—is its application, a realistic appreciation of the importance of the free market and an intelligent recognition of the legitimate role government can play in supporting and spurring its growth. While recognizing the limits of government, we must acknowledge that within those limits there is still a tremendous amount that government can do to help those who'll never be able to get by on their own and to encourage those who with some assistance can achieve independence and even affluence.

In the end, I think the New York Idea comes down to aspirations. We refuse to surrender ours. We refuse to stop believing that together—as a government, as a state, as a nation—we can build a future with more prosperity and more opportunity, even more justice and fairness, than we have now.

I believe that impulse, expressed in the state's motto—*Excelsior* ("Ever Upward")—captures what has made New York such a great place and may even help to explain why this state and its people have made such an immense contribution to America.

Freedom

The Idea That Gave Birth to America

In the hot summer of 1787, a New Yorker named Gouverneur Morris[1] put down the words that began the American journey toward constitutional government:

> We the People in order to form a more perfect union, establish justice, insure domestic tranquility, provide for the common defense, promote the general welfare, and secure the blessings of liberty to ourselves and our posterity, do ordain and establish this Constitution for the United States of America.

The result was an unprecedented adventure in democracy—a government that dared to bind together thirteen separate, often contentious colonies with the untried cord of one great idea. As bold as it was new and simple, the idea sprang from the conviction that we could create a society of unique freedom. Understanding from the history of Europe that oppression begins with repression, Morris and his constitutional colleagues were determined that the ability to think, to speak, to worship, and to act without unnecessary restraint by government would distinguish us from all other nations. For Americans, the guarantee of freedom would be not only a great privilege; it would be the very foundation of the country.

This freedom and the opportunity it promised were to be secured through the federal Constitution. But they depended as well on a silent compact, not written into law. As essential as the brilliant principles laid out in our Constitution is an idea that does *not* appear in its careful prose: the unspoken belief that the people will, in ways not commanded, continue to make democracy work; that freedom for each of us is guaranteed, and tempered intelligently, by our commitment to the common good. It is that instinct for mutuality, for community—for what we in New York have called "family"—that provides us with cohesion and coherence.

Though based on some of our deepest instincts, this idea of our common

---

[1]Morris was originally a New Yorker, but he actually represented Pennsylvania at the Constitutional Convention.

interest has always been harder to sell to the multitudes than the virtues of liberty. As summer gave way to fall, another document began to take shape.

"To the people of the state of New York . . ." So began the *Federalist Papers,* the brainchild of Alexander Hamilton, his fellow New Yorker John Jay, and the Virginian James Madison. Writing together as "Publius," they pursued their extended discourse on the American experiment with a wisdom and wit seldom equaled in the history of political letters. Their aim: to persuade the people of New York to ratify the United States Constitution and, in the process, to persuade an emerging nation of the advantages of a national government.

That a good deal of the debate that helped create the United States of America took place in New York, and was waged in part by New Yorkers, is more than a historical curiosity. In the late eighteenth century, New York was the center of American success and of the new civilization. Home to a fragile national government, it was also emerging as the country's business and financial capital. In the fall of 1787, the residents of Manhattan—free with their opinions even then—gathered in the streets and shops to study the latest newspaper entries from Publius and debate the rules the young nation should live by.

A decade after the Revolution, the states had found that their first common harness—the Articles of Confederation—was too loose to be useful. State had battled state in an atmosphere of mistrust and divisiveness; tariffs were raised in a spirit of revenge and undermined free trade generally. (New York, incidentally, was among the worst bullies, charging fees on all goods coming into its ports, no matter where their final destination.) This internecine warfare was making everyone poorer. Far more influential as Publius than as a delegate to the Constitutional Convention, Alexander Hamilton used the *Federalist Papers* to push New Yorkers and the leaders of the other states to tear up the Articles of Confederation and form a real national government. He understood that only a *national* government could promote the national economic interest; that independent states, squabbling over their separate interests, would ultimately undermine the prosperity of the country as a whole.

Ever since the *Federalist Papers* helped shape this first great debate in our country's history, New York, and New Yorkers, have played a big part in helping America define herself: what she ought to be as well as what she is. Having helped the country decide to become *united* states, New Yorkers moved unconsciously to a larger task, one we have yet to finish:

applying and improving on the spirit that said "All men are created equal."

The genius of this nation has been America's ability—not always exercised—to draw on a widening circle of talent, to open unlimited opportunities to people who never had any at all, and to be inspired and revitalized by what they achieve. The struggle to include the excluded—when the forces of the established order preferred to shut the door—has been the struggle for America's soul.

Perhaps there is no state that has embodied the principle of inclusion better than New York, from the first Dutch settlers who came here and created a colony free from religious persecution to the New Yorkers who led the campaigns to abolish slavery, give women the right to vote, and allow immigrants a chance to breathe free. Later, the impulse to include drove the crusade to protect working people from a ruthless economic system, and inspired the continuing struggle to extend civil rights, preserve religious freedom, secure real equality for women, bring down the barriers against those with disabilities, and keep our borders open to new seekers.

From the backlash against the gay rights movement to the rise of neo-Nazism, the headlines tell us that despite great progress, the story is not altogether one of triumph. But if the latest battles to include the excluded seem at times too hard or too divisive, we should remember the lessons New Yorkers have learned in the one great growth experience that has defined our state and molded much of the nation: immigration.

The Lessons of Immigration

Not all New Yorkers chose to come here as immigrants or were warm to people who did. Our native New Yorkers have always been here. They settled the continent generations before Columbus. Other New Yorkers are the children of ancestors who were dragged to this country in chains. For the most part, immigration has been the protein of American life, giving it sustenance and strength and the power to grow. All the immigrant children of America are part of that story, whether we trace our roots to Plymouth Rock in 1620, Ellis Island in 1910, or Kennedy Airport in 1990.

In New York, a vital piece of the story is told in the photographs on display at the Ellis Island Immigration Museum, the heart of the newly restored complex at the old immigration facility in New York Harbor. Its cavernous waiting halls and warrenlike dormitories served as the point of entry for the ancestors of more than 100 million Americans, or some 40 percent of the country's current population. In the years that Ellis Island was open, from 1892 to 1924, more than 12 million people passed through its gates to the promise of America.

But there was despair as well; Ellis Island more than earned its bitter alias, the "Island of Tears." Millions of prospective Americans saw their fate sealed in the registry room, where inspectors demanded flawless traveling papers and checked for any sign of illness. Tens of thousands were sent back to the countries they came from without ever setting foot on this continent—often separated from their families, sometimes deprived of their possessions. Today, if one visits the museum and looks into the weary faces of those ocean-tossed immigrants, past the babushkas and battered overcoats, past the pathetic bundles that held everything they owned, past the tags tied on them as if they were cattle, one can still see their enormous strength, their huge hearts, their vision.

The hands of these immigrants helped build the United States from the ground up—the Irish, the Germans, the Poles, the Asians, the Blacks, the Italians, the Jews. In the mid-nineteenth century, these desperate seekers fought hard for jobs as manual laborers, waiters, and servants. Americans feared at first that the newcomers threatened their livelihood. But there was plenty of work to be done—more, in fact, than Americans could handle on their own. Railroads, canals, buildings, houses, factories, stores, and farms were all multiplying. And because immigrants had often come from a routine of despair and poverty, they were willing to work at low wages to improve their lives.

The historian Oscar Handlin said that he once "thought to write a history of immigrants in America. Then [he] discovered that the immigrants *were* American history."[2] Handlin's sentiment is even truer for New York.

In this century alone, three great waves of migration and immigration have shaped and reshaped New York, especially New York City. The first, lasting until World War I, saw the influx of immigrants from Eastern Europe and the Mediterranean. The second migration began a decade later in 1924 and lasted until 1965—a period when immigration was restrained nationally.

---

[2] *The Uprooted: The Epic Story of the Great Migrations That Made the American People,* Oscar Handlin (The Atlantic Monthly Press, 1951).

While African-Americans migrated from the South and Puerto Ricans came up from the Caribbean, New York continued to welcome the shrinking numbers of new immigrants. The lifting of the "national origins" quota in 1965 ushered in the third great migration in this century, bringing more people from more different countries to America than ever before.[3] Millions of new immigrants, fleeing oppression, hopelessness, and poverty, uprooted by famine and civil unrest, came to New York from Vietnam, China, and South Korea; from the Dominican Republic, Haiti, and Honduras; and eventually from the then Soviet Union and the newly freed nations of Eastern Europe. In the past decade, 8.7 million immigrants found haven in the United States, the greatest wave since the first decade of the twentieth century.[4] Today, New York is home to representatives of some 178 different countries.

For several years I have had the privilege of administering the oath of allegiance to a corps of new citizens at the Flag Day naturalization ceremonies in the state Capitol. I wish every New Yorker—every American—could see what I see that day. Despite all their differences, these new Americans possess a common citizenship, proclaim a common allegiance, and profess a common faith in America—perhaps more fiercely than some of us who were born here. In the different shades of their skin you see the single magnificent face of our nation.

These new seekers are part of a living history—but how do we view that history and those writing its newest chapters? Should we preserve our fond memories of those immigrants who preceded us as nothing more than a curio, a pretty fable of how the American mosaic was made . . . and finished? Or is our history something more than that? Is it a challenge to do something more than remember the romance? Is the immigrant story a continuing one?

At times it is easy to forget how most of us got here. It doesn't take long before the children, grandchildren, and great-grandchildren of immigrants look at new arrivals—the new seekers—and come to see not one of us, but one of "them." Occasionally, those who have come here and made it have said,

---

[3] The Chinese Exclusion Act of 1882, repealed in 1943, was the first instance in which a particular nationality was barred from becoming naturalized citizens of the United States. However, Chinese-American families and communities were not allowed to develop freely until the 1965–1968 immigration reforms eliminated racially based quotas.

[4] The technical definition of an immigrant is "an alien admitted to the United States as a lawful permanent resident." It does not refer to those who have entered this country illegally.

illogically, "America is ours. It belongs to us. And we have to keep *them* out."
That sentiment has periodically been translated into laws that defined "them"
and then either excluded them or severely limited their access.

In an ugly symmetry of history, every surge in immigration has met a
countervailing tide of resentment and a self-righteous effort to bar the door.
In two centuries of this off-and-on xenophobia, the charges leveled against
America's new immigrants have varied in audacity and detail, but the essential meanness remains the same. In the nineteenth century, the attacks were
especially bold: "They are criminals," it was said, "drunken and licentious";
or "They're lazy," or "inherently inferior"; or "They couldn't be loyal."
"They're anarchists and rapists and subversives. Their language is different,
and their food and their music, their gods, their morals, and their manners.
They could never be real Americans. They'll ruin everything."

In Abraham Lincoln's day, the nativists wrapped themselves in the flag and
called themselves "the American party." Vowing never to reveal anything
about their organization, they also chose a nickname: the "Know-Nothings."
Some of our leaders, like Lincoln, saw that the Know-Nothing label declared
something deeper about these organized bigots. Support for exclusion, Lincoln said, was nothing less than "degeneracy." And, he warned, if

> the Know-Nothings get control, [our Declaration] will read, "all men
> are created equal, except negroes, *and foreigners, and catholics."* When
> it comes to this I should prefer emigrating to some country where
> they make no pretense of loving liberty . . . where despotism can be
> taken pure, and without the base alloy of hypocrasy [sic].[5]

Lincoln warned us of the shortsightedness and dangers of the politics of
exclusion. And group after group came to our shores, justifying his faith in the
American experiment and discrediting the nativists.

This history offers a sermon we still seem to need.

As recently as the 1950s, American intellectuals worried about the "mon-
grelization of America," about a "possible biological and cultural corruption

---

[5]Mario M. Cuomo and Harold Holzer, eds., *Lincoln on Democracy* (New York: HarperCollins,
1990), 83.

of pure Anglo-Saxonism by the Negroes, Asians, Slavs, Jews, and Mediterranean peoples."[6]

The punishing national recession of the early 1990s showed how angry and frustrated people become by losing their jobs, by that sinking feeling that elements of the American Dream are out of their reach, by diminished prospects for themselves and their children. It also demonstrated how quickly we can find someone else to blame for hard times. Immigrants, some charged, are the cause, or at least a cause, of the nation's economic and fiscal woes. Simpler and uglier versions of this same thought even emerged in the 1992 presidential primary, in the "America first" rhetoric of failed candidate Patrick Buchanan. Then several highly publicized incidents—the withdrawal of the nomination of Zoe Baird for hiring illegal aliens, the arrest of suspects in the World Trade Center bombing, and the arrival of a boatload of illegal Chinese immigrants in a ship that ran aground off the coast of Queens—brought immigration to the forefront of the national consciousness. These incidents, coupled with the strains of the recession, have resulted in strong anti-immigrant rhetoric.

The fiscal problems thrust upon California by the national recession have been complicated by an explosion of foreigners who many claim are draining the state's social service system. State officials there have speculated publicly whether they can afford to take care of the large influx of immigrants and are even calling for a federal constitutional amendment to deny the children of illegal aliens U.S. citizenship.

Although there is no question that illegal immigration poses problems for all states, we must be careful to avoid extremism in our rhetoric and in our response. I think back to the old neighborhood where I was born—South Jamaica, Queens. *Everyone* from South Jamaica came from somewhere else. I thank God that this country didn't say to them, "We can't afford you. You might take someone's job or cost us too much."

I'm glad they didn't ask my mother if she could count, because she couldn't. I'm glad they didn't ask my father if he could speak English, because he couldn't, or inquire about the special skills he brought to this nation, because there was no special expertise in the way he handled a shovel. And I'm

---

[6]Max Lerner, *America As Civilization* (New York: Henry Holt and Company, 1957), 81.

grateful that New York City's public schools didn't say to my parents, "We don't have the time or the inclination or the resources to teach your son, Mario, how to speak English. It's taking him too long."

I thank God for a government that was wise enough to see that the new immigrants were our future, strong enough to help them without stifling them, patient enough to give them a chance to earn their own way with dignity.

This is not to make a sentimental argument for "open borders." The truth is that we do not now have an "open border," nor have we ever had one. In 1990 the federal government reformed the nation's immigration laws, establishing two overall categories for new immigrants—those with specific family ties to an American citizen or permanent resident and those with desirable skills. While creating a strict formula for how many of each group we would admit each year, the new law will continue to admit immigrants from diverse backgrounds to the United States. The legislation was not perfect, but it was an honest attempt to be fair to all the legitimate and sometimes competing forces with an interest in American immigration. It was realistic about America's capacity and America's need.[7]

Especially in this context of fairness, the revival of anti-immigrant sentiment in America is sad to me personally and to millions like me who are the sons and daughters of immigrants. But at least for us in New York, there's another word besides "sad" to describe hostility toward immigrants: it's stupid. Today, New York is growing stronger and stronger through its immigrants; we need them more than they need us. We need their talent, their daring, their ambition, and their willingness to work.

We see the benefits most dramatically in New York City. From 1982 to 1989, nearly 685,000 immigrants surged into the five boroughs, helping to stop a pattern of population decline. Today, as many as one out of every three

---

[7]In 1986 I urged the Reagan administration to live up to the commitments it made to help states with the costs involved in the assimilation of refugees and of aliens who have attained legal status. Through 1992, the federal government had not lived up to its original agreements. The legalization program was never fully funded by Washington. New York State alone was left to cover $90 million in cumulative, unreimbursed costs. By failing to take responsibility for incarcerated undocumented immigrants, the federal government had cost New York State several hundred million dollars. The federal government, through cuts and failures like these, fostered resentment against legal immigrants and refugees by forcing some states and local governments to spend their shrinking resources to fill the gaps created by Washington's abandonment of its responsibilities. This is contributing to real friction, even hostility, between established and new Americans.

people living in New York City is foreign born, the highest proportion in sixty years.[8]

With so many newcomers, New York City's economy has been transformed. In the 1970s, the steady influx of immigrants helped New York through tough economic circumstances. Immigrants also had a positive economic impact here in the 1980s.[9] Part of the reason? In large measure, the newest generations of seekers are a ready-made middle class. Many of today's immigrants arrive with far greater education and skills than did those who came ninety years ago. Many bring with them medical, engineering, and other advanced degrees.[10] In fact, 22 percent of the immigrants in New York City's workforce are employed in white-collar and professional positions.[11] It is hard to imagine, for instance, how New York's health care system could continue to function without the immigrant doctors, nurses, and technicians who staff them today.

Many other immigrants find jobs in the factories, hotels, and restaurants on which we all rely. In fact, immigrants are credited with saving several indus-

---

[8]Changes in the 1965 and 1990 immigration laws have opened our doors to those who had formerly been excluded, making New York's immigrants the most diverse in the nation. New York City's latest immigrants come from all over the world. In New York, the restaurants serve practically every cuisine imaginable. Plays are performed in Korean, Chinese, Gaelic, Spanish, Italian, Yiddish. Church services are delivered in dozens of languages. A few years ago, half a million people marched in the annual West Indian–American Day Carnival, many of them recent immigrants from the Caribbean.

The mosaic is less varied in other states. In California, for example, Mexicans represent 62 percent of the immigrant pool. By contrast, the top three groups entering New York between 1980 and 1990—Dominicans, Jamaicans, and Chinese—together accounted for only 35 percent of the immigrants to our state. In 1991, 190,000 immigrants came to New York from over 165 countries, according to the Immigration and Naturalization Service (INS). The 1990 census counted 2,851,861 foreign born in New York State. In the past decade, the largest percentages of immigrants came from the Dominican Republic (17.6 percent), Jamaica (10.2 percent), China (7.6 percent), Guyana (7.5 percent), and Haiti (6.1 percent). Some 70,000 Irish émigrés have settled in the New York area in the recent years. Roughly 85 percent of the immigrants to New York State reside in the New York City metropolitan area. (Based on 1990 figures.)

[9]"Immigration and the Labor Force in New York State," a Report from the Chair, New York State Legislative Commission on Skills Development and Vocational Education, October 1991.

[10]The level of education ranges widely based on country of origin. While less than 5 percent of the immigrants from Mexico, the Dominican Republic, and Portugal had college degrees, the figure is more than 40 percent for those from Iran, India, Hong Kong, and Taiwan.

[11]"The Newest New Yorkers: An Analysis of Immigration into New York City During the 1980s," City of New York, Department of City Planning, 83.

tries in New York, such as garment manufacturing, which would have left the state—and probably the nation altogether—had immigrants not provided a new source of labor. If they are lucky, immigrants may get one of the few union jobs open to outsiders in the construction business. Among the most fortunate immigrants are those who can scrape together enough money to buy a small restaurant, a bodega, or a livery cab.

In New York City alone over forty thousand firms owned by immigrants add tens of thousands of jobs and $3.5 billion to the economy each year.[12] In Flushing, Queens, Sheraton has even built a new hotel to cater to the thriving new businesses, banks, and stores the growing Asian community has created. Forty percent of our gas stations are now owned by South Asians, according to the New York City Department of Consumer Affairs. Afghans and Senegalese are gravitating to and opening new fried-chicken franchises. Indians and Pakistanis dominate the newsstand business. Guyanese can be found behind the counter in the city's pharmacies and machinery repair shops. They also play a big part—along with the Jamaicans and the Irish—in the child care business. Eighty-five percent of the city's 1,600 greengroceries belong to Koreans.

As they struggle to build their futures, immigrants are also rebuilding New York neighborhoods—like Washington Heights, Sunset Park, and Flatbush. More than 17,000 immigrants from 112 countries have settled in one community alone: Elmhurst, Queens.[13] All over the city, thousands of new immigrants are renting and buying homes and apartments. In November of 1992, at the nadir of the region's real estate market, Dime Savings Bank reported that a startlingly large percentage of those who bought homes in the metropolitan area in the previous year—26 percent—were not born in America.[14]

The great majority of our immigrants live in the five boroughs of New York City, but substantial pockets of foreigners are living in other parts of the state as well. Many foreign families have spilled into the New York City suburbs. For example, Haitian immigrants have settled in Rockland County. The

---

[12]According to the New York Chinese Businessman's Association, despite the recession, not one of their two-hundred-member businesses had any layoffs.

[13]"The Newest New Yorkers: An Analysis of Immigration into New York City During the 1980s," City of New York, Department of City Planning, 119.

[14]"The American Dream: Diminished Expectations," The Dime Savings Bank of New York, FSB, 1992.

number of Westchester's Japanese residents nearly doubled in the ten-year period between 1980 and 1990. With its increasingly diverse clients, the Westchester County Health Department has translated its literature into Arabic, Mongolian, French, Creole, Portuguese, Farsi, and Japanese.

By citing some of the many benefits that this huge influx of immigrants has brought to New York, I don't mean to suggest that no new problems have been created. In 1992, 120,000 new immigrant students entered New York's public schools—at a time when one in ten New York public school students was already learning English as a second language and the system was already short on resources. But with the new pool of children comes an extraordinary quantity of talent that will ultimately elevate us all. In 1992 the New York Public Library held a ceremony honoring many of the city's high school valedictorians. Of the ninety-six who attended, at least forty-five responded that they had been born outside the United States.

Another problem commonly attributed to our most recent arrivals: the timeworn idea that they are stealing jobs from those who are already here. Yet this accusation overlooks an important point. Certainly the flow of immigrants increases the supply of workers, but it also increases the demand for goods and services that creates economic growth and job opportunities. A 1989 study by the U.S. Department of Labor reported that immigrants increase employment opportunities and wages of native-born workers.[15] In fact, because of their propensity to start new businesses immigrants tend to *create* jobs for U.S. workers. In 1990 former President Bush's Council of Economic Advisors reported that the long-run benefits of immigration greatly exceed the costs.[16] And in 1992 an article in *BusinessWeek* reported that immigration had a net positive effect on the U.S. economy. "On balance," it announced, "the economic benefits of being an open-door society far outweigh the costs. . . . In the 1980s alone, an unprecedented 1.5 million college-educated immigrants joined the U.S. work force."[17]

More, though, must be done to discourage illegal immigration and the hiring of undocumented immigrants, not only because it is unfair to those who

---

[15]"The Effects of Immigration on the U.S. Economy and Labor Market," U.S. Department of Labor, May 1989, 180.

[16]"Economic Report of the President," February 1990.

[17]"The Immigrants: How They Are Helping Revitalize the U.S. Economy," *BusinessWeek*, July 13, 1992.

wait years to get here, but because it creates an exploitable class of human beings—people too afraid of deportation to report to the police if they have been robbed or mistreated or witnessed a crime against someone else. To allow our country to be inhabited by millions who lack equal protection under the law creates a caste system that will ultimately damage our people and our democratic values. Ironically, it is also likely to increase resentment against immigrants in general, even those who enter legally and gain citizenship.

With all the social and economic challenges we face, neither New York nor the nation can afford to lose what immigrants bring to us—and those contributions cannot all be measured in dollars or jobs or talent. Different as they may be from those of my parents' generation, the new immigrants bring with them the same old-fashioned values: the eagerness to work and to achieve; the willingness to sacrifice for the next generation; a belief in family and personal responsibility; a faith in something larger than themselves—all positive values we need to replenish throughout our society. Add to these the principle of tolerance and a sense of shared fate, and you might have a prescription for healing much of what troubles America now.

The Politics of Inclusion

From the experience of immigration, we have learned—or should have learned—that our first impulses toward strangers are not always our best; that hatred is inevitable only if we fail to understand each other; that the diversity of our people is a strength, not a flaw; and that we *can* safely share the opportunity of America with those who seek to join us.

But despite the great strides made in our short journey as a people, the impulse to shun, to exclude, to hate, is still with us—along with the territorial fear it springs from.

Our society has periodically struggled to free itself from the sin of deprecating whole groups of human beings because of differences in how they look, what they believe, or where they come from. This assembled diversity has produced the most successful experiment in democracy ever conducted. But we have by no means achieved perfect harmony.

There have been moments of stunning failure.

We launched America as a unique bastion of freedom—but slavery was allowed to exist for almost one hundred years and legal segregation for one hundred more. Crosses were burned to terrorize outsiders in a twisted desecration of a symbol of holy love. A century ago Protestants and Catholics killed one another in the streets of New York City. In 1882 the Chinese Exclusion Act banned all but a very few Chinese workers from entry. During World War II Japanese-Americans were thrown behind bars on the chance they might forget their loyalty to their new home. At other times we sought to ban the teaching of foreign languages and to slam shut the doors of elementary schools sponsored by certain religious groups. Until rather recently, Americans hardly objected if people were fired or evicted on the grounds that they were homosexual; and today, too many are still willing to accept such discrimination.

Closer to home, visible to all of us, lies further proof that we have failed to create a world of safety and gentleness for our children. We may have discarded pernicious ideas like "separate but equal," but in the everyday reality of jobs and mortgages and the struggle for survival and dignity, routine discrimination still smolders. Despite all our very real progress, we remain a divided country. In inner cities across the nation, African-Americans, Latinos, and other minorities continue to be victimized by inferior schools and inferior housing, by chronic joblessness and poor nutrition, by the de facto denial of opportunity that still relegates them to the back of the economic bus.

A United Nations report released in May 1993 put the problem in unforgettable perspective: In terms of their quality of life—measured by life expectancy, education, purchasing power, and other factors—African-Americans and Latinos, on average, rank little better than citizens of the Third World.[18] Further evidence came early in 1992, in a joint report from the African-American Institute of the State University of New York and the Center for Social and Demographic Analysis at SUNY, Albany. The report, a compilation of recent statistics gathered by government, labor, and the federal census, reached distressing but not unexpected conclusions: African-American men are unemployed at a rate three times that of white men; the percentage of African-Americans in New York's prisons is about three times the percentage of African-Americans in the state's overall population; nearly three times as many African-Americans live below the poverty line as whites; African-American students score lower on standardized tests and drop out of high

---

[18]"U.S. Whites Top UN Quality-of-Life Index," *New York Newsday*, May 18, 1993.

school more frequently than whites. Finally, white Americans can expect to live considerably longer than their African-American counterparts. Allen Ballard, a history professor who helped prepare the report, summed it up this way: "Those figures are cumulative. That's a cumulative impact of hundreds of years of lack of inclusion in American society."[19]

Even if we don't see it every day, the immense misery in the ghettos of this country is still there, twenty-five years after the Kerner Commission report tried to sound the alarm. Even if we claim we've done our best, we know the suffering is there. Even if we say it's not our fault, we know it's there. Even if we are venal enough to try to justify it, we know it's there! Despairing of a solution, many have simply given up and sought refuge in the grassy bunker of suburban life. But what will we do when the despair and the violence start to spill across the city lines? Where will we move then?

For some of us, it is much too late to escape from America's problem with race. New York and the nation were reminded of that in 1989 when a sixteen-year-old African-American boy named Yusef Hawkins was murdered in Brooklyn, simply because he was walking through a white neighborhood at the wrong time. Three years earlier, in Howard Beach, Queens, white youths terrorized Michael Griffith, a black youth they felt had invaded their turf. They chased him into traffic, to his death. In 1992 a Hasidic scholar named Yankel Rosenbaum was set upon by a mob and killed after a Hasidic Jew driving through Crown Heights accidentally struck and killed Gavin Cato, a black child. These two latest deaths touched off a firestorm of misunderstanding and hatred between two peoples who have both known centuries of oppression from other groups. The situation became so volatile that some Hasidic Jews accused the then mayor of New York City, David Dinkins, of murder.

Bias crimes are not endemic to New York City—they happen all over our state, all over the nation. In Richville, in St. Lawrence County, a Hasidic rabbi and his wife wanted to purchase the house they had been renting. They were threatened with violence, so they abandoned the home. Gay students from Syracuse University were repeatedly harassed on campus—property damage, slurs, and threats occurred from other students. In 1991 a popular seventeen-year-old African-American at Lawrence High School in Nassau

---

[19]"Blacks Catching Up, Yet Many Are Left Behind," Tim Beidel, *Albany Times-Union*, January 23, 1992.

County was savagely beaten by three white men with bats and sticks. In 1992 a sixteen-year-old white junior at a high school in Bethlehem, not far from the city of Albany, was beaten up by two other youths for wearing clothing decrying bigotry.

Of course, resentment and violence, discrimination and despair, are not new phenomena, but they have never looked quite like this before—so pervasive, so damaging. I have lived in New York all of my life. And all of my life—and especially during my childhood—there have been around me faces of kindness and concern and love. My own courageous and sweet parents from Italy. The hardworking laborers, seamstresses, and shop owners of South Jamaica. The Irish and German schoolteachers at P.S. 50, who were especially kind to a child who did not speak the language well. The world of my childhood was a world unto itself, made up of people from all over the earth. Next to the store I grew up in lived a Greek woman named Mrs. Pedalis, and a Czech family called Suitkik. Next to them a Jewish family called the Ruhners, and the Fosters, and an Irish family named Kelly. Across the street lived Willie Gawolski and Emmanuel Desilvo, who worked in the Portuguese bar and grill. On the other side of my father's store was Lanzone the baker, Kaye the tailor—all of us together on the same block.

We were aware of our differences, but we didn't allow those differences to lead to hostility. Indeed, there was a commonality among us, a commonality of need and concern and striving. It was a magnificent polyglot neighborhood that had one thing in common: *everybody* was poor or struggling to get into the middle class. It was a good and unifying experience. Polish, Portuguese, Jewish, French, Irish, Italian, Black. It gave those growing up in that environment a broad and intuitive understanding of the different facets of our population, what we now call "diversity," both cultural and religious.

Even where the differences might have appeared most extreme—in matters of religion—we seemed to share more than you might think. On Sunday morning I served as an altar boy in little St. Monica's Church in South Jamaica, Queens. It was a Roman Catholic church where they said mass in Latin. On Friday night I served as *shabbas goy* in an Orthodox synagogue—turning out the lights and locking up because my neighbors' religion forbade them to work on the Sabbath. In many ways, the two experiences seemed more similar than different. Certainly the temple offered no kneeling, no nuns, and no collection plates. But the altars were similar; the vestments were similar. There was a language I didn't understand on Sunday morning and a language I didn't understand on Friday night, and I began to see how much was shared by these people of different faiths, despite their varying creeds.

But as I began to grow older, and to see more, and to travel outside my South Jamaica neighborhood, I began to see other faces: the faces of discrimination and bias; the face of envy; the face of fear; even the face of hate. We all grew up together in tenements when we were poor. But as we grew a little older and better off, our families moved to private houses in separate places, to new ghettos with nice lawns: Jews in one place; Italians in another; Blacks in their own communities. Differences that had been unimportant to us seemed suddenly significant to the people we met. Differences drew lines and created fences.

I came to learn the implications of difference, to know what it means to have a name and a face that some people find not quite acceptable—not "American" enough (that is, not enough like their name or their face)—when my family moved from South Jamaica to a so-called better neighborhood. I was stripped of the naiveté that instinctively accepted superficial discrepancies in color, language, and ritual as being irrelevant. I began to learn that the sophisticated world around me was not as smart or as good as the world we left in South Jamaica. I began to understand that in the "better" neighborhood, people treated differences almost always as dangerous, and sometimes as evil.

We had moved to a small house in Holliswood, another neighborhood in Queens, one that was then inhabited mostly by white Anglo-Saxon Protestants—no Blacks, no Jews, no Italians—and certainly no Italians who had once been poor and illiterate, who had come from the Mezzogiorno, the deprived area of Italy. I'll never forget the first meeting my mother had with our new neighbors. She was outside sweeping the walk. Three distinguished-looking women came down the hill to see her. They were a welcoming team of sorts, but they bore no gifts. She remembers them as *freddo*—cold, aloof. And they said to her: "You must be the Italian woman. Well, we want you to know you are welcome here, but please remember to keep the tops on your garbage pails."

It went through her like a knife! It left a scar that she could feel fifty years later. The insolence, the crudity, the arrogance—all born of an ignorance that permitted those people to believe that if it's different, it's inferior and somehow wrong. With maturity I came to the sad awareness that this kind of intolerance—this tendency to shun the alien, to be afraid, to be envious—lurks almost everywhere.

Unchecked, magnified, and sanctioned by the state, this impulse is what eventually produced the malignancy of the Holocaust and the "ethnic cleansing" we see now in the former Yugoslavia. In the intervening decades, we have seen similar organized atrocities—some carried about by independent groups, some sponsored by government—in both hemispheres and on practically every continent.

In recent years this corrosive tide of divisiveness and bitterness has scarred many parts of our society, threatening to turn our greatest potential strength—our diversity—into our greatest potential weakness. It's testing what we believe about ourselves; testing our willingness to stand up to defend one another. This resurgence of old animosities spawned by difference should concern everyone, especially those who have lived and flourished in a place as diverse as New York.

In 1992 millions of citizens who watched the Republican National Convention were shocked at its tone and disheartened at the sight of candidates for high office standing before national television audiences and asking Americans to condemn other Americans, cursing and castigating people, talking about "them" and "us." New York, with all its diversity, became a special target. The anger that spilled out from the podium was frightening. Fortunately, the convention's attempt to pit Americans against one another by provoking a "cultural struggle" or "religious war" was largely rejected as distasteful and wrong. Most Americans would rather be angry at their politicians than at one another.

Yet if the tone of the convention revealed anything about the state of the nation at large, it was a persistent sense of frustration with the present and anxiety about the future—bad omens for the prospects of tolerance and civility.

Despite all we gained in the civil rights struggles of the 1950s and 1960s, we seem to be losing ground. If we expect to reverse the slide, we will have to ask, and answer, some hard questions.

Why are we still fighting among ourselves? For bread?

For superiority? Do we mean the momentary advantages of one over another? Or do we mean the elimination of those differences? And how does bias become violence?

Is it still possible to do what previous generations have done to overcome tensions and disagreements, to forge out of our diversity a new measure of unity? Can we all pledge a common core of beliefs and rights, while preserving the ethnic, racial, and cultural identities that make each of us unique?

Today, with people coming to New York from all over the world, after a decade of record immigration, growing minority populations, and a new visibility for gay men and lesbians, the potential for a reaction against difference is as great as—or greater than—ever. There are people in this society who are still anti-Semitic; who will still beat you up—or worse—because you are gay or Asian; who will still deny you a job because you are a Latino, a Native American, or an African-American. How do we deal with the stupidity—and the danger?

Although I don't pretend to understand it completely, I believe the best weapon government can offer against this irrationality is rationality—education, the law, and opportunity.

We have to fight ignorance and hate every way we can—by speaking against it, by refuting it through our example. We must also expose hate for what it is, wherever we see it. In early 1992 Elie Wiesel wrote to me describing a series of conferences titled the Anatomy of Hate, which he had helped to arrange in several great cities—including Paris, Boston, Haifa, Oslo, and Moscow. We agreed that it would be a good time for New York to cosponsor such a conference, which we did later that year. Although no single gathering can begin to solve the problem, hate is one of those dark forces that tends to lose its power in the light of day. The more openly we talk about it, the less acceptable it becomes.

We also need what Martin Luther King, Jr., called a "revolution of values," a revolution that begins with individuals and extends to families, schools, churches, civic organizations, and our political institutions. We have to remind each other that there are plenty of ways to resolve conflict without violence. We have to teach our children about their moral obligation to each other as brothers and sisters and the inherent worth of each individual.[20]

---

[20]Beyond new laws, we must teach people new and better ways to get along with each other and to resolve differences nonviolently. In New York State we have an assortment of tools that the city and the state of New York have called on from time to time. For years we have had the Martin Luther King, Jr., Institute, a first of its kind in the nation. This state-chartered agency works to disseminate the views of Dr. King through training in nonviolent approaches to conflict resolution. Our Human

This effort should begin with those of us who have made it, who have been lucky enough to achieve some comfort, maybe even some affluence, prestige, and power. The worst sin of all would be if we responded instead by spreading the kind of hate that victimized our parents, by repeating the kind of stupidity that was used against our ancestors by the bigots and self-appointed aristocrats who lumped us together as "micks" or "wops," "chinks" or "kikes," "krauts" or "polacks"; by those who said, in effect, "Go home, you're not welcome here, you're not one of *us*, you don't belong." Having gone through it ourselves, and remembering all the biting words, we should realize that it would be a sin to sit around our own living rooms and talk about all those "others." What a sin it would be if we, who were the victims of racism and stupidity, should project it ourselves once we became secure. We must refuse to pass on the hurt and the injustice of bigotry; we must refuse to let it ricochet through our society, wounding other innocent victims.

For all of our differences over ideology, politics, and ethnicity, most New Yorkers are not as far apart on the dry substance of teaching tolerance and appreciation for other cultures as many in the current debate on "multicultural education" imply. Most New Yorkers stand somewhere in the broad territory of generally accepted common ground and common sense. Most of us understand both the need to recognize a broadened multicultural perspective and the need to make sure that these efforts lead to unity and an enriched sense of what being an American is, not to a kind of destructive factionalism.

What seems to have been lost in the debate is one of our most powerful and unifying values: diversity itself, the freedom to be different. The truth is, it is not the degree of our sameness that holds us together, but the degree of our commitment to the right to be different. What ties us together as a nation is not that we have all come to think alike, but that we agree to live by a system that allows us to disagree peacefully and gives us all a chance to be enriched from the free exchange of different ideas.

Ultimately, debates about multicultural education must start and end with what is in the best educational interest of our children. While multicultural education must not become a tool for fostering ethnic factionalism, we must also make sure that our curriculum does not perpetuate the sting of

---

Rights Division is also actively involved in reaching out to communities in conflict, helping to create better communication between parties on varying sides of tense issues. New York's Crisis Prevention Unit and antibias campaign help to get out our message that "New York's future comes in all colors."

exclusion by telling certain students that their ethnic heritage is not part of the American story.

Our efforts to widen our students' appreciation of different cultures will benefit all of them—even those in homogenous educational settings. To be a productive member of the workforce and a thoughtful and engaged citizen in the twenty-first century will require a highly developed ability to understand how others from different backgrounds—both within and beyond our borders—think and look at situations.

We need not fear the fact that the nation's composition and culture are changing if we remind ourselves that the nation's elasticity—her ability to adapt to changing times and changing populations—has been one of her greatest strengths and will continue to be as long as we are also mindful of the enduring consensus values—the mortar in the mosaic—that have helped hold us together.[21] Even here, in our uniquely free society, where diversity is protected and cherished, there is a rough but clear national understanding of what is right and wrong, what is allowed and what is forbidden.

We can find much of the consensus we require in the original documents that defined us as a people. The Declaration of Independence and the Constitution reflect values at the core of American life. We must not take them for granted or forget to point them out: an awareness of the profound ways in which we are all equal; reverence for the individual rights that issue from that equality—the rights of others as well as our own; a sense of the importance of working for a good greater than our individual comfort and success—a common good; and finally, a love for this place that has dared to aspire to these revolutionary insights and principles.

America's founders drew from a deep well of wisdom and history, from philosophical, cultural, and religious traditions that stretched from the Enlightenment back thousands of years to Rome and the ancient Greek city-states. These traditions yielded the other common values that guide us: a sense

---

[21]I have never believed that the United States was a melting pot in which individuals were meant to boil away their differences, a great, smoldering cauldron for cooking up indistinguishable new Americans. For years, whenever anyone has given me the opportunity, I have spoken about how, at our best, New York, like the nation, is a mosaic—a picture made up of many different pieces, each with its own shape and texture. When we carved *E Pluribus Unum* into our national identity, the aim was to unite all the bright, separate fragments into a greater beauty, a harmonious new whole.

of personal worth and the importance of each individual; dignity and integrity; compassion, service, and love of knowledge; responsibility, accountability, and the need for discipline and order.

These are the values that we ought to be teaching our people, especially our young. We ought to show them how equality, individual rights, the common good, the rule of law, and the love of country aren't just pat phrases to be wheeled out and paraded on national holidays. They are some of the assumptions on which our national life was founded, on which we have flourished, and upon which our future must be built.

Not all these values are written explicitly into our laws. But they are part of the consensus that underlies our nation's conscience. They all continue to play a crucial role in how we live, how we conceive of ourselves and of others, what we cherish, and even how we dream.

Conceived in these broad terms, education will do a great deal to advance the principles of tolerance and inclusion. But we will also need new laws.

Violence against groups because of who they are—bias-related crime—continues to rise throughout our society, as well as here in New York. When the usually snide insinuations of bias turn to violent attacks, none of us should remain silent. How could we, when fanatics who make a savage mockery of the rule of law take it upon themselves to attack individuals and, with them, the very ideals of equality that we profess? But our common voice—the state law itself—*is* silent on the subject of bias crime.

Although New Yorkers have avenues of legal redress through the penal law and the common law for acts of violence and intimidation, New York law does not recognize the particularly serious consequences to victims, the community, and public order when such acts are motivated by prejudice and hatred. Every commission that has studied the problem of bigotry and bias-related violence, including our own New York State Task Force on Bias-Related Crime, has told us the same thing: Any comprehensive response to bias-related attacks must have the force of law. If we fail to enact a proper legal deterrent, we fail not only those who become victims, but ourselves. Now more than ever, we need a law that establishes forcefully and unequivocally that our society will not tolerate bias-related violence or intimidation. Starting in 1987 and every year since, I've submitted legislation to provide for stronger penalties against those who commit bias-related violence or intimidation. Each time my proposal has been blocked by the state senate.[22]

Given New York's history, the Empire State will have a leading role in guiding the nation toward an intelligent multiculturalism. How well we manage the idea of America in a world of increasing cultural, religious, and ethnic diversity will be a defining question for the rest of this decade and into the new century.

A society that speaks out against and actively condemns discrimination, that teaches an appreciation for other cultures and a love for this country, and that passes laws to protect people from acts of hate will help create a more harmonious and tolerant America. But, ultimately, these efforts will prove fruitless unless both public and private sectors join forces to create a workable agenda that offers our young people fresh avenues to opportunity, dignity, and prosperity.

After the riots in Los Angeles in 1992, everyone asked, "What are we going to do about the inner cities? What are we going to do about race relations?"

The truth is, the eruption in Los Angeles was bigger than Los Angeles. It was Los Angeles, it was Howard Beach, it was all the little eruptions over the years. It was the people recognizing finally that "Los Angeles" can happen at any place at any moment.

Some people become so frustrated that they toy with the fantasy that locking up more of our citizens and electrocuting the worst offenders will solve everything. Others have become so pessimistic that they say there is no answer. Government, they say, can't help. Compassion doesn't work. Throughout the 1980s, all that the national government seemed willing to do was give better breaks to the people *outside* the ghettos and hope that by cutting down government involvement in achieving equal opportunity, the free market would suddenly do what it had never been able to do before—banish racial injustice.

Not surprisingly, nothing got better. The grim truth hasn't changed.

---

[22]In the absence of state legislation, I have used executive authority to direct the state attorney general to assist district attorneys in the investigation and prosecution of bias-related incidents. I've also followed recommendations of the New York Task Force on Bias-Related Crime in such areas as education and victim services. Working with local law enforcement agencies throughout the state, New York State has also started a bias crime data reporting system to accumulate more information on this shameful trend.

We still understand what must be done. We know it for certain because it rests on common sense. Maybe that common sense was never better expressed than in the simple language of *Brown* v. *Board of Education.* "It is doubtful that any child may reasonably be expected to succeed in life if he is denied the opportunity of an education," the decision says. "Such an opportunity . . . is a right which must be made available to all—on equal terms."

Those words mean as much now as they did in 1954. They state both the experience and the promise of the American experiment: the real meaning of equality is in equal opportunity. Where opportunity is denied, it is our responsibility as a people, as a government, to make it available. *Brown* v. *Board of Education* not only rejected the idea of American apartheid, it made explicit what had been a central truth of our history: equality of opportunity doesn't just happen; it must be achieved.

The private sector by itself couldn't overturn discrimination. It couldn't protect Black children from rock-throwing mobs in Little Rock in the 1950s. It couldn't force the integration of the University of Mississippi or face down segregationist governors. Free enterprise couldn't legislate or enforce fair housing laws. It couldn't teach children to read or make sure a pregnant woman had enough to eat.

Overcoming the threat to our magnificent diversity will ultimately require a greater commitment to dealing with the root causes of our societal vulnerabilities. We face a choice: we can bring the nation together to save our children, or we can watch this country be destroyed by explosions from Los Angeles to Boston.

What, then, should be done? If one took all of these complicated problems, and all the programs, all the laws, and all the speeches on love, if we had to pick one idea to be the focus of all our energy, it would have to be *work*—the good chance to get a decent job at fair wages, to rise on one's own merits and support one's family, and show the world what you can do. Work: it is what has drawn people to New York for centuries.

Work

Cultivating the Ingredients for Economic Growth

For more than ten generations, America has been an invitation to hard work and its rewards. That is the central idea in the American experience. Work helps define us. It instills in our people dignity and confidence, pride and security. It broadens our horizons and gives us a sense of purpose. And in this society predicated on the redeeming importance of work, it also provides a crucial sense of belonging. By the same token, those who cannot find work, or are underemployed, suffer socially and spiritually as well as economically. Their pain wears away at their families, their communities, and—when the lack of work is great enough—the entire nation.

In New York, government has been aggressively committed to the free enterprise system as the creator of economic opportunity, understanding that opening the world of work to those currently locked out is good for every part of our society.

Work is the glue that holds together our families and our neighborhoods. In the end, work is what makes society work for all of us. We believe that the availability of work with fair compensation and a chance for advancement may represent the closest thing to a panacea for the social and economic ills of the country as a whole. If it were possible with one wave of a magic wand to give this generation of Americans what my parents immigrated here to find—the chance to work and make their own way in the world—we would today have fewer people struggling on welfare, less drug abuse, less violence, less homelessness, fewer prisons, even lower taxes.

But today—in the most powerful nation the world has ever known—we are failing to provide opportunity for all who seek it. At this writing, close to nine million Americans—more than half a million of them New Yorkers—are unemployed, without the dignity of being able to support themselves through the labor of their own hands and minds and hearts.

What is the proper role of government in building that opportunity? The answer is not a special Democratic insight or a jewel of Republican wisdom; it's as plain as the crystal-clear common sense of Abraham Lincoln, who instructed us that government should do for the people what they need to have done, but which they cannot do at all or do so well for themselves. If it can be done by promoting the private sector, then it should be; if not, then government has a role. It is as simple as this formulation I used some time ago: "We should have all the government we need, but *only* the government we need."

Over the past eleven years we have pursued a comprehensive strategy for economic growth in the Empire State, a public-private partnership that builds on all our native strengths. New York continues to enjoy the contributions of tenacious entrepreneurs and visionary corporate leaders who have seeded so much of our prosperity. And we are blessed with a workforce that is among the most productive in the world. But despite all the talents of all these New Yorkers, and our proximity to some of the world's richest markets, the recipe for long-term economic growth calls for several other crucial ingredients that government can help provide or develop.

To restore our economic strength, we have a simple comprehensive strategy. Our plan profits from the instruction provided by the post–World War II economy, when our formula for economic development brought New York and America roaring into a period of industrial dominance.

The basic idea was this: We had to make things of value—goods and services—and sell them to the rest of the world. This is what made us great in the past, and this is what will do it again.

It requires the following ingredients: a high-tech capacity; superior higher education and job training; a motivated, well-trained workforce; the stimulus of massive investments in infrastructure; and ready access to the world markets.

All of these elements must operate in an environment of aggressive hospitality to the businesses that will create the jobs that are the state's lifeblood. We're working to reduce taxes, fees, and regulations and providing incentives so entrepreneurs and company presidents will see New York as a place where their dreams can flourish.

In some cases—like tax rates—we have had to work hard to correct mistakes made earlier in our history. In the 1960s and early 1970s New York State spent and taxed at an unsustainable pace. The adjustments downward have been difficult. In 1987 we cut the state's personal income tax rates deeper and faster than we should have, and for the past decade the legislature has consistently spent more than I asked.[1] But despite our failures, on the whole we have made the necessary adjustments and done the other things we must

---

[1] In 1991 I vetoed $899 million in additional spending that the legislature wanted but that the state could not afford.

do well, including developing all the ingredients necessary to thrive in the twenty-first century.

Right now, the elements of our plan are in place and operating. Some good results are already in. We have new job growth for the first time in years. Business and consumer confidence is on the rise. New business incorporations have increased, and so has personal income.

The struggle is not over. But we are clearly on our way back. Now we need to do more cultivating and nourishing. With hard work and sound investments in our people and the workplace, I am confident we will thrive in the twenty-first century.

Capital—Forging a Public-Private Bond Through Investment

During the credit crunch of the last few years, when many entrepreneurs were finding it impossible to get bank financing, our state lending programs have been their only resort. Putting tax dollars to work—leveraging and attracting new and additional private investment—is at the heart of our economic development strategy, the returns of which can be seen all around the state.

A modest but delightful example of the public-private partnership functioning as it should is a Ben & Jerry's ice-cream parlor that recently opened in New York City. Its owner, Joe Holland, a businessman who happens to be an African-American but who might have been of any race or background, is the kind of enterprising, modern Renaissance man who comes along rarely but has a tremendous impact on all the people he touches. He earned a Harvard law degree and became an attorney but gave up a successful practice to devote himself to the immediate needs of his home community—Harlem, at the northern end of Manhattan.

In a corner of the world racked with homelessness, joblessness, and despair, Joe Holland determined that he could make a difference. In the early 1980s he opened the HARKhomes shelter, a fifteen-bed drug treatment and housing center that supplies basic services for homeless New Yorkers. To provide employment and training for the people in his shelter, he started a travel business. Despite its success, Joe Holland remained unsatisfied. He still felt he could do more.

In 1991 he came up with another idea. He wanted to build an ice-cream parlor on 125th Street and Fifth Avenue, right in the center of Harlem. A philanthropist suggested he approach Ben Cohen and Jerry Greenfield, two former New Yorkers who had moved to Vermont and founded a now famous ice-cream company that grew into a huge enterprise, churning out thousands of gallons of gourmet ice cream every day. Ben & Jerry's liked Holland's idea enough to waive its $25,000 franchise fee.

But despite the strength of Holland's will, the merit of his plan, and the cooperation of Ben & Jerry's, he still needed the one thing almost no new business can do without: capital—capital no bank would risk on such an uncertain project.

For this visionary entrepreneur, the answer came from a source that most people would be unlikely to connect with business vision or canny investment: state government. Holland turned to the New York State Office of Economic Development (OED), which put up a $100,000 loan. It wasn't long before Joe Holland realized his dream: an old-fashioned parlor with mahogany booths, a soda fountain, a tin ceiling, and tiled floors.

In 1992, when I visited his ice-cream parlor on a balmy summer afternoon, I marveled at the improbability of this arrangement: a rural Vermont ice-cream company run by two expatriate New Yorkers, helping to open a business in an inner-city community with a New York State loan. Those who work in the fountain are formerly homeless people who merely needed an opportunity and the faith of someone who cared. Only six jobs were created, but each one was a precious act of defiance against the odds. Holland is still giving back to his community, earmarking 75 percent of the store's profits for his homeless shelter.

Over the past decade, New York State has made substantial public investments—hundreds of millions of dollars—in an impressive variety of businesses and industries that needed our help. Not every case offers a story as romantic and appealing as Joe Holland's, but every firm we help contributes to the prime mission of OED: to attract new businesses, keep current businesses here, and create jobs.

The scope of the Office of Economic Development is wide, from attracting movie production companies to welcoming tourists, from helping fledgling firms get started to helping established corporate leaders modernize their industries and generate thousands of jobs. Our ongoing agenda can be distilled down to doing more of what New York has already done to enhance our future prosperity: revitalizing our cities, building on our high-tech capacity, and retraining workers left behind by changing technologies. Though most New Yorkers are hardly aware of it, we sponsor hundreds of such OED projects every year. Between 1983 and 1993, more than five thousand projects were offered various forms of financial aid from the state, spurring companies all over New York to improve their capital value and develop the skills of their people. A custom chocolate company in Cheektowaga outside Buffalo received a $21,000 grant to improve its factory. A maple syrup company in Montgomery County received a loan to modernize its processing machinery. The National Soccer Hall of Fame in Otsego County won a grant for $81,200. And in nineteen economically distressed communities around the state, from Brooklyn to Batavia, we have created economic development "opportunity" zones—areas where the state works to attract businesses by helping with capital needs, reducing utility costs, providing wage and investment tax credits, and refunding sales taxes on building materials.

Another particularly satisfying story is the Cathedral Stoneworks, a stone yard at the Cathedral of St. John the Divine, a magnificent Gothic church built mostly in this century. Even those without much interest in cathedrals should make the pilgrimage to Morningside Heights in upper Manhattan just to see the quality of the carving. To help the stone yard buy high-tech machines for the job, the New York State Job Development Authority made $3.7 million in loan guarantees. An ancient art form was propelled into the era of "stone robotics" using computer-aided design. The real payback in our investment, however, came with the knowledge that we helped Cathedral Stoneworks grow from an apprenticeship program of seven people (five local young people and two English master masons) into a thriving multimillion-dollar enterprise that now employs fifty.[2]

Major institutions and large companies rely on us, too. In 1992 the state allocated $241 million to the Roswell Park Cancer Center in Buffalo to expand one of the finest cancer research and treatment centers in the nation. Dunlop Tire in Tonawanda borrowed $27 million from the state for a new plant, while Toshiba Westinghouse Electronics in Horseheads secured funding to train its workers.[3]

---

[2]Stoneworks also benefited from a UDC Regional Economic Development (REDS) Partnership Program training grant of $100,000.

[3]Toshiba also received a $7 million loan from the state to renovate its 250,000-square-foot manufacturing facility in Horseheads.

Our capital programs are also used to attract out-of-state businesses that are looking to relocate. In 1988 I welcomed the Spalding Company, a world-renowned sporting goods manufacturer, to New York State. Through a $4.3 million investment, we helped the firm relocate from Massachusetts to the upstate city of Gloversville, bringing a projected 250 new jobs to Fulton County.

In a healthy economy, the subagencies of the Office of Economic Development—the Urban Development Corporation, the Job Development Authority, the Department of Economic Development, and the Science and Technology Foundation—do the important work of helping firms relocate, invest in crucial equipment, and expand their payrolls. But when business is bad, as it has been in so many industries for the past three or four years, saving jobs becomes as important as creating them.

In 1992, when Morgan Stanley decided to carry out its two-year-old plan to relocate to Connecticut, we were being pinched by the economy as well as squeezed by the firm; it had long since become a buyer's market for real estate. The city and state of New York, together, granted Morgan Stanley nearly $40 million in tax incentives, provided the firm committed to New York. The immediate payoff was that we saved 4,100 jobs and retained the economic activity generated by the company's employees. Over the long term, Morgan Stanley should contribute $911 million in direct taxes to city and state government.

Similarly, when the five members of New York's commodities exchanges began to outgrow their current space in downtown Manhattan, we approved plans to allow the exchanges to construct a new building at a roomy site north of the World Trade Center.[4] The state and the city committed $100 million to help keep over 11,000 industry people in New York.

In 1993 we took an equally aggressive approach to keep CBS headquartered in New York City. Fifty million dollars in city and state tax and energy incentives committed CBS to invest more than $300 million to upgrade and improve its operations in New York—preserving jobs for the 4,600 CBS employees involved, fueling the region's economy, and maintaining New York City's status as a world hub for broadcasting.

---

[4]The five commodities exchanges are the New York Cotton Exchange; New York Mercantile Exchange; Coffee, Sugar and Cocoa Exchange; Commodity Exchange; and New York Futures Exchange.

Of course we would have preferred it if some of these businesses could have borrowed their capital from private banks. But the recent years since the stock market crash of 1987 have created a financial drought. We had to step in or see opportunities die. We couldn't do that: our people need the work!

In the past, the governors in the New York–New Jersey–Connecticut tri-state area could act as allies, banding together to lobby the federal government for aid during hard economic times. But more recently, especially in the wake of the New Federalism, the opposite has been true. We have had to compete with each other to keep businesses within our individual borders. I've said many times that I do not like bidding for business against New Jersey and Connecticut. I'm sure none of us likes to be in the position—but this auction-block atmosphere has become a cold reality. I would be pleased to see it end, and we have restrained our own enticement efforts to encourage that kind of comity. But our neighbors have felt compelled to work aggressively to seduce away our businesses, leaving us with little alternative.

We have lost our share of these battles. In 1985, for example, we did everything we could to dissuade Merrill Lynch from moving out of New York City to new headquarters across the Hudson River. New Jersey was offering tax incentives, low-interest loans, money for job training, tax credits, and sales tax breaks for newly hired residents. Despite our efforts to match any deal New Jersey offered, we failed. Merrill Lynch moved anyway, along with thousands of jobs—a loss that only intensified our commitment to working with the private sector to retain companies and preserve jobs for New Yorkers.

As their owners can attest, the help we offer individual businesses can be indispensable, but these efforts express only part of our broader economic agenda. In our support for certain key businesses and industries, we direct our aid to whole cities and regions, too.

For a decade or more, several cities across New York State have seen their downtown districts declining—a pattern familiar to cities across the country. Some urban planners attribute this deterioration to the growth of highways and malls—in general, to suburban flight.

In 1979 the McGill Commission was created by the federal government to study U.S. population shifts. A year and a half later it concluded that millions of Americans would migrate to the Sun Belt and that cities would continue to decline. I disagreed with the commission's conclusion when the report was made public in 1981, and I continue to reject its defeatism, the tacit assess-ment that if people are moving away from the cities, then we might as well abandon them. Jane Jacobs, a noted urban expert, has said that cities have a life of their own. They are living organisms, and we cannot afford to let them become extinct. I think she's right.

In New York City there is a clear pattern that does not support the McGill Commission thesis. To start with, the population is *always* in flux. Certainly there continues to be a consistent migration to the suburbs and to other states, for one reason or another—a job relocation, better schools, more space, cheaper rents, less crime. But there is at the same time a strong and revitalizing countermigration, as people—especially young people with education and ambition to spare—come to New York to work.

What can we do to maintain this vitality? In New York City our strategy with Morgan Stanley, the commodities exchanges, and CBS offers instructive examples. In other urban areas our tactics may be different, but the results are no less significant. A clear example is Syracuse, one of our largest upstate cities. In August 1992, Addis and Dey's, a well-known department store, decided to close, leaving the city's traditional shopping district with thousands of square feet of vacant space. The state provided the funding for the construction of the Onondaga Convention Center, or ONCenter—$40 million of a projected $82 million complex. It will help establish Syracuse as a northeast meeting place for major trade shows and breathe new life into the city's economy by helping to feed business to local companies, hotels, and restaurants.

Our many efforts to spur New York's economy have left us open to criticism—for example, to charges of being too generous to business at the expense of other pressing concerns. But the criticism has not changed my belief that maintaining the healthy interdependence of the public and private sectors is essential. We are irrevocably linked. We must continue together on a course that puts people to work, or we risk losing ground to our interstate and international competitors. I suspect Lincoln—given his view on the role of government—would have agreed.

Infrastructure—How New York Helped Build Its Economy

Few reasonable people would object to government's obligation to lay the physical underpinnings of transportation, sanitation, and other basic services that have taken on the ungainly name of "infrastructure." Yet despite the obvious importance of these efforts, they don't always receive the public's warmest welcome—perhaps in part because of the scale of the investments they require and the fact that their real economic benefits can be hard to measure in a satisfying way.

If we are ever tempted to underestimate the importance of a healthy and ambitious infrastructure program, we need only to remind ourselves of the pivotal event of New York's economic history in the nineteenth century—the building of the Erie Canal. Sometimes called the nation's first great infrastructure project, the Erie Canal offers a story that shimmers with Yankee ingenuity—that indefinable combination of stubbornness and inspiration that allows its practitioners to get hard things done. Like any grand project, the canal project had to endure skepticism and opposition, but in the end, vision and intelligence carried the day, which was a very good thing for the economy of New York.

To appreciate this story fully, one has to picture New York State in 1807, already teeming with business. Upstate dairy farming flourished. Dry goods poured out of the factories in New York City. Shops overflowed from their storefronts into the bustling streets of the Lower East Side. Street merchants sold cloaks and suits off racks on the sidewalks. The finance, securities, and real estate industries were beginning to blossom. Total deposits in New York banks nearly equaled those of the rest of the nation's banks combined.

De Witt Clinton, then the mayor of New York City, saw that the city he led—and the state he would one day govern—was quickly becoming the economic capital of the young nation. He also recognized that New York would possess a unique strength if it could create a transportation network that could open trade to the expanding western frontier. The network he envisioned would be a water and barge route that would enable shippers to come into New York off the Atlantic and transport goods cheaply and swiftly up the Hudson River and Mohawk River valleys to Canada, the Great Lakes, and the new worlds beyond. Clinton believed that such "internal trade" offered the best mechanism for building flourishing towns and cities across the state.

Hardly anyone else agreed.

The Erie Canal met staunch resistance from many factions, most notably downstate merchants who already earned a comfortable living without it. Arguing that an inland waterway would not help them, they told their legislators they would not support the canal if it were financed through taxes, which was how Clinton intended to raise the $7.6 million construction fund—an enormous sum in those days. Clinton dared to ask the federal government for financial assistance but was flatly refused. President Thomas Jefferson, who was scouting for a huge public works project that would promote commerce in his home state of Virginia, called the idea of digging through 350 miles of *New York* wilderness "a mad scheme."[5] Other cynics simply labeled it "Clinton's folly."[6]

Nevertheless, by 1825, seventeen years after Clinton articulated his vision, the canal was finally completed, and to great fanfare. Perhaps never have so many skeptics—the august Thomas Jefferson included—regretted their words. Only a few held out. James Fenimore Cooper complained that the canal was "artificial." And Herman Melville said it fostered "corrupt and often lawless life."

Unfazed by the naysayers, Governor Clinton marked the occasion by traveling the entire length of the system and on his arrival in New York City ceremoniously poured a barrel of Lake Erie water into the Hudson. The benefits of the canal were soon clear to all: travel time between New York City and Buffalo dropped from six weeks to ten days; the cost of shipping from Buffalo to Albany was cut nearly in half overnight; the cost of sending grain from Lake Erie to the Atlantic dropped tenfold; by the end of 1825, the Port of New York did a third of all the export shipping in the world and eclipsed

---

[5] Codman Hislop, *The Mohawk* (Syracuse: Syracuse University Press, 1989), 244.

[6] Clinton faced another hurdle: the massive scope of the project. When he had finally persuaded the state legislature to accept his idea, the canal commissioners concluded they lacked the expertise to venture much beyond the design stage. The world's canal experts were all in Britain. There weren't any trained engineers in New York who could actually push the project through to completion; besides, boats would have to be raised and lowered six hundred feet! Nobody knew if the eighty-three stone locks would work. Procedures for mass excavation—for a channel four feet deep and forty feet across—and blasting through limestone weren't yet refined. And where would Clinton get the tools to build it?

Part of the answer to these concerns lay in the nerve and inventiveness of the engineers finally hired for the job. When they ran up against huge trees that blocked the route, they realized it would take far too long to cut them down using ordinary methods. They devised a giant winch with a thirty-foot axle and sixteen-foot wheels that felled forty trees a day. Securing waterproof cement to hold the locks together was a particularly vexing problem. One engineer invented a waterproof material using limestone.

Wisely, the canal's architects also called on local farmers for help. Their plows could furrow the soil, bogs, and gorges for the good of the state. In effect, many upstate farmers developed second careers as construction workers.

Philadelphia as the premier U.S. port. Some five hundred new businesses hung out their signs in New York City as a result of new canal commerce.

Cities along the Erie Canal boomed—most notably Utica, Syracuse, Rochester, and Buffalo. Buffalo became the major port of entry to the American West, so its warehousing businesses grew dramatically. Rochester quickly became the milling center of the nation; it was known as "Flour City." The influence of the Erie Canal ranged to the Great Lakes and beyond. Wheat, flour, and lumber could now be transported there cheaply from upstate New York. Textiles flowed from southern New England; coal came from Pennsylvania via canal, and westering pioneers came from the rimland states, lured by the dream of virgin land.

In effect, New York accelerated the development of the American Midwest. It stimulated the growth of states like Michigan, Ohio, Indiana, Illinois, and Wisconsin. New York's daring experiment became a catalyst for territorial expansion throughout the United States. Without the canal, the nation would never have grown up so fast.

With time, of course, the canal lost its dominance in commerce as other means of transport took its place. But it remains an enduring example of what we can accomplish as a people, through our government, when we aspire grandly and sacrifice immediate gratification for the benefit of generations to come.

In New York, the Erie Canal was just the first link in a chain of public investments designed to make travel cheaper and more appealing—and by extension to make the state more prosperous. We pioneered a number of key transportation concepts—including the nation's first railroad in 1825. Near the turn of the century, New York City introduced rapid mass transit, a system of underground trains that wove through four of the city's five boroughs, making it possible for workers to travel quickly and inexpensively to jobs far from home. And the parkway, a highway combined with parkland and designed deliberately for its scenic value, made its first appearance on a stretch of public land along the Bronx River, between New York City and Westchester County.

But no single project could rival the impact of a huge initiative begun on the eve of World War II, under the leadership of Governor Thomas Dewey. The New York State Thruway, which would eventually expand into 641 miles of superhighway, was, like the Erie Canal, financed with public funds—a billion dollars' worth. It was the forebear of the nation's interstate highway system. Today it is the largest toll road network in the United States. For much of its length, the thruway actually parallels the corridor established by the Erie Canal. As the second great infrastructure project in New York history, it also produced a parallel, though less dramatic, surge in economic development.

Clinton and Dewey shared the view that public investment wasn't just a means to enhance public convenience or personal glory; it was an unparalleled and essential way for government to stimulate private investment. New York never would have attracted so many ambitious businesses, or achieved its phenomenal growth, without such huge public investments in its infrastructure.

Instructed and inspired by this history, New York has spent the last decade working to preserve and enhance the infrastructure we inherited. In 1983 we embarked on a ten-year, $10 billion initiative to rehabilitate and improve our roads, bridges, ports, railroads, and air terminals, through prudent use of user fees and two bond acts that won voter approval. That's a lot for most states, but consider the extraordinary dimensions of our highway system—a total of 110 billion vehicle miles traveled *each year*, the equivalent of more than five hundred round trips from the earth to the sun. I know that some people find it hard to get excited about investing in maintenance, but with that cosmic degree of wear and tear, the humble duties of reconstruction and repair become essential to both the safety of our citizens and the health of our economy.

In the 1980s New York State also approved a landmark $8.6 billion capital program for the Metropolitan Transportation Authority (MTA) to keep the subways, buses, and commuter railroads of New York City running smoothly and safely for the millions of workers, residents, and tourists who use them every day. By the end of 1991 the MTA completed one of the most ambitious public works rebuilding projects in American history. Miles of tracks were completely rehabilitated. New lines were installed to Roosevelt Island and Queens. Suburban train stations were refurbished for commuters from Westchester, Rockland, and Putnam counties. Subway cars and buses were cleaned of graffiti, and many were replaced. The new cars feature specially designed surfaces that are much harder to deface; so far, the crusade against the vandals has been remarkably effective. Through these and a host of other accomplishments throughout the metropolitan area, the system's users have seen real improvements. Ridership is up and subway crime is down, so our efforts seem to be working. And for the first time, instead of importing cars from other parts of the country, New York City is using subway cars made in New York State.

For New York to remain an international hub, we must also continue to move unprecedented numbers of airline passengers in and out of the New York metropolitan area efficiently. Even in an era when the nation's airlines have struggled with mergers, flight reductions, and bankruptcies, and despite slowdowns in 1990 and 1991, use of New York's three major airports is again on the rise. By 1993 JFK International Airport had regained its stature as the worldwide leader in cargo tonnage, outpacing Tokyo's Narita Airport by transporting 1.3 million tons of goods in the previous year.

As business recovers, we'll need a greater capacity for cargo and passengers. Some years ago we saw that part of the solution was to expand, slowly and carefully, a regional airport called Stewart International, a former air force base near Newburgh, sixty miles north of New York City. Understandably, the thought of more flights and the additional noise from regularly scheduled jet traffic did not endear the project to all area residents. But responsible, detailed impact studies were made, and the state withstood court challenges to the airport's development. In 1990 American Airlines ushered in scheduled passenger service at Stewart, and now eight carriers offer eighty daily departures and arrivals for mid-Hudson travelers. Passenger planes share the airport with cargo aircraft. International charter flights have begun. The airport has grown to ten thousand acres and is now one of the largest in the nation. Complementing the flight facilities is Stewart's nearby industrial park, which means jobs for the region. Anheuser-Busch, CRS Computers, and Federal Express are but a few of the tenants—and we're working to attract others.

Like that of so many of our infrastructure projects, Stewart's successful development illustrates the efficacy of coordinated public and private investment. In preparing our facilities to handle future economic growth, we are also providing New Yorkers with three precious commodities: safety, convenience, and, most important, work.

Energy—Fueling a Half-Trillion-Dollar Economy

If any subject is less inherently glamorous or more intensely important than transportation and infrastructure, it is probably our energy supply. Because the power of a free enterprise economy also depends on its physical power supply, for most of this century an overriding concern for the government of the Empire State has been securing a safe, affordable, reliable source of energy. In the process, New York has helped the country test and develop intelligent answers to the complex questions of generating and regulating power in a modern democracy.

In our early history, the legislature had granted franchises to private utilities to build power plants on the St. Lawrence and Niagara rivers. In return, the taxpayers got nothing—except the sky-high rates one would expect from such a monopoly. Conservationist and former president Theodore Roosevelt, speaking in Potsdam, N.Y., in 1914 put it this way: "You have in this section a most valuable asset in your natural waterpower. . . . Coal and oil barons cannot compare to waterpower barons. Do not let them get a monopoly on what belongs to this state."[7] The danger was clear. But the solution was a long way off.

In the 1920s Governor Al Smith mounted several campaigns to create a self-financing state department to regulate our power requirements, but he was continually rebuffed by the legislature. Smith, and later Governor Franklin D. Roosevelt, never lost sight of the need for a government partnership with "properly regulated private enterprise," as Roosevelt noted in 1929. At the time, the state already had formidable private power reserves available, but Roosevelt judged correctly that the private power sources needed to be supplemented—and closely monitored—because power was too important to the state's future to be left totally outside the public's control. In 1931 Roosevelt finally succeeded in persuading the legislature to create a public power entity that would not only produce more power, but would also act as a "birch rod in the cupboard"[8] to deter the forces of monopoly and protect the public trust: the New York Power Authority (NYPA).

Even after the birth of NYPA, Roosevelt's goal of cheaper electricity proved

---

[7]"Bold Dream . . . Shining Legacy: Sixty Years of Public Power for New York," New York Power Authority, 1991, p. 2.

[8]From an FDR campaign address on public utilities, September 21, 1932, Portland, Oregon.

elusive: the private utilities were vigorous opponents. Together with the Depression, war, and shifting politics, their opposition relegated Roosevelt's new agency to nothing but a paper existence for several decades. Although the idea of public power was later realized by *President* Roosevelt—through the Tennessee Valley Authority—public power in New York did not fully arrive until the 1950s, when Robert Moses and the New York Power Authority began construction of the St. Lawrence power project. Then, even before the St. Lawrence project generated its first kilowatt-hour, NYPA launched an even grander scheme to capture the enormous power of Niagara Falls. Finally, by 1961, New York's Power Authority was running at full speed, harnessing the power of both the St. Lawrence River and Niagara Falls.

Today these policy battles read like ancient history: How could there have been a time when our electric supply was almost entirely in private hands? It appears that just as we take electricity itself for granted, energy *policy* is a subject that springs to the surface of public consciousness only in times of crisis—when international politics register in higher prices at the gas pump or when a blackout leaves a city helpless.

On a hot July night in 1977, the lights went out on Broadway and in Brooklyn and the Bronx. For the second time in twelve years, New York City and much of the surrounding region fell victim to a massive power failure. A freak series of lightning bolts landed on successive high-tension power lines, starting a chain reaction that short-circuited New York's vast electrical system, throwing the sweltering city into darkness. It was as if Zeus had thrown a thunderbolt down from Mount Olympus and then, with one great breath, sucked out all the power and light from the city.

In some sections, what followed was a hellish night of looting, vandalism, and violence. Thirty-three hundred arrests. One hundred and ten police officers injured—some shot, others bruised by bottles. The city's major retail stores, according to some estimates, forfeited $20 million in business. Brokerage firms lost millions in daily commissions. The blackout's repercussions extended to the Midwest and the West Coast, disrupting business and canceling flights in and out of New York. It was one of the darkest twenty-four-hour periods in New York's history, but it made the unmistakable point that protecting the power supply was one of the most important responsibilities of the state.

We have found a way. Today there is an organization that manages our power supply, located just a few miles from the state capital, in a town called

Guilderland. The New York Power Pool comprises New York's seven investor-owned utilities and the New York Power Authority. Inside the huge control room, which looks like something out of NASA's Mission Control, engineers manage the daily operations of the electric system for the entire state of New York, monitoring electrical storms and other changing conditions that light up the panels on their vast electronic wall. These men and women stay in constant communication with New York's regional power providers, instructing them when to fire up generating stations—or shut them down—to meet the demand at any given hour in the most economic and reliable manner possible.

Seeing to it that electricity flows safely and dependably to our homes, apartments, and office buildings involves an elaborate network of utilities, owned both by the public and by private investors. They draw on raw materials from out of state and from abroad: imported oil from the Persian Gulf and Latin America; natural gas transported to New York through interstate and international pipelines; coal, moved here by rail and barge. The only major indigenous energy source New York has—its water—generates less than one-fifth of its consumed electricity.

Today we have fifty-three public power entities: forty-seven municipal electric systems, four rural cooperatives, the Long Island Power Authority, and Franklin Roosevelt's New York Power Authority. NYPA provides lower-cost electricity to all of the state's residential consumers and many of its businesses as well, and more people benefit from public power in New York than in any other state. In fact, public power accounts for about one-quarter of New York's total electricity supply, and it saves New Yorkers hundreds of millions of dollars and supports thousands of jobs every year.

When I was elected governor I pledged to support this tradition of public power. Through the New York Power Authority, New York has forged new contracts with all fifty-one of the state's municipal electric systems and rural cooperatives to ensure them uninterrupted access to hydroelectric power—the cheapest electricity in the country. NYPA has established new programs to allow these same players to use part of their allotted hydroelectric and nuclear power to spur economic development.

As part of my administration's commitment to expanding public power in New York, NYPA has also established an unprecedented public power franchise in the New York City metropolitan area, assuming responsibility for the present and future electricity needs of New York City's subway system, commuter trains, public buildings, streetlights, and other public facilities in the city and most of adjoining Westchester County. With this ambitious program, we will be able to save taxpayers and transit riders more than $1 billion in this decade alone.[9]

But being affordable and reliable are only part of our concern. Smog, acid rain, and global warming are stark reminders that we cannot develop an intelligent energy policy in isolation from its environmental impact. Nor can we deal with these problems on a piecemeal basis or postpone action in the hope that further research may minimize the problem. As the world has come to grasp the magnitude of the threats to our common environment, New York has tried to lead the way in forging a new consensus in public policy. We can no longer pursue energy policy on one track and environmental policy on another—not if we hope to maintain the quality of our lives and prosper in an increasingly competitive world.

Understanding the need for such coordination and synergistic thinking, New York in 1989 developed the nation's first integrated state energy plan, synthesizing the expertise and priorities of our energy, environmental, and regulatory agencies. For the seven preceding years, we had been unable to enact such a planning process because of legislative objections. Finally, however, in 1992 the legislature gave its approval to a comprehensive energy planning statute that has enabled us to harmonize all our energy, economic, and environmental needs.

The plan offers an integrated strategy built on four basic ideas: pursuing cost-effective improvements in energy efficiency; ensuring that all energy forms compete fairly in the marketplace, while encouraging those with the least damaging environmental effects; taking tougher measures to reduce emissions from the combustion of fossil fuels; and promoting a greater reliance on natural gas, while pushing to develop renewable energy sources—solar, wind, hydroelectric, and biomass power.

Efficiency is the cornerstone of our approach because of its many benefits: it saves energy, cuts costs, bolsters the competitiveness of New York's businesses, and improves air quality by reducing the emission of pollutants. Be-

---

[9]NYPA, as a nonprofit, public benefit energy corporation, does not use tax revenues or state funds or credit to produce the electricity it sells to public agencies, businesses, industries, and private utilities in New York. NYPA finances construction of its projects through bond sales to private investors and repays the bondholders with the proceeds from operations of the project. This allows NYPA to offer electricity to these customers at rates that are lower than those of investor-owned utilities.

cause actions speak louder than words, we have embarked on an extensive effort to make the state's own buildings more energy efficient.[10] In July 1993 I announced a $49 million program to help public schools pay for energy-saving building improvements and equipment, like new boilers and insulation. There is a certain justice to the funding process: the monies for the Energy Aid for Public Schools program were recovered from companies that violated former federal petroleum pricing regulations between 1974 and 1981. New York has invested $405 million of these funds for programs designed to address the energy needs of not-for-profit groups, homeowners, hospitals, and businesses. Our energy-efficiency programs save New Yorkers $1.5 billion annually in energy costs.

For example, the New York State Energy Office offers auditing services to determine how much energy businesses use and how much money they could save by becoming more energy-efficient. The office provides low-interest loans for consumers to invest in energy efficiency. And to make it possible for low-income New Yorkers to spend less of their income on energy, the New York State Weatherization Assistance Program provides insulation for those who lack it, blankets to make water heaters more efficient, and low-flow showerheads that use less hot water. (New York's privately held utilities, inspired in part by the state's efforts and encouraged by innovative state regulatory policies, also have aggressive programs to help customers reduce their electric bills.)

Today, because of our investment in programs like energy efficiency and mass transit, New York has the most energy-efficient economy among all the fifty states; the efficiency of our energy use is on par with Japan and Germany.[11]

---

[10]In a 1990 executive order, the state set a goal of reducing energy use in state facilities by 20 percent by the year 2000. A 1993 report by the New York State Energy Office found that state facilities' energy use per square foot of building area fell 5.6 percent from 1988/89 to 1991/92, exceeding interim goals for energy savings. Without this energy-efficiency effort, the state's energy costs would have been $28.5 million higher during this period.

[11]In 1992 the citizens action group Public Citizen reported that New York's energy intensity, which measures the amount of energy used to produce economic output, is much better than the national average. We use 47 percent less energy to produce the same amount of economic output on a per unit basis. Achieving this level of efficiency is important because our fuel costs are higher than those in most parts of the nation. Our overdependence on imported oil, the costs associated with implementing environmental protection regulations, and our great distance from petroleum and natural gas supplies have all contributed to higher energy costs in New York.

But there is still room to do more—especially on our highways. Traffic congestion, for instance, is a public nuisance with a serious hidden impact on our economy, raising the price of delivering goods and services in metropolitan areas. In wasted time and fuel, slowed traffic costs New Yorkers more than a billion dollars a year. One of the ways to dissolve this jam-up is to encourage car pools in "community lanes," as we are doing on the Long Island Expressway. When fifteen people ride in five cars instead of fifteen cars, the fuel savings speak for themselves, and the drop in congestion creates economic and environmental benefits for the whole state.

After energy efficiency, diversifying our energy supply and reducing our dependence on outside sources are our most important statewide energy goals. New York depends on oil to meet nearly half its energy needs, with three-quarters of that oil coming from foreign sources. That ratio is far too high, leaving us vulnerable to volatile swings in the price of oil. The solution? Developing new, renewable sources of energy. At the State University of New York at Farmingdale, the New York State Energy Research and Development Authority is helping the university develop one of the largest solar power facilities in the eastern United States. This seventy-five-kilowatt system consists of three separate photovoltaic arrays connected to the Long Island Lighting Company grid, supplying enough power to provide electricity for forty homes. Though the scale of the experiment seems small, it could have a substantial impact statewide if it's successful.[12]

In addition to producing less pollution, such innovations, when applied on a larger scale, should reduce the demand of businesses and consumers for more expensive, nonrenewable sources of energy—meaning that money once spent buying power will be freed up for investment and consumer spending, stimulating New York's economy.

We've achieved a good deal in energy management here in New York, though we're also realistic about how much more needs to be done. But no matter how vigorous our programs, or those of our sister states, even fifty

---

[12]New York has also been a leader in moving alternative-fuel vehicles from the drawing board into the showrooms. Research and development programs supported by the state have led to advances in alternative fuel technologies and vehicle components. In 1990 New York launched the Alternative-Fuel Vehicle Fleet Demonstration Program, which is road testing nearly three hundred vehicles fueled by methanol, natural gas, propane, and electricity. The results will help us decide which fuels can meet the state's transportation needs while also protecting the environment and reducing our dependence on petroleum.

states acting alone will not be able to meet the immensity of the national environmental challenge.

From 1981 to 1992, the United States did not have a national energy strategy. If you look in a library catalog, the gap is so glaring that it looks as if the file has been purged. During the same period, the consequences of that neglect grew increasingly evident: mounting pollution; faltering domestic energy production; dangerously dilapidated nuclear facilities; a growing reliance on Persian Gulf oil; swelling oil trade deficits. And perhaps worst of all: a potentially disastrous dependence on fossil fuels.

Finally, a few months before leaving office, President Bush signed the National Energy Policy Act. This was a good-faith but inadequate effort. We need a new national—and global—energy vision for the twenty-first century, and it should build upon the principles of sustainable development. We must reject the simplistic notion that we have to choose between a healthy environment and a healthy economy. Perhaps Norwegian Prime Minister Gro Harlem Brundtland put it best when she said: "The environment is where we all live; development is what we all do in attempting to improve our lot within that abode. The two are inseparable."

Beyond insisting on integrated solutions, conservation, and increased efficiency, the nation must make a longer-term commitment to reducing carbon dioxide emissions associated with fossil fuels—in transportation, in buildings, in industrial processes, and in generating electricity. The single most effective step our nation can take to reduce its dependence on petroleum imports—and also address the problem of greenhouse gases—would be to increase the fuel efficiency of its motor vehicles. If Detroit were to improve the average fuel efficiency of our cars and trucks by merely one mile per gallon over each of the next fifteen to twenty years, we would save ourselves, by the year 2012, 2.7 million barrels of oil per day—the rough equivalent of Mexico's current level of daily petroleum production.

Perhaps the most controversial energy source we have ever developed is nuclear power. When I became governor, New York State was already among the leading states in generating nuclear energy. We still are. Currently we have six functioning nuclear plants, generating about 20 percent of our state's total capacity. We have also had firsthand experience with a nuclear power plant in the wrong place at the wrong time at the wrong price. It was called Shoreham—a private nuclear facility whose opening we fought ferociously because some claimed it was poorly planned and not economical.

At the time the plant was conceived in 1969, planners thought Long Island's rapid growth would create massive power requirements. By the early 1980s the Long Island Lighting Company (LILCO), a private utility, planned to open Shoreham on the northern edge of Long Island. In the early stages of the project, many local residents urged that Shoreham not be built.[13] The forces that wanted the plant, including LILCO and the federal government, were more powerful than those that opposed it. LILCO had an obvious stake—it would eventually get to charge higher rates to pay for the construction. By the time I became governor, LILCO had all but completed the $5 billion–plus facility and was preparing to fire it up.[14]

A lot of people, myself included, argued that even though a huge commitment to the project had already been made, a nuclear facility on Long Island still threatened people's lives in a way that no responsible public official could tolerate. There was no way to evacuate the surrounding area in the event of an accident, and no amount of money could excuse the risk that this plant imposed on human life. Despite the opposition, most of the state's establishment forces, including our legislature, were afraid openly to oppose the plant or to commit themselves to opening it, either. The logic seemed to be "The best thing to do with a hot potato is not to try to catch it."

The federal government, however, very much wanted Shoreham to open. In 1989 I traveled to Washington and presented my case to President Bush. We talked for some time, but neither of our positions changed. The Nuclear Regulatory Commission (NRC) granted Shoreham a full-power license. However, before the company could act on it, New York won an appeal of the NRC ruling in federal court, giving New Yorkers a final chance to scrap the project.

In the end, Shoreham was not stopped by any act of the legislature. Shoreham was not stopped by any executive order of the governor or any act of the Office of Economic Development or the Long Island Power Authority,

---

[13]The Shoreham plant, in many ways, was doomed from the start. First, it was planned for a site that had far too many people living near it. It was a plant that had deficient technology. It lacked an adequate evacuation plan. The construction delays and problems caused incredible cost overruns: the plant was supposed to cost $2 billion; instead the final price tag was $5.3 billion.

[14]Eventually LILCO would be licensed to run Shoreham at 10 percent of its operating capacity. While the state was negotiating a settlement, there was a strong possibility that Shoreham could have received federal approval to go to 25 percent operating capacity. Had this occurred, it would have been much more difficult to stave off the inevitable—the sanction for full-capacity operation.

or even by the protests of local residents. Ultimately it was stopped by those people with a financial stake in operating Shoreham. They decided it no longer made economic sense, as we had suggested all along. LILCO's management and shareholders concluded that opening the nuclear facility would have been more expensive in the long run than closing, decommissioning, and converting it.

Yes, billions had been spent; but if Shoreham had opened, over the next thirteen years it would have cost Long Island ratepayers $2.5 billion more than it cost to shut it down.[15] It was, in the end, a case of LILCO not wanting to throw good money after bad.

Industry, Ideas, and High Technology

Today, New York's economic stature far outpaces its relatively modest size. We have less acreage than a nation like Taiwan, yet we have the tenth largest economy in the world, with an annual gross state product totaling $481 billion.[16] Only four European countries, Japan, Canada, Brazil, California, and the United States as a whole produce more goods and services than we do. And the chronicle of our commercial success offers endless reminders that in the next century, America's prosperity will depend on our ability to turn new ideas into profitable products faster than anyone else.

The first lesson comes from the late nineteenth century, when New York

---

[15]With the help of the New York Power Authority, we are breaking new ground by decommissioning Shoreham, an effort that will help other utility systems—both public and private—in the future. Decommissioning nuclear plants will be one of the most challenging power activities of the next couple of decades. The contribution even of New York's current nuclear facilities is expected to decline, since there are no plans for any new nuclear plants to be built. If nuclear power is to reassert itself as a viable option in the United States and elsewhere, the industry must solve several problems. The next generation of nuclear plant designs must be standardized and plant safety margins increased. The licensing process warrants reform, and there must be a responsible and credible solution to the issues of waste disposal and decommissioning plants. Currently, the tremendous pileup of nuclear waste material, due mostly to two generations of weapons building, is a national problem beyond the scope of engineering and civic planning. We have too much of it; nobody is sure how or where it should be buried; and, understandably, nobody wants it in their backyard. Finally, if nuclear power is to be considered a viable power supply option, it must demonstrate its economic feasibility in competition with other energy-delivery systems.

[16]New York State Office of Economic Development, 1991.

State, in part through advanced policies on infrastructure and energy, developed a reputation as a place where business could flourish. The payoff? We attracted some of the greatest thinkers and doers of America's Industrial Revolution—inventors, investors, manufacturers, and merchants. Through their impatience with the status quo and their patience for trial and error, they turned New York into the leading commercial and industrial state in the country. A key factor was the synergy possible because so many gifted people came together in the same place at the same time. In 1879 Thomas Alva Edison had the idea for the incandescent lamp, but he had no bulb. It wasn't until New York's Corning Glass Works created a satisfactory blown-glass sphere that the invention could be developed, perfected, and marketed.[17]

In this heady industrial period and the decades that followed, New York produced or attracted an extraordinary percentage of the ideas, individuals, and industries whose products made modern life modern: Samuel F. B. Morse, inventor of the telegraph; Alexander Graham Bell and Antonio Meucci, the two people credited with making telephone communication possible; George Eastman, who established Eastman Kodak and made photography widely available through the invention of the portable, automatic camera; General Electric and its universe of consumer and industrial products; Carrier Corporation, the pioneers of air-conditioning; Thomas J. Watson and IBM; Chester F. Carlson and Xerox; Corning Glass and modern fiber optics. The collective impact on the quality of human life—and the economy of New York State—is incalculable.

The technological inventiveness embodied by individuals and companies like these has been paired in New York with equally innovative corporate management. An early and unsung example: George F. Johnson, a young man who started out with big ideas but no money and went on to create a minor empire based on shoe manufacturing. Johnson made his mark in the late nineteenth and early twentieth centuries, in the region of upstate New York known as the Southern Tier. His motto displayed all his brass and ambition: "As long as people are born barefoot, Endicott-Johnson will sell shoes."

But George Johnson was more than a driven entrepreneur. He was an inspired and progressive leader of people. Drawing his workers from the area's

---

[17]Fifty-five years later, Corning built the largest piece of glass ever made—the two-hundred-inch telescope mirror disk that went into the observatory at Mt. Palomar in California.

growing immigrant population, Johnson promised them a "square deal" and practiced what he called "welfare capitalism." As his company prospered, Johnson made sure that the local community was buoyed up, too. He built playgrounds; donated money for hospitals, libraries, and public schools; and he ensured that his employees could buy homes at below market prices. He paid good wages, provided health care benefits, and instituted "employee profit-sharing"—one of the first programs of its kind in the nation. He also championed the eight-hour workday, a radical idea for its time. Because of these practices, the Endicott-Johnson factory never had a strike or a shut-down, and the company grew to be the nation's second largest maker of shoes.

Our future prospects continue to rest in our technical base—computers, software, electronic products, and high-speed fiber-optic information path-ways—and in our ability to manage these resources imaginatively. Fortu-nately the legacy of our first great inventors translates into a remarkable population of ready talent. If you put all of New York State's engineers and scientists together in one place, they would make up a good-size city, some 360,000 strong. Of all the states, we have the second largest concentration of doctoral computer scientists, life scientists, and engineers—and the largest concentration of Ph.D. chemists and mathematicians. In the second half of this century, New York schools have produced 13 percent of the world's Nobel laureates in science. Today, seventeen science Nobelists live and work here. We nurture our talent early, too; we regularly have a disproportionate number of Westinghouse Science Talent Search finalists and semifinalists in our high schools.

To capture all the dividends of this native talent, we're strengthening the connection between our universities and our high-tech corporations—attract-ing corporate funding and expertise for academic research centers while targeting our own substantial research dollars toward those technologies with the greatest commercial promise.

The modern practice of research and development was actually born in New York in 1900, when General Electric's consulting engineer, Charles Proteus Steinmetz, lured to his staff Willis R. Whitney, a highly talented thirty-two-year-old from the chemistry labs at the Massachusetts Institute of Technology. For GE, hiring Whitney was a coup, but Whitney himself was uncertain about his new post: Would GE continue to support his work if he didn't produce immediate, tangible results? Refusing to give up his MIT appointment, Whitney chose to work for GE just two days a week until the company was certain that the shareholders would sit still for the idea of pure research.

By 1902 Whitney had reason to feel more secure; the company's annual report declared, "It has been deemed wise during the past year to establish a laboratory devoted exclusively to original research. It is hoped by this means that many profitable fields may be discovered." GE's patient backers would not be disappointed by the remarkable stream of inventions that poured out of Whitney's first lab—including the most efficient light bulb since Edison's.

Today there are hundreds of industrial R&D facilities throughout New York. Some are the corporate R&D labs of industrial giants like IBM, GE, and Xerox. Some represent the cutting-edge facilities of new leaders in emerging fields, like the Pall Corporation in biotechnology and Symbol Technologies in bar code scanning. This breadth of established and emerging activity in New York, and the accompanying investment it attracts, puts New York among the top industrialized nations of the world.

Public support of R&D also accounts for New York's world-class innovation. In a decade, New York State's Science and Technology Foundation has supplied nearly $180 million to support 1,230 technological research and development projects across New York. This sum has garnered more than half a billion dollars in matching funds. From efforts like these come ideas like a paperless braille machine for the blind. Special bathtubs for people in wheelchairs. An interactive video machine that can teach sign language to deaf children. A special electronic mat that can stimulate learning-disabled babies to crawl and disabled people to move on their own. Advances in superfast computers that can make billions of calculations in a second. A new kind of plastic that can withstand extremely cold temperatures in outer space. A tiny width of cable that can faultlessly transmit data at high speed for thousands of miles. All these ideas and products are being developed and refined now in New York—to create the jobs of tomorrow. And all of these were partially funded and nurtured by state programs.

It disappoints me that our state's high-tech reputation is not better known beyond our borders. Part of the explanation for that may be the fact that our leading high-tech companies are not crowded together in a single region with a convenient label, like "Silicon Valley" or "Route 128" or the "Research Triangle." In New York, high-caliber technical research takes place all across the state. A vivid reflection of this shows up in the sheer variety of sites and specialties of our thirteen Centers for Advanced Technology, or CATs. First funded in 1983, the CATs are cooperative research partnerships among universities, industry, and state government. The idea is to pool our resources—helping students connect their work with the needs of the real world and allowing companies to reap the rewards of the latest research.[18]

For example, the CAT at Cornell University in Tompkins County focuses on applications of biotechnology to agriculture, the environment, food sciences, nutrition, and health care. Researchers there are experimenting with a full range of applications, including new ways to increase crop efficiency, to produce pesticide-free foodstuffs, and even to grow better grapes for our burgeoning wine industry. The University of Rochester CAT, in Kodak's backyard near Rochester, is one of the premier sites for electronic imaging and optics research.[19]

At Syracuse University, scientists have spent years working on artificial intelligence, or AI, in pursuit of a "thinking machine" that could mimic the human brain. Though it sounds like science fiction, there is practical appeal as well.[20] At Rensselaer Polytechnic Institute in Troy, the CAT specializes in robotics. Artificial intelligence and sophisticated robotics will make our factories more efficient and will eliminate many dull or dangerous procedures, from sorting trash for recycling to repairing downed power lines, cleaning hazardous waste sites, and performing maintenance tasks deep inside nuclear power plants. Certainly some jobs may be lost to these "intelligent" machines, but there will be a tremendous need for skilled workers who can build, program, maintain, repair, and operate them.

Our CAT investment has been substantial: since 1983, $82 million in state

---

[18]The state's thirteen CATS as of September 1993 were CUNY (ultrafast photonic materials and applications), Cornell (biotechnology), NYU (digital multimedia production, publishing, and education), SUNY Albany (advanced thin films and coatings), SUNY Binghamton (integrated electronics and engineering), SUNY Stony Brook (medical biotechnology), Syracuse (computer applications and software engineering), Rochester (electronic imaging systems), Columbia (computers and information systems), Polytechnic (telecommunications), Clarkson (advanced materials processing), Alfred (advanced ceramics technology), and RPI (automation and robotics).

[19]The optics labs in Rochester provide research into many wide-ranging applications, including information processing based on light to the construction of better binoculars, microscopes, and robotics vision systems.

[20]Also at Syracuse University, CAT researchers developed an expert computer system that helps Niagara Mohawk, a central New York utility, automatically adjust its power load requirements based on changing weather conditions.

support has been matched by over $131 million from industry and has generated an additional $127 million in federal funds. CAT research has produced more than sixty-two patents and hundreds of technology licenses, as well as over fifty start-up companies.

The next step in our high-tech strategy is to make sure that once firms like these start up, they have the strength to stay up. That's where our "incubators" come in. One example sits at the midpoint of Long Island, at the State University of New York at Stony Brook. In October 1992 I paid a visit to the spotless new one-story building in a wooded corner of the campus. The paint on the walls was scarcely dry; it was a bright new place for an even brighter new venture. The event was the opening of the Long Island High Technology Incubator, a special shared headquarters facility for a group of fledgling businesses—including firms involved in biotechnology, computer software, electronics, advanced materials, and environmental testing.

Our business incubators—which are usually sponsored jointly by government and a university—are designed to give a boost to start-ups with promise. The approach is not unique to New York; indeed, there are some five hundred incubator programs throughout the United States. But there are thirty-five in New York State alone. In this case, Stony Brook and the state offer competitive rents, a broad range of research facilities, a communal answer to overhead costs, and immediate access to a network of business and financial professionals. By making it possible for these firms to share basic costs, services, and equipment while they get on their feet, the state helps them face down many of the early practical threats to their survival.

The concept is working. While the mortality rate among ordinary new businesses is high—with only one out of every ten surviving—seven out of ten "incubator" companies defy the odds. The Stony Brook incubator program began in 1985 when the state committed its first $700,000 planning grant. The following year five companies moved into an interim campus facility. Today those firms, which started with ten employees among them, now provide 275 jobs on Long Island and occupy one hundred thousand square feet of space in a high-tech research park two miles from the campus.

Many of these companies have become part of the "Biotechnology Corridor"—a miniature Silicon Valley with an organic twist. New York State is home to about two hundred biotech companies—firms whose research and products will help define the next generation of medicine.[21] Forty percent are clustered in the Biotech Corridor, drawn there by the magnetic forces of top-flight university research, the Cold Spring Harbor Laboratory (where Dr. James Watson, the DNA pioneer, holds court), and a plethora of hospital facilities—the core market for biotechnology products and services.

The work of these firms holds great promise for improving the quality of our lives. I may seem a little optimistic, but I have been spoiled by one particularly gratifying success outside the Biotech Corridor: Regeneron Pharmaceutical, a Tarrytown-based company whose research may someday serve to prolong our lives and solve the mysteries of various brain-related disorders.

Regeneron began in 1988 when Dr. Leonard Schleifer and two assistants began a series of highly sophisticated experiments—conducted out of an apartment on York Avenue in Manhattan. Like many of his colleagues in neurology, Schleifer was attempting to develop drugs to treat crippling diseases like Alzheimer's, Parkinson's, Huntington's, and Lou Gehrig's disorder (amyotrophic lateral sclerosis).[22]

To develop nerve growth proteins, the building blocks of his biogenetic treatments, Schleifer needed a proper facility and a full staff—and for that he needed capital. When he turned to the state for help, I said, "Our deal is this: We'll put up the money, but we're going to take a little piece of the action." So the state provided the seed capital—$250,000. In return for our risk, New York State now owns 66,774 shares of stock in the company. (At this writing, those shares were worth more than $1.2 million.)

Along with the loan, the company also accepted an additional responsibility: to raise another $750,000 in matching funds from private investors. It managed to raise $5 million. Part of the reason: The publicity surrounding the Regeneron stock offering opened the eyes of investors beyond our borders. In California, Amgen, another biotech giant, made a multimillion-dollar, multi-year investment in Regeneron. The Sumitomo Chemical Company added

---

[21]One of them, Curative Technologies, already has developed commercially successful products that help treat wounds for diabetics and chronically bedridden patients.

[22]Alzheimer's alone has leaped up the list of priorities, as more than four million people are now affected, most of them elderly. In addition to the cost in human suffering, Alzheimer's and other neurological disorders cost the nation billions of dollars a year. Clearly this is an area where new treatments can reduce costs.

another $10 million for the rights to market Regeneron products and technology in Japan.

As Regeneron has grown, it has found new ways to demonstrate its commitment to New York State. In June 1993 I joined corporate executives and local officials to announce a major expansion of the firm to facilities at the former Sterling Winthrop Drug complex in East Greenbush, just across the Hudson River from the Capitol. Regeneron is buying a $7 million building at the site for manufacturing, warehousing, and distribution.[23] By September of 1993 a total of 225 Regeneron employees were working diligently to develop nerve growth factors. In a year they expect to hire another 50 people, some of whom will move into a twelve-thousand-square-foot state-of-the-art research lab to continue their steady search for treatments and cures for some of humanity's most devastating neurological disorders.

The story could end right here, and any executive fortunate enough to strike such a deal would be grateful—perfectly content to wait until Regeneron comes up with its first marketable drug. But the story also has a rewarding subplot. For Schleifer's scientists to do their work, they need totally antiseptic environments—the so-called clean rooms where you see technicians working in head-to-toe white jumpsuits. One big maker of clean rooms is another New York firm, Clestra Cleanroom Technology, in Syracuse.[24] When Regeneron saw how good Clestra's clean room technology was, it placed an $800,000 order.

The kind of synergy we see with Regeneron and Clestra should become even more common as our technology programs continue to play off each other's strengths. One example: a sixty-mile stretch of countryside between Corning and Alfred that the state has formally designated the "Ceramics Corridor." (Ceramics ranges from simple materials like glass and porcelain to highly sophisticated and advanced substances that include fiber optics and

---

[23]The firm also plans to invest an additional $7 million in the building for improvements and to lease $5 million in high-tech equipment for the facility. The state provided Regeneron with a $2 million low-interest loan from the Urban Development Corporation, and as I write, an additional $5 million in assistance was approved by New York State's Job Development Authority. The company anticipates adding 250 jobs at the capital district site over the next three years and as many as 450 total jobs there in the next five years.

[24]Clestra was helped, coincidentally, with a venture capital investment of $90,000 from New York State. The state's investment in Clestra was eventually repaid with a $185,000 check, representing a 100 percent return.

other electronic products.) The corridor is anchored by a unique partnership that features an incubator and a Center for Advanced Technology—yet another important collaboration among the government, the private sector, and academia. Alfred University's College of Ceramics supplies the brainpower. Corning Incorporated, once known mainly as the maker of Steuben glass but now a leader in industrial ceramics, provides the business expertise, the R&D, and a skilled work force. The state provides the seed money—in this case $10 million, an investment we think will generate some $2 billion in related business activity by 1996.

The Ceramics Corridor already boasts an interesting mixture of firms: Corning, IBM, Westinghouse, Toshiba, Kyocera, and many smaller operations, all intent on developing new building and manufacturing materials that are stronger, lighter, less expensive, and environmentally sound.[25] Our investment in helping them is crucial for New York's future. Ceramics is now a $50-billion-a-year industry nationwide, and there are predictions that it will grow at a rate of 15 percent a year for the next two decades. With our commitment, we are staking a claim in what should be a substantial market share of this business.

CATs. Incubators. Technology corridors. Just three elements in our strategy to make sure that our state will continue to be a source of new opportunities for the next generation of New Yorkers. But while we help build on the promise of new industries, we can't afford to ignore the troubles of some traditional pillars of our economy. One of them is the defense industry.

The Cold War ended faster than any of us were prepared for. America now faces a major new challenge: how to rechannel the wealth once funneled into creating exotic instruments of destruction toward productive new investments. In the long term, this change will have a positive effect on our economy, but in the interim, reductions in the defense budget and the resulting layoffs in the defense industry will continue for some time to cause pain

---

[25]One small firm doing important work in this field is Poly-Ceramics. This story began in 1989 when I first met Kevin Hayes on a visit to Alfred University. He was then a bright and energetic student there, and I sensed he might do great things. He was earnest about pursuing an engineering career. I encouraged him to remain in New York and build his future here. Later he founded Poly-Ceramics, along with his partner, Peter Roberts. Their new company will be developing ceramic metals, composite materials, and even hydroponic growing techniques.

throughout the nation. That's certainly true in New York.

For nearly 2 percent of the entire American workforce, the Cold War may end at a cliff called unemployment. By 1998, as U.S. military spending continues to decline, 2.6 million Americans may have been pushed over the edge—200,000 in New York alone. At the federal level, until recently, the response was well intentioned but reactive—like watching the plunge and then calling an ambulance. In New York we thought we had a better idea. By intervening before the layoffs start, through sophisticated programs to retrain workers and help defense firms diversify into commercial markets, we are building a bridge to the other side of the canyon.

New York has already lost nearly one hundred thousand jobs since 1987 because of cutbacks in military spending. Today, thousands of defense engineers and technicians, accustomed to steady jobs and middle-class lives, are threatened with layoffs in a world that offers little in the way of comparable work. Communities that once drew life from military bases and defense factories face dislocation and distress. Defense firms, with advanced equipment and high-technology expertise, must find new directions or go out of business.

No doubt these losses are predictable in a free market economy where there are few guarantees when it comes to demand, but we would be foolish to allow this looming calamity to run its course. Our government has an obvious interest in helping these firms make the transition, partially or entirely, to commercial production. Defense workers who have lost their jobs should be eased into other activities that will make good use of their talent and training, compensate them fairly, and strengthen this nation's ability to compete globally. If we fail to act, the dramatic change in Pentagon spending habits will translate into further pink slips and shutdowns across New York and America.

Once again, our motivation here should be a mixture of compassion and common sense. Obviously, business bankruptcies and unemployment are painful for our citizens. They are also costly for the state—in this case costly enough to counter any laissez-faire argument for letting "industrial Darwinism" take its course. But just as important, if New York and the nation are to stay competitive in the global marketplace, we need healthy, forward-looking companies and an intelligent, adaptable, highly trained workforce. What better source than our home-grown defense contractors looking for a new role in the world?

State government can be of particular service to many of those who are most vulnerable: small- and medium-size defense firms that often lack the resources and in-house expertise to transform themselves into players on the open market—or to survive in the meantime.

To help our defense firms and their employees make the transition to peacetime production, in 1991 we established our Defense Diversification Program (DDP), an umbrella initiative embracing a wide range of services for defense contractors seeking to convert all or part of their operations to peacetime purposes. Through DDP, we start by helping each firm create a comprehensive, custom-made strategy for converting or diversifying its business. Then, depending on their individual requirements, companies can choose from a menu of DDP services—whether they need to improve productivity, retrain workers, buy new equipment, adapt to new production techniques or technologies, penetrate overseas markets, adopt commercial business practices, or learn to market themselves.

One example of our success is Dayton T. Brown, Inc., a Bohemia, L.I.–based firm whose 330 employees provide the military with testing and engineering services and specialty test products. The company recently received assistance from New York State to develop a strategy for diversifying its operations, including six months of training in statistical process control and total quality management skills. The training project helped Dayton T. Brown achieve two vital "firsts" in 1992: the firm received its first export order—a $375,000 request for dual-use equipment—and its first major nondefense contract. The contract not only helped Dayton T. Brown hold its own, it allowed the firm to create ten new jobs when virtually all its competitors were shrinking. Brown, which takes pride in the way it tested the strength of materials on submarines, can now take pride in the way it tests the durability of beverage containers.

New York State also provided crucial financial and technical assistance so that Hazeltine Corporation could build new research facilities and secure the training needed to implement total quality management and adapt to a new production system. In this case, the training costs, borne largely by Hazeltine, were more than $500,000—but in the first year the investment saved the company more than $5 million in reduced defects and waste. Today, Hazeltine continues to make steady progress toward the goal it set at the beginning of the project: reducing defects by at least 20 percent each quarter. The result will be a business armed to do battle in exciting but unforgiving global markets.[26] Hazeltine is also diversifying, attempting to shed its image as solely a defense-based company. While it specializes in advanced radar technology for military use, it is now developing technology that will broadcast news programming on commercial airliners.

While not every company can be saved, our results have been impressive, especially given the modest size of our investment: so far we have provided assistance to more than one thousand firms and fifteen thousand workers through our DDP and skills training programs.[27] Despite our success—and because of it—the demand for our DDP services continues to outweigh our resources, and the same is true across the country. Ironically, many states, including my own, were unable to devote as many resources as we would have liked to worker training and industrial modernization programs—because the recession devastated our state budgets.

We need federal cooperation. Unquestionably, the fastest, most effective mechanism for preventing the personal and societal catastrophe of massive layoffs and business shutdowns will be a strong partnership between the states and the federal government—a program that matches the nation's dollars with the states' expertise and existing agencies, a program geared to retraining people before they lose their jobs and to saving companies before they lose their footing. From coast to coast, the states are, I'm certain, ready to help.

---

[26]The state also helped Hazeltine finance a new research facility.

[27]One of our best state programs to improve workers skills and competitiveness is the Industrial Effectiveness Program (IEP), which has helped more than 450 manufacturing companies improve quality, productivity, and competitiveness. IEP's potential customers are the almost thirty thousand companies and one million people employed in New York's manufacturing industries. By helping them to improve their productivity, profitability, and competitiveness, IEP and other economic development programs are helping to modernize our state's industrial base and preserve a high living standard for our citizens. One example is Standard Motor Products in Long Island City, Queens, which makes automobile parts. With 650 employees, Standard is one of the larger manufacturing companies in New York City. Recently, increased competitive pressure on the factory was coming from out-of-state competitors and even from the firm's other production operations in Kansas, Puerto Rico, and Hong Kong. Without major changes, the Queens employer could easily have been forced to shut down and transfer production jobs out of our state. IEP experts went to Queens and concluded that the company could save money by better managing its inventory. With the endorsement of Local 365 of the United Automobile Workers, the firm launched a program to reduce inventory by introducing "just in time" management techniques throughout the plant. Standard put a new emphasis on training, developing the skills of executives, middle managers, supervisors, and floor workers. The labor-management teams worked together over an eight-month period to save the firm several hundred thousand dollars.

At the moment, our skills training efforts and similar programs in other states are distinguished from the federal approach to worker assistance by a focus on existing workers. On the whole, federal support is available only after the pink slips arrive—when people begin to seek unemployment or federal funds for dislocated workers. Unfortunately, only 5–10 percent of those eligible for such federal assistance are receiving it. And the forty states that have skills training programs for existing workers spend on them, altogether, only about a quarter of what the federal government pours into aid for dislocated workers. This is not to suggest that funds be shifted from programs serving dislocated workers or that those programs are adequately funded now. But we do believe that new monies could productively be spent on preventive measures: helping companies stay in business and helping workers keep their jobs.

By establishing a partnership with the states, the federal government could make a difference for the millions of Americans whose livelihood is threatened by the otherwise welcome miracle of superpower peace. Such a partnership offers other practical advantages as well: by building on existing state programs and staff, it eliminates the need to wait for the conclusions of routine demonstration projects and makes it possible to expand federal assistance without expanding the federal bureaucracy. In this urgent moment, one thing the managers of small- and medium-size defense firms do not have is the time to track down answers in the endless corridors of Washington.

Both President Clinton and several congressional panels have cited New York State's DDP and skills training programs as so well conceived—so efficient, so useful—that they could serve as models, both for other states and for future federal efforts.[28] The same might be said of many other state-level programs, such as Florida's Sunshine State Skills Program or California's Employment Training Panel. Today, U.S. Secretary of Labor Robert Reich and others in Washington have the opportunity to turn our old-fashioned, reactive federal training programs into the proactive, preventive, state-federal services the country so desperately needs—for both momentary rescue and long-term redemption. I am confident they will seize the chance to help.

---

[28]In July of 1993, the U.S. Commerce Department awarded a $4.5 million defense diversification grant to New York, the largest federal grant ever awarded for such purposes.

Preparing New York's Changing Workforce for the Twenty-first Century

With so many Americans out of work—from the highly skilled, former employees of our defense contractors to the desperate kids on our street corners who have never had a job—it's hard to believe that the country could face a labor shortage any time soon.

But it's true. By the year 2000 we'll need between 450,000 and 750,000 more chemists, biologists, physicists, and engineers than we will have. At the same time, upward of one million American students drop out of school every year—the equivalent of the entire state of Rhode Island. And private employers have to spend billions each year on remedial training, trying to impart the basic skills they wish they could have hired.

If current trends continue, we will simply not have the workforce we'll need to sustain American living standards in the next century. Those who have studied the composition and compensation of the American workforce know that the United States is rapidly becoming more and more a nation of two cities—separated increasingly by the quality of their educational and economic opportunities. We face profound problems that undermine our economic strength and our future—problems we have barely begun to address.

Today in America we are making do with an educational system designed to serve a low-skill, high-wage manufacturing economy that has nearly evaporated. To sustain a first-string position in the global marketplace, we will need to invest more—and more intelligently—in educating and training our people for the world they actually live in.

The persistent success of our foreign competitors should make that clear. The workers who come out of high schools in Germany, Japan, France, and Sweden are better trained and more highly skilled than ours. Because these workers can handle more responsibility and execute more than one role, it's easier for our competitors to streamline operations. They need many fewer supervisors, fewer quality checkers, fewer production schedulers, fewer maintenance workers—so they become more efficient, more flexible, and better able to make quality products in a changing world. Because they are more productive, they can set lower prices and sell more products. Because they can sell more, they can expand. Because they can expand, they can employ more people, even while increasing wages—thus creating new jobs while raising the standard of living for all their people.[29]

There is no magic to their formula. Much of the success of foreign education can be traced to logic so simple, it's embarrassing that America has failed to apply its lessons before now. The Japanese send their children to school for 240 days a year; the Germans, 220. We send ours to school for 180 days. This means the typical Japanese child will have received one-third more classroom time than the typical American child—or *four more years*—from kindergarten to the end of high school.

Here at home, some New York companies such as Xerox, Eastman Kodak, and Corning have recognized the obvious value of a well-educated workforce and are investing substantially in training while encouraging the public education system to do more and better at the same time. We need to encourage other American firms to follow their lead—increasing the quantity and quality of worker training, and expanding the role working people can play in designing better ways to get things done.

But we also need to remember that with all the workplace reforms in the world, America will continue to languish, dead in the water economically, unless government can repair the aging hull of our educational system.

Perhaps no other state puts as high a priority on education as we do in New York. We regard quality education as a long-term investment to develop our most precious resource: our people. In New York we have some of the finest public schools in the country. Elementary and secondary school students consistently earn high honors for educational achievement. But we also have hovels called schoolhouses, where students and teachers are in desperate need of the most basic assistance. In effect, today we have a two-tier educational system; one is good to excellent, the other is mediocre to poor. The great gulf in income and opportunity that widened in the 1980s between economic classes has also carried over to the school system.

Today, New York's public schools, the primary tool for educating our students and democratizing our society, serve 85 percent of our children, many of whom come from poor and lower-income families. Regrettably, too many of the second-tier public schools are not educating or preparing their students as well as we need. The severity of the problem is now pushing

---

[29]*America's Choice: High Skills or Low Wages? The Report of the Commission on the Skills of the American Workforce*, National Center on Education and the Economy, June 1990.

parents, educators, and lawmakers to ask a radical question: Should we launch a new effort to rebuild these public schools on their existing foundation—or is it time to quit pretending that we can turn a propeller plane into a space shuttle. Is it time to start again from scratch?

Much of this debate revolves around the idea of applying free-market principles to the world of education, allowing parents to choose where their children go to school and thereby forcing schools to compete for students. In the public schools, within school districts, I believe "school choice" can be an intelligent idea if applied equitably, so that it increases educational opportunity for all students, not just those with the most motivated parents or easiest access to private transportation. We must also design our programs so that "choice" does not lead to schools segregated by race or class.

Through the use of incentives instead of mandates, New York State has freed local districts to proceed with school choice programs at a pace appropriate to their needs. One result: We have actually been able to use the choice mechanism—especially in the form of "magnet" schools—to combat racially imbalanced institutions. For example, when the Buffalo schools faced court-ordered desegregation more than a decade ago, they decided against forcing the children to be bussed to schools they might not want to attend and opted instead to allow parents to choose from an array of intriguing "theme" schools, ranging from highly traditional institutions, with students in uniforms, to schools linked with an important local institution, like the Buffalo Zoo or Museum of Science. It worked: middle-class white families who had been abandoning the city proper because of the poor quality of the schools suddenly had a reason to stay. Other districts, in Albany, Yonkers, and East Harlem, have had similar success. An experimental magnet school in Rochester was lauded publicly by President Clinton as a model for the nation. Recognizing the promise of these programs, we have worked hard to increase their funding. When I came to office, there was no state support for the magnet school program. Today we provide more than $85 million across fifteen districts.

New York is already proof that public school choice can work, and we intend to do more of it; but, increasingly, the argument is shifting to the idea that "choice" should include private schools as well, which would then be subsidized with public funds according to how many students they could attract.

The Empire State is blessed with some of the finest private elementary and secondary schools in the nation, and we are grateful for the role these sectarian and nonsectarian schools play in educating our children. We support private schools as much as any state and will continue to support them in every way that is constitutionally permitted, including funding for textbooks, library materials, computer software, testing, and transportation. However, I believe subsidizing private education with further large injections of public money would not be good policy, especially in these already austere times.

Even apart from the significant constitutional question it would raise, I believe such a plan would cream away a small fraction of the most able students from the public schools, while leaving the vast majority—many of them the most disadvantaged—behind, with no new commitment to help them. At the same time, it would increase the tax burden on the residents of those districts whose schools are most troubled, since they would lose whatever state aid was channeled into vouchers for those children headed for private institutions.

Those who advocate a voucher system argue that the best way to improve the quality of education is for public schools to compete directly with private ones for support. But that suggests there would, in fact, be competitive schools competing on an even playing field. Would non-public schools be required to accept *all* applicants if there were room, regardless of academic or disciplinary history, as most public schools must today? Would non-public schools have to accept children defined as having "handicapping conditions"? Would the value of vouchers increase for those students who are harder to educate? Are non-public schools prepared to accept all state regulations and court decisions against discrimination?

In addition, there could be unanticipated new costs to the state if a voucher system were implemented. For such a system to work, parents would have to be given information about the quality of education being provided by every school. That would entail creating a new state-level bureaucracy to administer a voucher plan, to oversee how local tax dollars are spent, to monitor accountability and performance, to make sure that profiteering schools did not "defraud" educational "consumers." If government issued vouchers for some students to attend non-public schools, it would be compelled to extend vouchers to middle-income and wealthy families. And how could the state avoid granting similar subsidies to all the children already enrolled in private schools?

Ultimately, instead of encouraging benign pluralism, issuing private school vouchers would lead to malignant neglect of the public schools.

Behind the argument for private school choice is the premise that we have done everything we could to reform and improve public schools, and it hasn't worked. I reject this assumption on two counts: first, because we have certainly not exhausted every promising avenue of reform; and second, because much of what we have tried is working well—though its effects are not yet reaching enough students.

How can we extend the benefits across New York's public schools? To start with, we must continue to implement the ideas spelled out in "A New Compact for Learning," a comprehensive strategy for reforming New York's public schools adopted by the New York State Board of Regents in 1991. The compact specifies reforms like these: using incentives to encourage greater accountability and better performance from our schools; relaxing certain state mandates so that teachers, parents, and administrators can work together to shape programs to achieve better results for their children; developing new ways to measure how well students are performing; and continuing to train and develop public school teachers.

After these structural questions, the second issue is sustaining proper funding. Between 1983 and 1993—a period that featured two national recessions—we raised state aid to public education from $4.6 billion to $8.8 billion, an increase of 91 percent, more than twice the cumulative inflation rate for that period.[30] Today, state aid to education accounts for nearly one of every three dollars we spend from our General Fund.[31] We've increased state funding for prekindergarten education, put nearly two hundred thousand computers in the classrooms, and increased teacher salaries to attract and retain the best teachers possible. We have also pushed for a renewed emphasis on the fundamentals—reading, writing, arithmetic, science, analytical thinking, and problem solving. Test scores and attendance are both up, and by 1990–91 we had brought the statewide dropout rate to a twenty-year low.[32]

---

[30] Over the same period, New York's public school population, grades K–12, stayed relatively constant at 2.6 million students.

[31] In 1991–92, New York ranked third in the nation behind New Jersey and Alaska in total spending per pupil, averaging $8,658 per student in grades K–12, nearly $3,200 above the national average.

[32] Results in standard tests given in grades three through six in reading, writing, and math have shown improvement, with students scoring up to twelve percentage points above the state reference point. Average daily attendance rates have also increased by a full percentage point from 1982–83 to 1990–91. In 1991, the latest year for which we have data, 91 percent of children grades K–12 were attending class on any given school day.

But for all this progress, it's clear we must find a way to do more.

In the past, our most glaring failure was that children living in poorer districts did not receive the same educational funding as their peers in wealthier districts. This has changed in New York City. At $7,512 per pupil, the $7 billion New York City spends on its 972,146 students is higher than it has been. In fact, if New York City were a state, it would rank fourth in overall school spending per student (after Alaska, New Jersey, and New York State). But New York City schools still don't receive as much funding as other middle-class suburban districts, and a greater portion of the per pupil figure goes to administration and overhead—not in the classroom, per se. Clearly, we need to do better.

It should come as no surprise that many New York City schools are overcrowded. Some have been forced to convert bathrooms, gymnasiums, hallways, and closets into classrooms. In some schools children go without textbooks and without adequate heat during the winter. In poor rural areas with small, widely separated schools, the cost of busing alone is staggering. For our smallest rural schools, it is a struggle just to provide the basics—a gym, a principal, a library, support staff—and at the same time to live up to the regents' mandated curriculum.

Faced with these conditions, the legislature and I created a special temporary commission in 1988 to assess the rules for apportioning state school aid. In a year's time, the Salerno Commission—named for its chairman, Frederick V. Salerno, the former president and CEO of New York Telephone—reported the troubling details of a problem we already understood in principle: that the needs of poor students across the state were being neglected. Every year since, I have pushed the legislature to pass the Salerno recommendations into law; until 1993 the state senate had steadily resisted. But in the spring of that year, we began to see some movement toward the light. The legislature simplified the school aid formula, put a greater emphasis on at-risk students, and agreed to allocate more state education aid to some poorer school districts.

I'm confident that the next few years will produce more victories on the road to fairness, perhaps spurred by legal decisions that conclude the fundamental lack of fairness in school system funding violates our state constitution. At the same time, to make sure that all our education dollars are serving the needs of children, we need dramatic new efforts to root out waste and abuse.

In 1993, spurred by reports of egregious overspending on executive salaries in certain school districts, I decided to use the strongest investigative device available to a governor—a Moreland Act Commission[33]—to conduct a comprehensive review of the education system in New York State. With a special focus on local spending patterns, the commission was instructed to hold public hearings to unearth specific problems in the system; consult with the labor and business communities to determine the skills the marketplace will demand in the future; and review financial controls and management practices to determine exactly how our educational dollars are being spent. At the same time, I have asked commission members how to replicate those parts of the system that are operating successfully.

Regrettably, it seems clear that in the end, even our best efforts at the state level will not do enough to revitalize our educational system without more resources from the national treasury. A longer school year costs money. Computers and science labs do, too. So does rebuilding aging facilities. Magnet schools cost money. So do Head Start and Pre-K. It takes money to hire more teachers or to run special programs for children with fetal drug and alcohol syndrome. And Liberty Scholarships would certainly cost money, too.[34]

Anyone who wants to see significant money well spent ought to visit the new $150 million home of Stuyvesant High School, which New York State helped to build on the banks of the Hudson in lower Manhattan. Since Stuyvesant first opened its doors in 1904, it has been geared to serving the city's intellectually gifted students. In the words of the day, the Stuyvesant mission has always been to ensure that "every boy, no matter how poor his parents may be, may have opportunities equal to those given the sons of the rich." (Girls have been admitted since 1969.)

Providing an intensive science and mathematics curriculum for teenagers from every borough of New York City, Stuyvesant is widely recognized, along

---

[33]The Moreland Act Commission was created in 1907 and revised several times since then. It gives the governor broad investigative powers, enabling him to probe the administrations of the various departments under his command—and also those not directly under his command, such as education. It also allows him to appoint a special commissioner in cases where malfeasance is suspected.

[34]The Liberty Scholarships program, which I announced in 1987, would guarantee that every young person who qualifies for college—every child, no matter how poor—will be afforded the means to earn a degree. The Liberty Partnerships program would provide counseling, mentoring, and other support services for students when they are still at the junior high school and high school levels. Regrettably, because of fiscal realities, we have had to defer this dream in New York for the time being. But the idea is one we should work to realize as we pursue our agenda for the twenty-first century.

with Bronx Science and Brooklyn Tech, as one of the best schools in the United States. It has led the nation in the number of National Merit Scholars it produces. More graduates of Stuyvesant have earned Ph.D.'s than those of any other secondary school in the nation.

New York chose to build this temple to the education of such high-caliber students because the old Stuyvesant facility at Fifteenth Street and First Avenue had deteriorated badly. In 1987 the Battery Park City Authority, using New York City funds, began to build the new school. Less than five years later, in September 1992, the new Stuyvesant High School opened its doors—the first public high school built in New York City in over ten years.

Even from the entrance, with its polished gray and black granite columns and its Latin inscription—*Pro Scientia Atque Sapientia*[35]—you can tell that the school takes its mission seriously. As you pass through the quiet, secure, graffiti-free hallways, you enter a world we should seek to replicate for all our public schools. Accommodating nearly three thousand students, the ten-story academic tower houses seventy-seven classrooms and laboratories, an 866-seat auditorium, a swimming pool, two gymnasiums, art and dance studios, a dining hall, and a nine-thousand-square-foot library stacked with forty thousand volumes and with computer terminals that connect students directly to the New York Public Library.[36] The quality of these facilities speaks eloquently to the students about our respect for their work and their ideas—a priceless boost for them in the uncertain atmosphere of adolescence.

In May 1993 I spoke to some five hundred Stuyvesant students in the new auditorium and to the rest of the student body through a closed-circuit television system that carried my remarks to every classroom in the building. I explained why New York was willing to support such an expensive investment in their future. Quite simply, New York *needs* them to realize their full talents. We need them to develop so that one day they can return some of that strength to the place that helped them grow.

I asked the students at Stuyvesant never to forget what New York's public

---

[35]"For Science and Knowledge"

[36]The school also features computer rooms, photography labs, ceramics and robotics shops, and a weight room. Stuyvesant publishes twenty different magazines and fields twenty-three separate athletic teams. It boasts a symphonic orchestra, symphonic band, chamber music group, stage band, and gospel and Renaissance choir. Its students participate in more than eighty clubs, including astronomy, chess, computers, cycling, debate, Frisbee, German, golf, hockey, martial arts, Ping-Pong, rockets, skiing, and world affairs.

education system was making available to them. I reminded them that in a world on the verge of quantum advances in science, information technology, and medicine, no one would be better equipped than they to help all those who may never have the opportunity to attend a school like Stuyvesant. I asked them to remember, once they began to achieve professional success, that the money they would give back to the state through taxes would help us afford new schools, smaller classes, better-paid teachers, and more modern and dignified places to learn for all of New York's children.[37] And I beseeched them to succeed—because our future depends on it.

For the students at Stuyvesant and other prestigious schools around the state, attending college and earning a four-year degree is a strong probability. Through both public and private channels, we are serving this elite group rather well. But the 70 percent of high school students who will never earn a four-year college degree deserve more of our attention.

By the year 2000, 70 percent of the jobs in America won't require a college education—but they *will* require technical skills that too few of our students now possess.[38] As old-fashioned corporate hierarchies give ground to a self-directed workforce, our young people will need to be comfortable working in teams, solving complex problems, and making decisions that support larger strategies. If we want something better for our children than the dead-end jobs of the future, we owe them an educational system that will stimulate them to reach the highest standards they can.

The solution? Bringing the classroom closer to the workplace—so students are exposed to the challenges and standards of the working world while they still have time to prepare and so employers can begin to choose and train the workers they'll need in the future.

One step is to encourage apprenticeship programs for young people who leave school early. In the construction industry, for example, most training comes through apprenticeship to a master in the trade. Why can't we replicate that relationship in industries all across the country? In the former West

---

[37]New York State is also helping New York City rebuild the physical facilities of its public school system through a special School Construction Authority. The authority has issued $500 million in Municipal Assistance Corporation (MAC) monies to improve the learning environment of other students in other districts.

[38]*America's Choice: High Skills or Low Wages? The Report of the Commission on the Skills of the American Workforce,* National Center on Education and the Economy, June 1990.

Germany, apprenticeships have been the basis of industrial success, measured in a massive trade surplus in high-quality manufactured goods. Plant workers there are the best compensated in the world.[39]

But to build a better bridge between school and work, we will need to do so from the school side, too. Starting in 1995, we expect to put in place a dramatic new program called Career Pathways. The program will reorient our school system to a new milestone besides graduation: a set of specific proficiencies in language, reading, math, science, and certain workplace skills that students should be able to attain by about age sixteen. Having mastered these skills, they will find it much easier to get their foot in the door of a prospective employer. At the same time, the final two years of high school will be redesigned to help students prepare for the careers they have in mind. As they work toward their diplomas, they will participate in a flexible program combining academics, work skills training, and actual workplace experience.[40]

By offering a challenging, bread-and-butter answer to the familiar adolescent lament that schoolwork is pointless, Career Pathways should help keep more students in school longer—long enough to be well prepared for the work they choose to do, whether that requires a college degree or not.

Until almost the middle of this century in America, college was an opportunity largely restricted to the very few families who could afford it. Scholarships were long shots and loans virtually unavailable. But with the end of World War II and the passage of the GI Bill of Rights came an explosion in enrollment, a flood of students eager to seize the unprecedented opportunity their government offered. This resulted in a dramatic democratization of the whole idea of higher education—and a highly motivated generation of engineers, scientists, artists, accountants, technicians, teachers, and business leaders from across the social spectrum who would, together, transform our economy.

With the GI Bill, a college education joined a house of one's own as a crucial ingredient in the American Dream. With that stimulus, higher educa-

---

[39]According to federal data, in 1992 the German factory worker had the highest level of wages and benefits in the industrialized world. "International Comparisons of Hourly Compensation Costs for Production Workers in Manufacturing," Report 844, U.S. Department of Labor, April 1993.

[40]The Department of Labor also holds annual career and education expositions. These expos, held all over New York, show teenagers and young adults the wide range of career choices available. Young people meet with potential employers, receive career information, and are given advice on financing a college or technical education.

tion naturally flourished and diversified—and nowhere more fruitfully than in New York. Today, few other states—indeed, few other nations—can match our system of higher education, the variety and quality of our institutions, the range and learning of our faculty. In education as in our economic system, and our cultural inheritance, New York's strength dwells in our diversity. We rely not on either the private or public sector alone, but on a balance between institutions public and private, religious and secular, and between small, specialized colleges and large, comprehensive universities.

With this array of alternatives, we use our resources to pursue two complementary goals: helping to sustain the strength of New York's private institutions and, at the same time, developing superb public university systems.

Statewide, we have nearly one million students pursuing degrees at more than 250 colleges and universities. Forty percent of all college students in the state enroll in independent institutions—nearly twice the national average. The best of our private institutions rank among the best in the world: schools like Ezra Cornell's land-grant legacy, Cornell University in Ithaca, or Columbia University, dominating the northern end of Manhattan. The University of Rochester and the Rochester Institute of Technology (RIT) in Monroe County, and the Rensselaer Polytechnic Institute (RPI) in Troy offer three of the most prestigious engineering programs in the nation. Syracuse University is home to one of the finest communications schools. Vassar College, a few miles from the Hudson River in Poughkeepsie, and Colgate University, couched in the tranquil hills of Madison County, excel in the liberal arts. New York University, the nation's largest private university, is blessed with internationally renowned research and professional schools as well as a fine undergraduate college that offers the added education of living in the heart of the Big Apple. Founded as religious institutions, Yeshiva, Fordham, St. John's, Manhattan College, Canisius, Le Moyne, St. Francis, Siena, Concordia, Houghton, and several others have trained hundreds who would later join the state's political leadership.

Our appetite for academic prestige might be satisfied by New York's network of private colleges and universities—but not our desire for democratic access. Fortunately New York also enjoys a magnificent system of *public* higher education, in New York City and across the state.

No system of higher education has ever done more to bring aspiring peoples into the mainstream of American professional life than the City University of New York (CUNY). Astonishingly, more of the nation's CEOs graduated from the City College of New York than any other college. By combining academic distinction with low costs, urban campuses, and a tradition of tolerance and respect for people from every nation, race, and creed, CUNY has opened doors to thousands who might not have succeeded elsewhere.[41] In effect, it has served as a kind of educational Ellis Island—a gateway to the opportunity of America.

The Free Academy, which began in 1847, changed its name to City College in 1929, and it eventually became the City University in 1961. From the late 1920s on, college after college emerged on the scene—senior colleges, community colleges, professional schools—peppered throughout the five boroughs of New York City.[42] Today, City University receives almost $883 million in state support and serves over two hundred thousand students. CUNY institutions, and especially CUNY's community colleges, help tens of thousands of New Yorkers improve the hand they've been dealt—from a newly appointed supervisor who wants to master the skills of managing people, to an unemployed laborer gearing up to start his own small business, to a woman preparing to rejoin the workforce after several years at home with her children.

The community college operates as a kind of custom tailor, adjusting its curriculum to regional, cultural, and occupational needs. For example, LaGuardia Community College routinely seeks counselors who speak Greek because its Long Island City turf is a traditional point of arrival for Greek immigrants to America. Kingsborough Community College employs professors of history and politics fluent in Yiddish and Russian to help reach the scores of Russian Jewish immigrants who have settled in the neighborhood called Brighton Beach.

By dissolving the barriers of language for these newcomers, CUNY is honoring the original impulse behind public higher education in New York: the desire for equal access to opportunity. In the late 1940s the state realized that it was important to expand the capacity of its public colleges to ensure access for underrepresented groups, whether they happened to be Jewish, "Negro," or Catholic—and certainly those who happened to be poor. Combined with the sudden return of thousands of college-hungry GIs, this led to

---

[41]Until the 1976–1977 academic year, attendance at CUNY was tuition free. Even today tuition remains remarkably low.

[42]In 1983 the School of Law at Queens College welcomed its first class.

the creation of the State University of New York (SUNY).

Founded in 1948 from a loose confederation of teachers' colleges and assorted institutions, SUNY is actually the newest state system in the continental United States. Starting from a full-time enrollment of just over twenty-five thousand in 1949, SUNY has transformed itself into the largest, most comprehensive state university system in the country, serving four hundred thousand students with sixty-four campuses and an annual budget of more than $3.1 billion.

Though SUNY was designed to serve as many students as could qualify, it would never have sustained such success if it were little more than an educational last resort. In fact, understanding that the promise of access would be hollow without a guarantee of excellence, SUNY has pushed relentlessly to achieve both goals at once. One annual survey ranked five members of the SUNY system among the nation's top fifty "best buys" in colleges and universities: Albany, Geneseo, Stony Brook, Binghamton, and Buffalo.[43] For SUNY Buffalo, the honor came for the fourth consecutive year.

To keep open the doors of New York's colleges and universities to as many students as possible, the state maintains the most generous financial aid program in the country. Through our Tuition Assistance Program (TAP), the state provided an estimated $614 million in fiscal year 1993–94, to help more than a quarter million students from New York attend college and graduate school. That's the most financial aid awarded by any state, and it's about as much as the sum of grants and scholarships provided by the next three largest states *combined.* Because of the help we provide, nearly one-third of our full-time undergraduates attending classes in our state and city universities have all but $75 of their tuition paid in full.

Over the course of the 1980s, as costs and demand continued to rise, New York doubled the resources devoted to SUNY and CUNY.[44] In infrastructure improvements alone, we invested more than $2.1 billion in SUNY and $1.3 billion in CUNY.[45] But, more recently, under the steady pressure of recession we have been obliged to reduce the state's higher education budget. SUNY and CUNY have, in turn, been forced to cut back on some programs

---

[43]*Money Guide: Best College Buys,* September 1993.

[44]New York State funding for postsecondary education rose from approximately $1.5 billion in fiscal year 1980–81 to $3.1 billion in fiscal year 1992–93.

[45]These were the capital projects appropriations between fiscal years 1983–84 and 1993–94.

and to raise tuition—though it is still lower than at comparable four-year public universities in our neighboring states.

Any rise in tuition inevitably endangers access for at least some students, but we're proud that we are winning the battle on the whole. As the economy recovers, ensuring SUNY's and CUNY's future health will be a major priority.

Though the recession still pinches our immediate ambitions for our public universities, we have not let it cramp our commitment to strategic planning. Beyond the fresh horizons that a college education opens for individual students, our colleges' greatest service may be in training New York's future workforce. Through the SUNY 2000 plan and CUNY's Workforce Development Initiative, we are already working to make sure that we will have all the talent we need in crucial fields like environmental conservation, social services, and health care. And to help us maintain our leadership in high tech, we established HEAT, the Higher Education Applied Technology program, which supports advanced research at eleven public and independent universities.

It shouldn't be too much to ask for—a government that can make strategic decisions in advance, geared to respond to changing realities. But the old habits and hierarchies and procedures and precedents infect every bureaucracy on earth, no matter how well intentioned. Without proper treatment, they produce a certain listlessness in the patient—though not a loss of appetite for funds.

To help our public universities make the best, most efficient use of tax dollars, we must continue the movement I began a few years ago to give SUNY and CUNY the power and flexibility to make more of their own decisions. And we need to work harder still to extend that principle across the spectrum of government operations.

Other Strengths to Build On

I am a long way from understanding all the science behind New York's advanced technologies and all the languages through which students converse with computers, but their economic potential is clear. Dozens of drawing-board ideas in the last two decades—the personal computer, the compact disc, the fax machine, the cellular phone—have transformed the way we work and live. At the same time, we shouldn't mistake the extraordinary powers of new science for the whole answer to our economic future.

In fact, though even most New Yorkers might find it hard to believe, two of our state's most significant industries, now and in the future, are two of its oldest and most familiar: tourism and agriculture. And though each may appear to be a realm that can "take care of itself," we know that we cannot afford to take either one for granted.

Like all my fellow governors, I have a full-time, year-round responsibility to be an unabashed pitchman for our state. It's part of my job to get people to come to New York. If I can't persuade you to move here, then I'll settle for getting you here for a vacation. I'm constantly promoting New York as one of the world's great tourist destinations, and it's frankly a pleasure. But it is also very serious business: ninety *million* people travel through New York State annually. At $20 billion a year, the travel and tourism industry creates jobs for nearly seven hundred thousand New Yorkers.

Since the recession that began in 1989, tourism has suffered along with the rest of our economy. New York is the same gorgeous, vibrant, varied place it always has been, but fewer people have the money and leisure time to spend in our restaurants, museums, and theaters, in our hotels, country inns, and campsites.

The decline in revenues and attendance reminds us of the practical power of advertising. In recent years, sustained pressure on the state budget has left us slim resources for promoting the excitement and charm of New York, and the industry has sustained extra pain as a result, from the hoteliers in the Catskills to the carriage drivers in Central Park. State tourism budgets peaked in 1987 at $15.8 million. By 1991–92, we had been forced to slash the amount to $3 million. Frankly, we made a mistake. We should have found a way to keep the advertising high when we need it most. We are beginning to compensate: this year we earmarked $7 million, and next year I hope to do better still.

With the funding in place, the hard part is choosing what to feature. The Empire State offers more to see and do than most countries, from the craggy rocks at Montauk Point on the eastern tip of Long Island to the awesome, swirling curtain of Niagara Falls. In between lies Manhattan, where the twin towers of the World Trade Center stand watch over New York Harbor, the majesty of the Hudson River Palisades, and the sweetly scented firs of the splendidly wild North Country.[46] We can't lay claim to the best snow or the highest peaks in the country, but we have more downhill ski trails than any state in the Union. We do not have a longer coastline than more widely known resorts in other countries, but many thousands of European tourists flock to our shores every summer because our beaches rival the beauty of the Riviera. I've seen both, and while I cannot claim objectivity, my preference is the Long Island beaches.

And, of course, there is the phenomenon that is New York City, the Big Apple. As the symbol of America's sophistication and her diversity, it is perhaps the most traveled city in the world. If all New York City had to offer were the inexhaustible variety of its nightlife and neighborhoods, its restaurants and retail stores, it would still be a magnet for people from all over the world. But it also remains the capital of American culture, a fact that is as important to our economy as it is to our soul.

A Vibrant Culture That Is Good for Business

In fact, art and culture simmer and sizzle everywhere in New York State. Once again, the magic is in our diversity: from the great institutions like Carnegie Hall, Lincoln Center, the Metropolitan Opera, the New York Philharmonic, the New York City Ballet, and the Metropolitan Museum of Art to the most defiant individual artists in every field. There are world-famous collections like the Guggenheim, the Whitney, and the Museum of Modern Art and their more retiring—but abundant—upstate counterparts like the Albright-Knox Gallery in Buffalo, the Memorial Art Gallery in Rochester, and the Everson in Syracuse. And so much more. The affluent Establishment auction houses. The sleek downtown galleries and impromptu sidewalk displays. The comforting dazzle of Broadway and the dazzling challenge of places like the Public Theater. The inspired fashion designers on Seventh Avenue and the designers of their inspiration on Avenue C. The feature films shot in front of our inimitable urban backdrops or in our Hollywood-scale sound stage in Astoria, Queens, and the experimental pictures shot by film

---

[46]See appendix A for a regional description of each part of the state.

students all over the city. Ghosts of giants, shadows of the living masters, and hints of the genius yet to come—at SUNY Purchase and NYU, at Juilliard and Cooper Union, at the Eastman School of Music and the Fashion Institute of Technology, and on the city streets.

All this intensity and talent seem natural to New York. But as governor I know that the arts are in an unusual position: they are essential to our economy, creating tens of thousands of jobs for New Yorkers and drawing millions of people here as spectators, students, and fans. But they also need government's help to survive.

Despite our state's immense cultural inheritance, we were not the first to decide that the arts deserved public support. That distinction goes to Utah, which came up with the idea of an arts council in 1899. Other states like Virginia and North Carolina financed museums, theaters, and touring symphony groups long before the idea was applied here. Cities, too, were supporting the arts before most states chose to. New York, however, was the first state to make a large, strategic commitment to the arts, realizing that the vibrancy of our artistic and cultural institutions was essential to our strength as a people, to our quality of life, and to our long-term economic prospects.

Of all New York's governors, perhaps Nelson Rockefeller had the most intense personal interest in the fine arts, and his recognition that New York State could and should take an active role in nurturing them became one of his enduring legacies. In 1960 Governor Rockefeller freed up the first funding—$50,000—to begin a temporary state commission on the arts. Five years later the legislature made the New York State Council on the Arts a permanent fixture, budgeting nearly three-quarters of a million dollars for its annual operation.[47]

The state's commitment started modestly, but it climbed steadily. In the 1970–71 fiscal year, New York's arts budget exceeded that of the federally funded National Endowment for the Arts. In 1989–90 we reached our high-water mark: $55 million. Then, once again, we felt the chill of recession. How could we maintain our commitment to the arts when more and more of our people needed state assistance just to get by? State council chairwoman Kitty Carlisle Hart, who has served with stubborn exuberance and indefatigable

---

[47]The council's founding chairman was Seymour Knox, the well-known philanthropist and collector whose paintings make up the bulk of the collection at the Albright-Knox Gallery in Buffalo, the nation's first museum to be devoted exclusively to modern painting.

charm since 1976, constantly reminds me how much her budget has suffered during the past four years. But I believe we have turned a corner: despite recent reductions, for fiscal year 1993–94 the council will receive $26 million, a 14 percent increase over the previous year. This is still the highest allotment of any state in the nation and ranks us fifth in per capita spending on the arts, behind only Delaware, Michigan, Alaska, and Hawaii.[48]

An important part of the council's role is the appealing but delicate job of giving most of that money away. The recipients may be any nonprofit group connected to the arts who can present a compelling application, and the range is tremendous. (Individual artists also may apply if they are sponsored by a nonprofit organization.) The council comprises more than a dozen programs that fund various disciplines, including folk arts, dance, literature, music, electronic media and film, and theater. Others focus on museums, arts in education, and architecture. Approximately 1,300 groups around New York receive some council funding in any given year.

A few examples to illustrate: The State Council on the Arts provided funds so that the New York Philharmonic could perform free parks concerts in every borough of the city. Poetry readings, a traditional mainstay of Manhattan's 92nd Street YMHA, also receive grants. We contributed $8 million toward restoration and construction of the National Museum of Native American Culture. We provide funding for Hospital Audiences, Inc., a group that gives New Yorkers with serious illnesses or disabilities the opportunity to create their own artwork as part of the process of healing. Other recent initiatives include a million-dollar folk arts program; a national architecture competition; new support for literary magazines, translators, and writers of nonfiction; the Frédéric Chopin Singing Society of Buffalo; the Rochester Association of the Performing Arts; increased funding for cultural festivals; and the Pocket Orchestra Program, for small dance and opera companies that could not otherwise afford to hire musicians.[49] And we have supported countless individ-

---

[48]Regrettably, as the recession dried up state tax receipts, we've also been forced to discontinue the Governor's Arts Awards, sponsored in the past by New York Telephone. Recipients have included distinguished New Yorkers such as novelist Toni Morrison, film director Sidney Lumet, playwright Neil Simon, singer Lena Horne, the late trumpet player Miles Davis, and painter Willem de Kooning. Another indicator of tough times: the New-York Historical Society, repository of many important documents about the founding of our nation and our state, needed a last-minute bailout by Albany's legislators in the spring of 1993 just to keep its doors open.

[49]We're committed to the vast and diverse resources the state has to bring art to as many different

ual artists, many in the difficult early stages of their careers—film director Spike Lee, video artist Nam June Paik, Academy Award–winning documentary filmmaker Barbara Kopple.

The council has also achieved exciting results through efforts that compound the positive effects of the individual grants by making the public realm more attractive. For instance, through the council's twenty-year-old Architecture Planning and Design program, we funded a study for the Bronx River Corridor Preservation and Development Plan. Eventually the plan generated $13 million in New York City funding for design improvements that made the area far more appealing and accessible for the people who live nearby. The council also has supplied a grant to hire a planner to do a study called Hamlets of the Adirondacks, which has served as a blueprint for sensitive development in the North Country.[50] Today, the Architecture Planning and Design program has by far the largest public funding for design of any state arts council, and has served as a model for other states.[51]

Despite all we've done for the arts since Nelson Rockefeller's first initiative, it has not been enough. As our economy begins to repair itself, I am committed to reinvigorating our state backing for the arts. And to skeptics who still argue that the world of art and culture is no place for state government, my reply is simple: explain to me why the state shouldn't be involved in any activity that enriches the lives of New Yorkers and sweetens the invitation of the Empire State to people beyond our borders.

---

ethnic groups and institutions as possible. And that is why we make money available to the Art Appreciation Guild of St. Nicholas Ukrainian Orthodox Church, the Polish Community Center, the Dance Theater of Harlem, the Jewish Museum, the New York Buddhist Church, the Irish American Heritage Museum, the Institute for Italian-American Studies, and the West Indian–American Day Carnival Association, to name just some of the dozens of deserving applicants.

[50]Through the Lighthouse for the Blind, the council has supported the publication of guidelines for designing playgrounds for visually impaired children. We have given money to People for Westpride, a small neighborhood organization, to develop positive alternatives for the redesign of the Penn Yards site. State funding has been provided for a book on architecture in the Hudson River valley. We've also asked architects to design new housing prototypes for people with AIDS.

[51]The council's twenty-year-old Architecture Planning and Design program has received the Thomas Jefferson Award from the American Society of Interior Designers, the Citation Award from the New York State Association of Architects, and the Public Trust Award from the Preservation League of New York State.

Strengthening the Economy Through Sports and Recreation

Like so many other states, we've discovered that this same reasoning applies to another "industry"—the world of sports. Organized athletics have been important to New Yorkers at least since 1839, when baseball was born in the upstate community of Cooperstown, home to the Baseball Hall of Fame.[52] But in the century and a half since, several sports, including baseball, have been transformed from casual pastimes into huge enterprises that deserve our encouragement and demand our oversight.

One example should demonstrate both the depth and the value of that conviction. On a cool mid-October day in 1992, Vincent Tese (the state's commissioner of economic development), Mayor David Dinkins and Deputy Mayor Barry Sullivan of New York City, and I flew down to Atlanta to meet with Ted Turner about the 1998 Goodwill Games. In the 1980s, before the collapse of the Soviet Union, Turner devised this athletic contest between the United States and the USSR as a gesture toward world peace. His first run at it lost millions of dollars. It didn't bother him at all. He stuck with the idea, no matter what the state of world affairs, every four years. The Cold War barriers have melted since then, but Turner believes, and I agree, that we still have an obligation—perhaps stronger now than ever—to help these two great peoples understand each other. Sports, with its universal language of sweat and strain, of strength and shrewdness, offers a useful beginning.

Spurring our trip was the fact that New York City had found itself ranked as a finalist to host the 1998 event, along with Dallas, St. Louis, and Miami. In a race with such strong contenders, it was crucial that the mayor and I appear personally to represent the New York City area as the ideal venue. When we met with Turner in his office, it was clear that he didn't have any aversion to holding the games in New York City, but he needed us to give him a positive argument—one factor that would convince him our site would be better suited than our competitors'. Dallas looked to be the most imposing

---

[52]Recently this popular museum began a capital program to raise funds for expanding the exhibition space and the library—a move that should ensure its financial health and create a few jobs, too. Also, we are well aware that historians have argued whether New Yorkers or New Jerseyites can lay claim to the birthplace of baseball. It may be one of those baseball arguments that is never resolved. Until absolutely proven otherwise, we will side with those historians who say the first game was played in upstate New York.

rival. While Turner stood and paced among his numerous yachting trophies, a thought occurred to me.

"Ted, you know that New York City has one thing that Dallas doesn't have," I said.

Turner, intrigued, asked, "Oh, what's that?"

"Water," I said. "We have water and Dallas doesn't. Where would you go sailing in the middle of Texas?"

I don't know if I made any difference in his thinking, but the following day Mayor Dinkins and I were able to hold a joint news conference at Madison Square Garden to announce that we had won the competition.[53] (Dallas got even: the Cowboys killed Buffalo in the 1993 Super Bowl!)

Though the athletes will be amateurs, the Goodwill Games themselves mean big money for New York. The 1990 games held in Seattle brought that city a $300 million boost in business. As a much bigger market, and with the added advantage of being a major tourist attraction in 1998, New York City is poised to benefit from the projected half billion dollars in economic activity the games will create.

It will hardly be the first time we have been lucky enough to sponsor major amateur competitions. In 1932 the Winter Olympic Games came to Lake Placid, a charming resort town in the Adirondacks. When the Olympics returned in 1980, it was in the Lake Placid arena that the U.S. hockey team won a gold medal against the Soviets in an emotional final game. Every winter Lake Placid is also host to the Empire State Games, which pit top amateur athletes in downhill skiing, ski races, ski jumping, speed skating, and other sports; the summer version of the games is a yearly fixture in cities like Albany and Syracuse. In spring we look forward to the annual New York State Parks Games for the Physically Challenged, the first of its kind in the nation; fall brings the magnificent spectacle of the New York City Marathon—the world's largest—with thousands of runners pounding through all five New York City boroughs. And in the summer of 1993, Buffalo was host to the

---

[53]The other thing I thought useful to mention in making our case was that I would do my best to help promote the 1994 Goodwill Games, scheduled for St. Petersburg. I wanted to make it clear to Turner that while we did have an economic interest in the games, we realized that the first priority was the games themselves—that it was just as important to promote unity and harmony between the United States and the former USSR. I explained to Turner that I had been to St. Petersburg before, and I would make every effort to attend the 1994 Goodwill Games.

World University Games, a college-level Olympics that attracted the best athletes from dozens of nations.

Like all these amateur contests, professional sports in New York supply a powerful package of entertainment, inspiration, and economic activity. At the top professional level, one football team, the Buffalo Bills, plays its home games in New York. There are also two baseball teams, the Yankees and the Mets; three hockey teams, the Sabres, the Islanders, and the Rangers; and in basketball, my favorites: the beloved New York Knicks. New York leads all states with fifteen minor league baseball teams, from A to AAA level, with clubs like the Rochester Redwings, Albany-Colonie Yankees, Buffalo Bisons, and Syracuse Chiefs. Regrettably, the eagerness of other states to share the delights of our superb sports franchises has produced a string of seductions; the Giants of baseball and football, the Dodgers, the Nets, and the Jets were all born in New York.

Queens boasts the U.S. Open tennis championships, one of the two crowns, along with the All-England Championship at Wimbledon, that every great player covets. We have two major auto racing circuits, in Bridgehampton and Watkins Glen. Madison Square Garden in the heart of Manhattan, home to the Rangers and Knicks, also hosted a world heavyweight title boxing bout in 1993. The Nassau Coliseum on Long Island is home to the Islanders. And New York has four Thoroughbred racetracks—Finger Lakes, Aqueduct, Belmont, and Saratoga—and also harness tracks for Standardbreds, including Yonkers and Monticello raceways.

In all these incarnations, professional sports in New York tend to flourish without our support or interference. But a few prominent exceptions have demanded our attention. For example, because of new standards imposed by professional baseball, thirteen of New York's fifteen minor league teams must upgrade their parks by April 1995. Proposals have been made by some legislators to seek state aid to help finance some portion of the minor league park refurbishing, in part as a way of stimulating the local economy.[54] In July 1993, along with the legislature, we created a $60 million Sports Facility Assistance program to address these issues.

We have also been drawn into the sporting arena on the volatile subject of

---

[54]The idea is a good one. The state helped to support building the Buffalo Bisons' and the Binghamton Mets' new parks.

legalized wagering on horse and harness racing. This industry is important to the economic security of thousands of New Yorkers—the breeders, owners, trainers, jockeys, drivers, and track workers, and all the businesses, especially in the graceful resort town of Saratoga—who depend on the tourist trade the races bring to town. In fact, the racing industry in New York supports forty-seven thousand jobs and produces a revenue stream of $160 million annually for state and local governments.[55]

Thus it has been a subject of real concern that in the last few years the New York Racing Association (NYRA) and the Off-Track Betting (OTB) Corporation, two of the operators for legalized wagering on horse racing in New York, have come under attack. They have been charged with permitting gross inefficiencies and exorbitant management salaries, while producing patronage jobs for both political parties. It is no coincidence that these abuses surfaced as the economy plunged into recession. As people had less to wager, purses were reduced—but not management salaries, which remained at their high levels, producing an operating loss of $6.7 million for NYRA in 1992.

To study the problem and propose solutions, we convened a panel of experts, the Governor's Advisory Commission on Racing in the 21st Century. Since OTB has for years been luring away customers who once visited the racetrack, one conclusion might be that the state could consolidate NYRA and OTB into one public agency and then sell the entire racing franchise to a private operation, thereby providing steady tax revenues.

A combined agency theoretically would operate much more efficiently. A merger would eliminate the tension of competing for customers; operating costs—including the marketing expenses to woo new customers—could be reduced greatly. A single entity with an improving balance sheet would be attractive for a private buyer.

In private hands, NYRA and OTB could become profitable once again. In the fall of 1993 New York City already had begun negotiations with Ladbrokes, an English betting concern. There is no doubt that a private company would further streamline operations, eliminating much waste, including needless management jobs that were once the province of political appointments.

I certainly favor privatization if it means that the wagering public will be

---

[55]This is based on a betting handle of nearly $3.1 billion in 1992. Adjusted for inflation, the revenues realized by the state are far below the levels of those garnered in the early 1970s.

getting better service and the state's revenues can once again become constant and predictable.[56]

Agriculture—One of Our Oldest and Most Valued Industries

Not much more than a century ago, there were still farms on the island of Manhattan, and the truth is that New York is still primarily a rural state. Lewis County actually has more cows (32,000) than people (27,000). Eighteen percent of our state's population, 3.2 million people, live in our long, quiet miles of country—the sixth largest rural population in the nation. Taken together, rural New Yorkers would constitute the twenty-sixth largest state in the Union.[57]

My mother, who grew up on a farm in Italy, has a saying that always returns to me when I visit the state fair in Syracuse or any of the various rural counties of upstate New York. "The farther you move from the land," she'd say, "the farther you move from God." On a farm you can see how people rely on one another, how all of nature moves in cycles, and how we, too, must pay homage to that rhythm, working with it, not against it. Through the remarkable work they do every day, farmers teach us the values they live by: respect for the land, for the animals, for the power of nature. And they remind us that local agriculture produces more than sweet vistas.

It produces economically, for certain. Farming has been the industry most responsive to technological and scientific change, and New York's $3 billion agriculture and food industry outstrips every sector of our economy in its ratio of workers to output. Today our thirty-eight thousand farmers and their families cultivate about 27 percent of the state's land area, or 8.3 million acres,

---

[56]My support of sports in New York and the racing industry should not be construed as blanket support for casino gambling, which has become a popular method of plugging gaps in public budgets across the nation. Personal feelings aside, on a practical level, it would take at least three years to be approved in both houses. Also, many religious and civic groups are opposed to casino gambling. Finally, there is a respectable body of economic thought that holds that casino gambling is actually economically regressive to a state and a community.

[57]Over the past decade New York's rural counties grew more than twice as fast as the rest of New York's counties.

producing a wide variety of food products: meat, apples, potatoes, eggs, onions, grapes, cabbage, sweet corn, green beans, dry beans, grain, maple syrup, tart cherries. Milk is the leader, accounting for more than half of the state's farm cash receipts.

With its fertile soil, abundant water supplies, and diversity of crops, New York emerged early as one of the nation's leading food producers. Our history presents a slowly expanding partnership between the state and its farmers, as people gradually grasped that new techniques and technologies could protect them against many of nature's whims.

For centuries, of course, New York's farmers were on their own. But with the 1840s and 1850s came a rush of new mechanization and a cascade of agricultural reforms that promoted stricter production standards and made it suddenly important for farmers to have a technical education. In no time New York's farmers were rotating their crops, adding gypsum and lime to their soil, and trading their goods to a string of blossoming rural communities connected by the Chenango Canal & Erie Railroad. But we had only begun to realize the full potential of our land and our people.

The challenge was much the same across the country. In response, President Abraham Lincoln signed the Morrill Land Grant Act of 1862, creating the nation's land grant university system. In the western states, where the federal government had substantial holdings, the land grant process was simple. But in older states like New York, Washington didn't have the land to give away. Instead it issued scrip that entitled such states to land farther west; New York got a million acres of northern Wisconsin. The eastern states were then meant to sell their parcels and use the proceeds to start their colleges, but because they all put their holdings on the market at once, prices plummeted—to fifty-five cents an acre. Ezra Cornell, an upstate farmer and member of the New York State Senate, had lobbied hard for the federal legislation. It matched his own priorities: he was already planning to donate his Ithaca farm and $500,000 to create a new upstate university. When Cornell saw the corner the state was in, he sensed an opportunity for both parties. He offered sixty cents an acre if the legislature would use the funds to launch his new school in Ithaca, an institution that would "teach agriculture and mechanical arts to the sons and daughters of the masses." Cornell got his deal, and the state gained another extraordinary institution—a magnificent public-private partnership, even before we had the jargon to describe it.

By the turn of the century, Cornell's College of Agriculture was offering scholarships for agricultural students and exploring new ways to disseminate farm technology throughout New York. Cornell professors traveled by train to speak to farmers; they published in agricultural periodicals; they held annual "farmer's weeks" in Ithaca, where farmers from all over the state could take courses on farming principles and techniques.

In 1914 the federal government joined the state to fund Cornell's Cooperative Extension Service. County farm bureau associations sprouted up in fifty-six counties within five years, replacing the old "farm trains" armed with professors. From Nassau to Niagara counties they quickly disseminated new ideas about milk production, fertilizers, plant diseases, and tractors. During World War I, county agents worked through these bureaus to help farmers secure capital, preserve food, and train their laborers in techniques to increase production.

As farmers became more specialized during the 1930s, the extension service emphasized improving their commodities rather than just their yields. In 1935 the College of Agriculture took a key role in researching the use of artificial insemination, a revolutionary technique pioneered in New York that would improve the quality of dairy herds and have other far-reaching consequences. By 1940 the research had moved to the farm and New York farmers led the way for the nation's dairy industry. From 1946 through the 1960s, New York's farmers used the college's expertise to cut their production costs and make improvements in feeding, fertilizer application, leaf and soil analysis, and marketing methods.

More recently, the Cooperative Extension Service has reached out to educate people not directly involved in farming, like buyers, retailers, and consumers of farm goods, as well as ordinary New Yorkers interested in landscaping and gardening. Today, through television, radio, newspapers, newsletters, seminars, and meetings, Cornell University's Cooperative Extension Service gives food and fiber producers a competitive edge by introducing them to the latest innovations developed by Cornell's scientists. In recent years, for example, agricultural research, disseminated through Cornell, has helped to improve the color, size, and quality of New York's apples.

The lesson of the last century is that, like the land itself, the agriculture industry needs steady cultivation and protection. We cannot afford to treat agriculture as a quaint relic of our rural past, to be preserved for the serenity its scenery brings to people who spend most of their time in a world of concrete. New York's dairy farmers, grape growers, and winery owners don't represent some special interest. Developing our agricultural industries is in the best interest of *every* part of this state.

For the past two decades, New York State has been putting in place a modern agricultural policy to help our farmers meet the challenges of late-twentieth-century farming. By the early 1970s it had become clear that farmers needed special treatment from the state legislature, or the escalating real estate taxes on their farms would quickly put them out of business. In 1971 New York enacted the Agricultural Districts Law—the first of its kind in the nation—to maintain farming and farmland. Without the legislation, farms would have been valued like all other real estate—at the "highest and best use for development purposes"—which would have made it impossible for thousands of farmers to pay their taxes.

In recent years, as business conditions for some sectors of the industry worsened and pressures grew from residential, commercial, and industrial development, the state has helped orchardists and vineyardists by amending the Agricultural Districts Law to eliminate additional assessments for fruit trees and grape vines. And in 1992 the state passed the Agricultural Protection Act, a comprehensive bill that will reduce nuisance lawsuits against farmers; provide greater protection for farms against most public development projects; help counties develop farm protection programs; and revise certain property tax provisions affecting farming.

These measures were all designed to relieve the mounting legal and financial pressures our farmers face. But we recognized the need for more affirmative steps as well. Although the occasional downstate legislator will make the argument that "there are no cows in Brooklyn," New York State has made an aggressive, bipartisan commitment to a nationally recognized plan called New York Agriculture 2000, created to improve business opportunities for the state's food and agriculture industry. Under its auspices, our Seal of Quality program has channeled millions of state dollars toward marketing our home-grown food products, and through our Wine and Grape Foundation we promote New York's world-renowned wines and champagnes—a $40-million-a-year industry. Our Farmers' Market Coupon program strengthens us two ways: by helping the poor and the elderly buy fresh fruits and vegetables at 115 farmers' markets around the state, the program gives them a way to improve their diets while upping the demand for local produce. One hundred and three thousand New York families are participating in this program today, directly benefiting seven hundred farmers, who have received more than $5 million in additional sales since the program began.

But just as it was in the nineteenth century, some of our best work has been in education. Through New York's Integrated Pest Management program, we have been able to help farmers involved with any of twenty-five different crops adopt techniques that allow them to use smaller quantities of pesticides— saving them money and reducing the toxins in the soil and water. Part of the concept is a simple, ingenious matter of timing: by applying pesticides precisely when destructive insects are most vulnerable, an apple farmer, for instance, could easily save half his annual expense of $30,000 for buying and applying pesticides.

Because the dairy business dominates the farm scene in New York, we have designed several programs to serve this group as well. New York's Pro-Dairy project helps dairy farmers boost their profits by acquiring modern management skills. Today, four thousand dairy farmers take advantage of this program, many of them young farmers who represent the future of the industry. Another program, the Milk Producers' Security Fund, protects dairy producers from milk dealers who default.

Anyone who doubts that these programs and policies are making a difference need look only as far as Syracuse. In 1990 the Dairylea milk cooperative built a new headquarters in the region—citing the state's support for a competitive dairy industry as one of its prime reasons for making an additional capital investment in New York. Today the Dairylea facility employs seventy-five to eighty people in Onondaga County, generating $4 million a year for the region's economy.

Over the next forty years, as the population of the globe doubles, some experts suggest that the planet will have to yield as much food as it has produced in the last ten thousand years. Meeting that challenge will require a revolution in the way we organize and disseminate our agricultural knowledge around the world. In Ithaca, Cornell's Food Processing Laboratory and Biotechnology Center, opened in 1987 with $33 million in state money, is turning New York into a global center for designing practical ways to apply state-of-the-art findings in biotechnology. In just one hundred thousand square feet, scientists, farmers, businesspeople, and students are working together on research that will transform the way we grow food and produce biological substances for commerce and medicine. They may even spawn a new industry or two.

In a world where many millions go to sleep hungry, New York's scientists and New York's farmers continue to work diligently as they have for more than a century to find the scientific miracles that will help feed the world in the twenty-first century. To aid and encourage this legacy, I called for a conference on agricultural science and technology in my 1993 State of the State Address. This conference explored new scientific research in agriculture so that New York's leadership will continue into the new millennium.

Creating a Leaner, More Responsive Government

In the seventeen years I spent as a lawyer in the private sector, I had plenty of chances to observe government mechanisms that had become shortsighted, wasteful, corrupt, inept. I began to study the reasons why. I asked myself and others: Why are government agencies different from my business? I served on corporate boards. I ran a law firm. Always we tried to work efficiently, always looking for a better way, hiring the fewest number of employees we could. What was different about political and governmental systems? I brought my experience—and my questions—with me to government.

By the time I came to the governorship in 1983, it was clear that the demand for government services was growing faster than our ability to respond. At the same moment, like the shareholders of a major corporation, the taxpayers were also demanding that government become leaner, more productive, and more responsive. In New York we would have to remember that no economy can thrive under a government that is grasping, obstructive, or intrusive. If we wanted a world with enough work to go around, we would have to take a few cues from the private sector, managing our precious tax revenues as intelligently as possible.

We started where any corporation might start: by tracking down those cases where we were operating less efficiently than we could. One of my early acts as governor was to establish the Governor's Office of Management and Productivity (MAP). Over the last decade my productivity program, monitored by MAP, has helped save the taxpayers $690 million—$54 million in 1992 alone.

Through an ongoing series of detailed investigations and audits, we have discovered a number of inefficient and inappropriate practices that we have moved promptly to correct. Among them are inappropriate Medicaid billing to nursing homes; the failure of businesses to remit immediately to the state sales taxes they had already collected; inadequate collection of delinquent child-support payments; the failure to recycle massive amounts of newsprint, polystyrene cups, stationery, and junk mail within state agencies; the use of two people on snowplows when one would do; and unproductive superintendents at our military armories. In the end, nobody is writing headlines reading, STATE GOVERNMENT SAVES MORE THAN HALF A BILLION DOLLARS, but that's what we've done. Maybe the reason they're not writing those headlines is that they know there are still a lot more efficiencies that ought to be made and haven't been yet: we're working on it.

It's also been important to make sure that we employ only as many people as we need to get the job done. The pressure was especially intense as we were buffeted by the second recession of the decade. Through a prudent mixture of attrition and layoffs, since November 1990, New York has reduced its General Fund workforce (employees paid through tax collections) by about 14 percent, saving the state approximately $1 billion annually. In fact, with just 142 full-time state employees for every 10,000 New Yorkers, we ranked forty-fourth out of all the fifty states by 1991, the latest year for which comparisons are available from the United States Census.[58] Only six states run their operations with proportionately fewer employees.

At the same time, we have given our workers new incentives to help the state strengthen and streamline its operations. Since 1985 our Productivity Awards Program has offered state employees a chance to win cash bonuses, currently $1,500, $1,000, and $500, for their cost-cutting ideas. Over the life of the program, we have recognized eighty-three individuals from twenty-one agencies. Together they have saved taxpayers $19 million.

To help build productivity, morale, and performance throughout the state workforce, we have also begun to apply our own version of the "total quality management" techniques being pursued at private firms around the world. In 1991 we launched a six-agency Quality Through Participation pilot program

---

[58]This is an improvement since 1983, when we ranked thirty-second.

to improve the way the state delivers services and regulates small businesses. Each agency was assigned a private-sector partner and went through a rigorous period of self-examination and outside critique by the people it is supposed to serve. A key goal is to give lower-level employees the power and confidence to make many day-to-day decisions, reducing the number of cases in which citizens are tossed from department to department until by chance they find someone with the authority to act.

One test case is the Department of Motor Vehicles (DMV), long criticized and even ridiculed for its inefficiency and long waits. I challenged the DMV to "reinvent" itself and to start viewing the drivers and owners of motor vehicles as customers we wanted to keep. In response, the DMV has teamed up with Kodak Corporation, which has donated the time of some of its total quality specialists to train DMV officials, who in turn can spread the quality message through the agency. Twenty-five district offices have participated in the program, and by the spring of 1993 about half had already achieved substantial reductions in customer waiting time.[59]

"Privatization" has become something of a shibboleth in recent days. Like the words *empowerment, paradigm,* and *workfare,* it is taken by some to connote a discrete new approach to public policy. Maybe this illustrates one of the problems we have today—words have become more important than ideas and action. Here is my view of "privatization" as a practical reality: I have said repeatedly that we will entertain all offers of privatization. And we have. If they work better than government in meeting our people's needs, then, of course, I will favor them. We do a great deal of "privatizing" in our government already.

Routinely, state agencies contract out an extensive variety of services to both not-for-profit and private organizations. A few specific examples around the state: the rest areas along the New York State Thruway and at Jones Beach, which were refurbished by private contractors; Stewart and Republic airports, located in the Hudson valley and Long Island, respectively; the Gideon Putnam Hotel at Saratoga State Park, the hotel at Bear Mountain

---

[59]The Rochester facility is currently being redesigned to be the DMV "office of the future," which will include a neighborhood service center that can be used by local community groups. Other district offices will also undergo complete overhauls, if necessary. The agency seems to be well on its way to making substantial improvements.

State Park, and the Glen Iris Inn at Letchworth State Park, all of which are privately operated through franchise agreements. The pro shop at Montauk Downs, a state golf course, is contracted out.

The state has been exploring other imaginative ways to use the private sector where such use can eliminate state bureaucratic inertia, save money, improve services, and meet the standards of public safety. As of this writing, the state was looking at options to lease vehicles for the state fleet. On a much larger scale, we would like to explore the possibility of selling the World Trade Center to a private interest, and we have publicly invited anyone interested in our airports or in providing health insurance through private companies to talk to us.

Such collaborative exposure reminds us of government's tendency to take on a life of its own, proliferating procedures and regulations, occasionally without enough regard for their side effects or the quality of their intended results. As part of the ongoing effort to make government more productive, we are also taking aggressive steps to limit government regulations to only the essential. For example, since 1978, the state has relied on the Office of Business Permits and Regulatory Assistance (OBPRA) to provide comprehensive license and permit assistance to new and expanding businesses and, more recently, to review and reform outdated or unnecessarily onerous state regulations.[60] Emphasizing this direction, we merged OBPRA with the Office of Management and Productivity in 1993, creating a new agency, the Office for Regulatory and Management Assistance. One of its goals will be to improve the regulatory climate in New York—making it easier to do business in New York—without compromising public health and safety.

To understand the need for such work, it helps to look at what we've already achieved. By eliminating 4,875 forms, and simplifying 938 others, we saved the state $85 million since 1989. Recent progress in regulatory relief has targeted specific industries: food processing, trucking, day care. For example, we eliminated duplicate federal and state inspections of food processing plants, excessive fees food processors had to pay before they did any business, permits for frozen desserts, and landfill permits for food processors that

---

[60]The regulatory impact on small businesses is far greater than on large ones, and the fact is that the vast majority of our 468,000 private-sector companies—about 98 percent—employ fewer than one hundred workers. Small businesses need the most help in wending their way through the regulatory labyrinth.

dumped pure food sludge. In the trucking industry, we got rid of several permits and used the federal requirements instead. In addition, we revised the licensing of crane operators and asbestos handlers.[61] The changes may seem insignificant to people outside the affected industries, but by making it easier for these businesses to operate profitably, we make it easier for them to grow, invest, and hire.

At a more fundamental level, we are also reforming the process we use to develop regulations in the first place. Through our new procedure—nicknamed "neg-reg," for negotiated regulation or rule making—debate will now come *before* and not after a new regulation is adopted. We will invite businesses in before the die is cast, and with the assistance of neutral arbitrators, we will work together to come to an agreement on what shape a new rule will take. Our goal is to balance the regulatory process, apply it fairly, and work out the disagreements before we pass the point of no return. The interested parties are encouraged to pledge that they will not litigate the issues on which they've previously reached a pact. This process has already been used successfully by the federal government. The 1990 Federal Clean Air Act was adopted only after a negotiation process between the oil industry and environmental groups, presided over by a disinterested arbiter.

New York was one of the first states in the nation to adopt the federal program. We have begun our first neg-reg on a controversial pesticide application notification rule being considered by the New York State Department of Environmental Conservation. We're convinced that with input from consumers, labor groups, and the industry—hotels, motels, restaurants, and hospitals—we'll be able to agree on a fair and reasonable rule, one the industry can respect and the state can enforce. If the experiment proves successful, we'll introduce neg-reg broadly throughout the administration.

Because of the scope of our mission in state government and the changing needs of the people we serve, the opportunities to make our operations more reasonable and more responsive seem almost infinite. Certainly the job will never really be complete. We can always make our system better at reducing costs and improving quality—as fundamental an obligation as winning the war against upwardly creeping taxes.

---

[61]We are also looking at ways we can reform the Department of Environmental Conservation's landfill closure requirements to relieve the burden many towns face in disposing of their garbage. A complete discussion of New York's solid-waste policies is contained in the "Beauty" section.

Wealth, Taxes, and Fiscal Responsibility

A few years ago I gave a speech on federal tax policy and federalism to an outdoor audience at Harvard's Kennedy School of Government. Halfway through my address, I peered into the crowd, comprised of some of the most distinguished and learned men and women in America, and said, "This stuff is really boring, isn't it? Just imagine: If you find it so tedious, and still don't understand it, how am I ever going to explain it to the rest of America?" A few years later, even the chairman of the Senate Finance Committee, New York's Senator Pat Moynihan, while considering President Clinton's plan to reshape America's tax policy, grumbled about the "impenetrable language of the budget clerisy."[62]

Though tax policy makes for dreary conversation, the effects of fiscal choices at the local, state, and federal levels often have far-reaching consequences that affect millions of lives. Obviously, if taxes are raised too high, they can depress business activity and consumer confidence. In deciding where to locate, companies and individuals take into consideration the tax climate in a particular city or state. As we have discovered in New York, even the lingering perception of brutally high taxes can hurt a state's economy.

Nearly two decades back, New Yorkers were extravagantly taxed. In 1975, after four terms of the so-called Rockefeller years, New York State saddled its top earners with the second highest personal income tax rate in the nation, 15.375 percent, along with a state sales tax that had increased to 4 percent. But that era is long over. My predecessor, Hugh Carey, a Democrat, not only stopped raising taxes he reduced them by $2 billion. Since 1983 we have reduced the top income tax rate further—from 10 percent to 7.875 percent by 1993, roughly half of what it was eighteen years earlier. In fact, our top personal income tax rate is down to its lowest level in more than thirty years. At the same time, we have held the state sales tax rate at 4 percent, just where it was in 1974. Overall, the burden of total *state* taxes on individual New York taxpayers has *fallen* since I've been governor: we've improved from the fourteenth-highest-taxed state down to the twenty-fourth. Although this reality often eludes our critics, the CATO Institute, a conservative think tank in Washington, was honest enough to admit in 1992 that "the governor who has

---

[62]*The New York Times,* June 3, 1993, p. A20.

cut tax rates the most, perhaps surprisingly, is Cuomo."[63]

The truth is, New York State is becoming a more competitive place to do business because of our commitment to hold the line on our competitive broad-based tax rates and our willingness to work with businesses to address their regulatory concerns. Here in the Northeast, Connecticut was recently forced to enact a new income tax. In 1990 New Jersey doubled its top tax rate on personal income to 7 percent. And a 1989 study, done by the Tax Department of Wisconsin, designed to evaluate how much tax a hypothetical corporation would pay if it decided to locate in a major industrial state, concluded that manufacturing companies would pay less in state *corporate* taxes in New York than in Texas, Ohio, California, Michigan, Minnesota, Arizona, Louisiana, or Indiana.[64]

These facts point to a self-evident but important observation: governors can control taxes levied only at the state level. They do not control taxes at the *local* level, nor can they exert great influence over what taxes are raised at the federal level—usually. A striking exception to this rule might rank as the least visible but most important victory we've achieved for New York at the federal level: the battle we waged and won in 1985 to preserve the deductibility of state and local taxes. It was an important issue and will remain so, not just because the federal government flirted with the idea again in 1990 when it needed to raise new revenues, but because it raises questions at the heart of our Federalist system of government.

In the beginning, the United States Constitution reserved to the sovereign states the authority to raise their own revenues. In 1913, the federal government, anxious to impose a new national income tax, made a covenant with the states: it was agreed that people should not be penalized by losing their right to deduct the taxes they pay to state and local governments. That was the *quid pro quo* without which the states would never have consented to a federal income tax.

Seventy-one years later, a "conservative" White House—which had always before deferred to states' rights—tried to break a commitment that had lasted nearly three-quarters of a century. In December 1984, shortly after President

---

[63]"A Fiscal Policy Report Card on America's Governors," Stephen More, *Policy Analysis* 167, January 30, 1992.

[64]"Maze of Regulations Blurs State's Corporate Tax Picture," *Albany Times-Union,* September 28, 1992.

Reagan's reelection, then Treasury Secretary Donald Regan unveiled a tax reform plan. A key provision: the "disallowance of the deductibility of state and local property, sales and income taxes." The phrase, meant to be lost on most people not familiar with an accountant's lexicon, represented a real and potentially devastating threat to middle-class New Yorkers and to state and local governments across the nation. The White House wanted the additional revenue to cover the deductions the president's Treasury secretary and future chief of staff wanted to preserve: capital gains, the oil depletion allowance, foreign tax credits for large corporations, depreciation, and other tax advantages for the well-to-do.

From the beginning I regarded the proposal as devastating, unfair, and possibly unconstitutional. The question of deductibility was not some esoteric matter that we could leave to economists, lobbyists, or tax lawyers. At its core, it concerned more than what we pay to this or that level of government. It affected, in a real way, New Yorkers' prospects of finding a job, buying a house, or starting a business.

Under the Reagan administration plan, middle-class homeowners from Long Island to Buffalo would have been deprived of deducting from their federally taxable income the money they paid for local property taxes—the difference for many of them between owning a home and losing it. Those who survived the loss of deductibility and managed to meet their mortgage payments would have been left with considerably less personal income. With the burden of state and local taxes no longer cushioned by the federal deduction, people would have demanded a reduction in public expenditures at both the state and local levels—and not just in New York, but in states such as Massachusetts and California as well.

Consider what that would have meant when taxpayers voted on local school budgets or when their representatives in Albany, Boston, or Sacramento voted on state aid to education. The Reagan-Regan plan would have penalized and punished states that tax themselves to provide public aid to private universities, provide scholarships and tuition assistance, maintain quality public universities, help children born to lead lives in wheelchairs, build prisons to house criminals the federal government didn't catch, or help poor people the federal government failed to take care of.

To an objective analyst our arguments were sound; but politically, the president's position was clever. It divided the country into what he called "high tax states" and not-so-high tax states, ignoring the fact that the high tax states were also high need states.

The proponents of the elimination of deductibility argued that those who did not itemize deductions—especially deductions for state and local taxes—were subsidizing those who did. In fact, administration advocates went out of their way to make New York State a target of their attacks. They said it was unfair for the "elite" and the "special interests" to benefit at the expense of the majority of taxpayers. But the elite, in this case, was America's middle class, and the special interests were state and local governments struggling to provide essential services to their citizens. And the deduction these "elitists" were taking was by far the *most frequently used* deduction in the entire federal income tax system. An estimated 44 percent of taxpayers across the country used it in 1984.

We made the case all across the state and through the halls of Congress, and by the fall of 1985 President Reagan's plan ran into trouble—not because the middle class refused to give up an alleged loophole, but because they saw the fallacy in the president's reasoning. Led by New York's delegation, Congress voted to preserve the deductibility of state income and local property taxes. Although the deduction for state and local *sales* taxes was taken away, by winning 87 percent of the fight, we estimate that our victory saved state and local taxpayers throughout the United States nearly $41 billion in 1993 alone.

The failed attempt to disallow these crucial tax deductions was merely a part of the federal supply-side economic policy that affected the quality of life at the state and local levels all across the land. In fact, by the early 1990s, the shift of the tax burden had become so egregious, the social needs so immense, and the fiscal imbalances so pervasive, local governments were forced to pass record tax increases. In New York this has led to our having one of the highest *combined state* and *local* taxes in the country.[65]

Not surprisingly, disgruntled local officials and opinion leaders around New York often make the argument that the reason local taxes in New York are so high is that the state shifts its burdens to the localities or is balancing its budget by cutting aid to education. But the truth is that while the federal government spent a decade reducing the portion of its budget granted to state

---

[65]The reason this is so is that New York City, Nassau County, and Suffolk County have some of the highest local taxes in the nation.

and local governments, New York State has tried to relieve the burden it places on its localities. The part of our budget that we send in local assistance aid has increased dramatically since 1983. The share of the state budget that goes to localities has increased from 60 percent to 68 percent during my administration. I have taken money that traditionally went to pay state workers and run state agencies and given it to the local governments, school districts, and other service providers at the local level. And during the brunt of the recession, from November of 1990 through the 1992–93 fiscal year, our state workers were denied an increase in salary, and thousands were released from the state payroll.

Given the fiscal climate, how could we *not* work to contain the largest single expenditure in the budget—education? With state education aid increasing at nearly twice the rate of inflation over the past decade, local governments cannot reasonably blame local property tax increases on state actions involving education. But in politics, the rule of reason is often inapplicable.

The problem is one of communication. An example: New York State offers financial incentives to encourage school districts to merge, with an eye to relieving the burden of local taxes. But if particular districts refuse to consider such a change, how do we explain it to the people? How do we explain to New Yorkers whose local taxes are rising but whose services have been reduced that Nassau County's school population is now roughly half what it was in 1972 and Suffolk County's is two-thirds, but the number of districts—with all the overhead of districts—has remained virtually the same: 123?[66] (I'm pleased that we're finding a warmer reception among local governments for another property tax relief idea—our recent proposal that school districts be allowed to pay for education through local income taxes instead of the current regressive property tax if they and their constituents choose to.)

Here is another fact that some local officials have rarely conceded, as they blame the state for local tax increases: employment by *local* governments is about one-third higher in New York than the national average and higher than any of the states in our region. In fact, in 1991 New York ranked number two in the nation, with 480 *local* government employees per 10,000 people, at

---

[66]I have pushed local governments to consider merging and sharing services where appropriate, not just in school districts, but throughout the more than 10,000 units of local government and special districts that have developed in New York over the last 215 years.

the same time that the state employed 142 workers per every 10,000 residents.[67]

While localities appear in no hurry to cut back themselves, local government officials often complain to their constituents about the money they must devote to mandated Medicaid services, as if the state had abandoned its responsibilities on this score. Actually the trend is in the opposite direction. The state's share of Medicaid costs has gone up and the local share has gone down because the legislature and I chose in 1983 to pick up most of the local governments' costs for long-term care—Medicaid money that goes to caring for the elderly and the disabled. When I became governor, the state paid nearly 28 percent of the cost of Medicaid, and local governments paid approximately 26 percent (the federal government paid the remaining 46 percent). In 1991 the state paid more than 35 percent, while local governments paid less than 21 percent. Local governments once spent a dollar on long-term care for every dollar spent by the state. Now they only have to pay a quarter for every dollar the state pays. Local governments have saved *$6 billion* in Medicaid costs because of this change, and I have proposed that the state assume *all* local costs for Medicaid.[68]

While neither the governor nor the state legislature can single-handedly keep local taxes down, this "Medicaid pickup" is one way we can lighten the load. I have proposed additional ways for the state to relieve mandates on localities and offered other measures to help local governments save money for their taxpayers. Repealing the obsolete Wicks Law, for example, would save local governments hundreds of millions of dollars each year. Most local governments want the Wicks Law repealed, but the state legislature has refused to get it done.[69]

---

[67]"Big Government, It's Local in New York," Associated Press, May 25, 1993.

[68]As of 1993, local taxpayers were paying Medicaid bills because the New York State Senate refused to let the state take over the local governments' Medicaid bills.

[69]The Wicks Law basically mandates that the state and other local governments must parcel out building contracts in excess of $50,000 to four separate companies: one each for plumbing, air-conditioning/heating, electrical, and general, which covers everything else. The result? Projects take longer; they are more cumbersome to manage; culpability for problems is harder to discern; and perhaps worst of all, they cost more. The New York City School Construction Authority estimates that building takes almost 16 percent longer and costs 13 percent more because of the Wicks Law. The law is antiquated—it was enacted nearly half a century ago—and puts New York far behind forty-five other states and the federal government, which uses one contractor to oversee an entire project.

It's all part of a broader effort to help local governments control their spending, beyond the example we try to set at the state level. In New York, where the recession struck early and hard, we have been charting a more conservative fiscal course for years. Especially as compared with other states, ours is a record of restraint—one that began long before the latest recession. From 1983 to 1993 we held the rate of growth in taxpayer-supported spending far below the national average and below the average for other states in the region. Between November 1990 and April 1992 we reduced the projected spending of New York State by more than $7 billion.

But no matter how tightly we restrain our annual spending, the most important issue for us to tangle with at the state level remains our debt. Many New Yorkers worry that the debt we have outstanding—more than any other state's in terms of raw dollars—is unaffordable. But, like a wealthy corporation, we can afford it because of the revenues generated by our $481 billion economy. I would also propose that a far fairer measure is to examine our debt on a per capita basis. Moody's Investor Services publishes statistics measuring the debt burdens of states. According to Moody's, five other states carry more debt per capita, and seven other states have a higher debt burden as a percentage of their revenues.

How much debt one can afford is something that can be measured arithmetically whether you are talking about a state or a county or a city. It is done much the same way a bank makes a home loan. At a bank they find out how much you earn a month and how much the debt service would be for the kind of mortgage you want, and they then tell you, by a formula, whether you can afford it. New York and the rest of the states go through much the same process.

Experts have told us that debt service ought not to exceed 10 percent of tax receipts. Moody's reported that in 1992–93, the state used just 5.6 percent of its receipts to service its debt. And according to what is regarded by many as the most direct measure of debt burden—the weight of state-related debt on personal income—New York's burden declined from 1982–83 to 1992–93.

Although the state's indebtedness increased in the 1980s, the crucial questions, after whether one can afford to borrow, are "What did we use the debt for?" and "Could we have afforded not to?" Just as few Americans could afford to buy a house without taking out a mortgage, we cannot run a modern government without debt. While borrowing from the future to pay for *current expenses*—the way the federal government does and as New

York City did in the early 1970s—is courting catastrophe, taking on debt prudently to invest in our future is both an acceptable and an inevitable part of modern governance.

For example, since 1983 we have embarked on a massive building program, financing essential projects that could not have been paid for in cash. If this state were permitted to invest in its future only with cash, it would not have been able to preserve some lands or fund the $241 million Roswell Park Cancer Center, or our other hospitals, or our state university system, or our housing or prison programs. To finance all these programs with just the taxes we collect in a year would demand such a huge income tax increase that it would bankrupt the state. We would drive out businesses and individuals in droves. So we issue debt—the way a family takes out a loan to pay for a college education or a business borrows to purchase new equipment—so that essential investments for future generations are made now and paid back over decades.

One of the most criticized state actions with respect to issuing debt was the use of Urban Development Corporation bonds in 1983 to build additional prisons after the voters had rejected a state bond issue expressly for that purpose. Although what we did was legal, it was not the ideal way to use the state's public benefit corporations. But at the time, we had no other choice. The voters were convinced that we should not borrow to build prisons, as if the prisons would appear by magic (or the need for them would disappear). Not enough people were asking the question "What happens if we don't issue debt to build new prisons?" What would the state have done with the new prisoners? Would those legislators, who criticized our financing method, have voted for tax increases to build new prisons? Or would they simply have chosen to let the prisoners out? When the choice came down to issuing debt, raising taxes, or letting convicts free, the state chose to borrow.

Fortunately, though we face complex indebtedness questions, we do not have to face an acute deficit comparable to that of the federal government, which must allocate nearly 14 percent of its budget to paying interest on our national debt. By law, we always balance our budgets. What we do have is an annual cash flow problem that started in the Rockefeller years and that we are now working to correct. The issue was this: Each spring at budget time, because we were required to pay out assistance to local governments *before* we received tax revenues, we had to borrow short-term. The historic fiscal reforms I have implemented through the Local Government Assistance Corporation will gradually reconcile these periods, eliminating the thirty-year-old practice of borrowing in April simply to balance the ledger. In 1993–94 we reached the lowest level of spring borrowing since 1969.

The financiers who know the business also know that the strength of New York's bonds is unsurpassed. In 1975 and 1976 we proved that even in the face of the bankruptcy of New York City we did not consider defaulting as an acceptable alternative, as some had recommended we do. To help restore New York's stature as a place of opportunity, we will need to remember that in fiscal affairs, discipline and restraint are always a good idea—even when your pockets are full.[70]

The Bitter Fruit of the New Federalism

A 1992 *New York Newsday* headline asked the question WHO IS CHEATING NEW YORK OUT OF $136 BILLION? Senator Moynihan provided the answer in a report his office issues each year, analyzing how much states pay to the federal government in taxes and how much they get back in federal appropriations. By the end of the 1980s, New Yorkers were paying $21 billion more a year in federal taxes than they were receiving in federal aid. Senator Moynihan estimates that since 1976 the cumulative imbalance of payments is more than $150 billion. So much for the illusion that New York siphons away wealth from the rest of the country.

It is impossible to speak intelligently about the fiscal convulsions states and cities suffered in the early 1990s without viewing the crisis, in part, as the bitter fruit of the New Federalism. By 1993 the nation was left with a "fend for yourself federalism" that forced the states to fill national needs without national resources. This has created a tension between the needs of the states to raise revenues for unmet social problems and their need to create congenial tax policies to attract and hold increasingly mobile businesses.

There is a crucial distinction between taxation at the state and federal levels. For example, a progressive tax increase on individual income at the national level does not drive droves of wealthy Americans to relocate in Canada or Mexico. But states face a different economic reality. If we raise our

---

[70]For a full discussion of New York's debt reform efforts, see "Toward an Investment-Led Recovery" in the "Hope" section.

state tax rates too high—especially after we have improved our competitive-ness by lowering the state's income tax rates by nearly half since the Rockefeller years—we risk driving away business and residents.

That's one of the reasons I have resisted calls over the past few years to "soak the rich." Ultimately a strategy like that would have soaked all New Yorkers because it would have suffocated our economy. Hiking the state income tax would have hit New York City's economy especially hard—a part of the state that is hurting now and that we need to bring back. Raising the rates on our broad-based taxes would have driven businesses and jobs out of New York, by the thousands, so I did everything in my power to keep a lid on the taxes that affect our ability to compete with neighboring states.

Even in difficult times—despite the thousands who marched on the mansion and spit on me for reducing the state workforce when they thought new taxes could cure us—New York State's budgets over the past five years have shown that we can achieve a balance between keeping our tax rates competitive and investing in all the areas necessary for increasing the opportunity to work. Because we understand that many factors determine why businesses and individuals decide to come to New York, we have continued to invest in our infrastructure, our schools, and the skills of our workforce.

Today, in New York, even after all the spending restraints we have instituted over the past five years, 99 percent of the state's pupils will continue to attend schools in districts that spend at or above the national average per pupil. We still have one of the best and most affordable systems of higher education in the country. Not a single SUNY or CUNY campus has been forced to close. We remain at the vanguard of preventive and primary health care for children. We have not cut aid to poor women and children or to people with AIDS. We still provide more drug and alcohol treatment than any other state in the nation. We continue to run one of the best-managed prison systems and have one of the largest and most attended systems of parks in the country.

Taken together, we've still managed to provide a great many services, despite our tendency to overuse and overstress them. We have continually looked for new means and methods to solve problems without going to the well so often that we run out of resources. Although we have been forced to change our ways, we've done so without losing our way.

Justice

In a democratic society like ours, we can have neither order, nor justice, nor progress without a respect for the law, a willingness to keep strong its protections, and a clear realization of how central it is to all our values. Our commitment to the rule of law has helped us become the democratic envy of much of the world. Without it there would be no real hope for predictability and assurance that produce both domestic tranquillity and effective international dealings. The United States Constitution and the process of public debate that it safeguards have served us so well that we are tempted to take them for granted. We shouldn't. They are together a miracle of political history. No other place in the world has ever been gifted with a pattern of government as intelligent, farsighted, and successful as the one that is embodied in our Constitution.

Ever since 1777, other states have looked to New York—and to New Yorkers—not just to help construct the federal Constitution, but to ensure that the opportunity it promised is extended to all Americans, so that one day everyone would be sheltered, protected, and empowered by it. Just as New York preceded the United States of America, the New York Constitution preceded the federal document. In fact, the New York Constitution helped inspire—both in its language and in its basic principles—the Constitution that stands above all Americans.

New York, a "reluctant pillar" of the American republic, was actually one of the last states to ratify the U.S. Constitution, in part because New Yorkers wanted to make sure that the new federal Constitution contained a Bill of Rights as comprehensive as their own, with explicit safeguards, including freedom of speech, freedom of religion, freedom of the press,[1] freedom of

---

[1]The principle of a free press was pioneered in New York fifty years before we adopted a state constitution. John Peter Zenger, publisher of the *New York Weekly Journal*, had vigorously attacked the governor of the province, whose administration was graft-ridden. Zenger had published articles alleging that all governors whose names began with a "C" were corrupt. Although I'm personally certain that Zenger's generalization was irresponsible, it seems that he was correct in the case of Governor Cosby. Even the *Journal's* advertisers agreed with him; they paid for notices mocking the rotten practices of the administration. Outraged by the criticism, Governor Cosby threw Zenger in jail. But Zenger prevailed at his trial, and "absolute truth" was established as a defense against charges of libel.

Similarly, New York was one of the first states to offer constitutional protection to ensure "the free exercise and enjoyment of religious profession and worship without discrimination or preference." This clause not only guaranteed that religious beliefs would be *tolerated*, but that they would be absolutely *free of interference*. Because New York State was so diverse, there were other important

assembly, freedom from unlawful search and seizure, and freedom from military tyranny.[2]

New York also provided some structural inspiration for the national government as well: the basic philosophy of checks and balances, which established the three branches of government—executive, legislative, and judicial.[3] This governmental trinity created a unique mechanism for balancing the competing interests of all our citizens.

Such constitutional structure and principles have, over time, helped to shape a system where order is balanced with justice; where all—black and white, poor, rich, middle class—can enjoy a reasonable degree of freedom; where an individual's rights are safe against the whims of its rulers or the

---

religious freedoms in the constitution—including allowing Quakers to be exempt from the militia (though they had to pay a special tax instead). Unlike many other states, New York did not have a provision for a religious test as a requisite to hold office, nor did it insist on making the Protestant religion supreme.

[2]Ironically, a Bill of Rights was not included in the original draft adopted by the framers of the New York Constitution. Apparently the framers felt they had drafted enough language within the original forty-two articles to preserve civil liberties. It wasn't until 1787, two years before the federal Constitution was ratified and ten years after the state's constitution was adopted, that New York legislators felt the oversight was significant and passed "an act concerning the rights of citizens of the state." This amendment protected the rights of the accused by ensuring "due process of law," protected New Yorkers from excessive bail and unjust fines, and limited the courts' power to impose "cruel and unusual punishments." It also guaranteed citizens the right to petition while securing free speech.

[3]The New York State Constitution established a government that was closely modeled after that of the New York colony, though it was pathbreaking in many ways—further establishing both an administrative structure and a code of intelligent laws. The legislature was composed of two houses: the senate and the assembly. Members of the senate were elected from four senatorial districts and held office for four years. Each county was allotted a quota of assemblymen based on its population. Members of the assembly served terms of one year. The New York Constitution provided for the first popularly elected chief executive in America—a governor. The powers vested in the governor were limited, much less than those granted to later governors, probably because of the prevailing distrust of royal and executive authority. The governor's power included commanding a militia and granting pardons except in cases of murder or treason. It was Gouverneur Morris, at the prompting of Joseph Smith of Orange County, who drafted language that would allow the executive branch the power to approve or reject a law. Known as the Smith-Morris amendment, it gave the governor a strong voice in the adoption of a new statute, yet his power to approve was not absolute in any way; it was diminished by a council of revision. The council comprised the governor, the chancellor, the judges of the New York State Supreme Court, and four senators selected by the assembly. The last word, of course, was given to the lawmakers themselves. Vetoed bills could be adopted by a two-thirds vote of the senate and assembly. This idea was ultimately adopted by the national government and has endured ever since.

prejudice of its majority. By adopting a government based on the rule of law, we created a society in which the simplest of powerless people, willing to strive, could achieve freedom, security—and even affluence and power—beyond anything possible for them anywhere else in the world.

Part of the secret, I believe, is contained in the preamble to the Constitution, the implicit promise that we would work as a people to create a "more perfect union." Acting on that inspiration, ten generations of Americans have used the law to advance the concept of liberty, to secure civil rights to all citizens, to protect the sanctity of conscience.

The law is designed to protect life and property from the oppressor and the offender. While we apply it firmly through our criminal justice system, it has a broader use. As we approach the twenty-first century, we must continue using the law as a progressive instrument: to protect the natural beauty of the world around us; to protect us from the technology that could destroy our privacy; to protect us from the tyranny of the gigantic, powerful institutions in both the private and the public sectors that find it difficult to constrain their power; to secure the rights of those who, for much of our history, have been denied the full benefit of our Constitution—African-Americans, Latinos, and other minorities; women; gays; the physically challenged; the poor and powerless.

That progressive impulse, to use *government* to help "perfect the union," has been an incalculable part of our nation's success. And in no place were those impulses ever more developed than in New York, the heart and soul of American progressivism in thought and action.

A Century of Social Justice

In the nineteenth century New York State was transformed economically by Governor Clinton's soaring vision, the Erie Canal. But in our time New York's great economic and social progress has been born out of crisis. By 1900 the free enterprise system was creating great wealth for a relative few who occupied "Millionaires' Row" on Fifth Avenue. It was also forcing the tenement dwellers—and the scattered homeless across the city—to labor ceaselessly under inhumane conditions for wages that doomed them to permanent poverty. American men, women, and children were being forced to work every day of their lives for a single, heartless employer and live a whole lifetime in poverty. Owners could set their own "minimum wage," meaning as little as they could get away with. Children and women could be treated like beasts of burden, and hundreds of people could be forced to work in conditions so bad that fatal accidents were almost routine.

A stroll through the Lower East Side Tenement Museum at 97 Orchard Street in New York City gives a glimpse into the conditions that working men and women struggled under at the turn of the century—toiling for low wages to put food on their tables, crowded like cattle into sweatshops or into their own small bedrooms. If they had a spare quarter, they could feed the electric meter to light up their tenement flats; otherwise they spent the evenings in darkness. One can still see the vestiges of hard times scrawled on the door-jambs, a long list of notations and check marks indicating completed tasks: "27 jackets, 50 shirts, 43 pants, 18 suits, 16 top coats."

All of this happened despite a government that could have legislated an end to such servitude; despite wealthy owners who could have stopped it; despite the churches, synagogues, and charities; despite even prayer . . . nothing stopped the exploitation until the working people decided to organize and do it for themselves, starting through the struggle that has been the union movement.

Much of the struggle was fought in New York. Union organizing in New York State had its roots in the early nineteenth century when skilled crafts-men, mechanics, farmers, and shoemakers banded together to demand a decent wage. In 1864, as the New York State Senate considered legislation that would have punished striking workers organized into trade unions, workers around the state united and rallied in protest. The largest demonstration took place in New York City, where fifteen thousand workers denounced the bill.[4]

What began in New York and elsewhere in the Northeast soon spread across the country, picking up speed as the union movement became the voice of justice and decency, demanding that those who were building the nation—the farmhands who tilled the soil in California, the men who poured the steel in Pennsylvania, the coal miners who worked the mountains of Appalachia,

---

[4]*Stand Fast! A Chronicle of the Labor Movement in New York State,* New York State Department of Labor, 1993, p. 2.

the women who sewed the clothes in New York—should be dealt with as human beings, with dignity; that they be paid a decent wage and allowed to work decent hours; that they be protected against accidents and provided for in their old age.

The union movement pushed forward in fits and starts.[5] It took a few well-publicized tragedies to galvanize public opinion and finally compel government to guarantee more humane conditions for working men, women, and children. The Triangle Shirtwaist factory fire in 1911 ignited a passionate outrage across the state and nation. The burning building in New York City's Greenwich Village took the lives of some 146 workers—mostly Jewish and Italian women and girls—and it happened mainly because the owners had locked the doors and blocked fire exits; they were afraid that their employees would leave the premises early or take scraps of fabric home. After the tragedy, workers who feared for their own safety realized, many for the first time in their lives, that their future depended on their banding together to push management and government to secure a safer workplace.

Much of the early legislative work was led by Al Smith, one of New York's most productive legislators and, later, one of its greatest governors. Smith was a son of the people, a man who dedicated his entire life in public service to creating a better life for the have-nots. Growing up poor on the third floor of a tenement in the slums of the Lower East Side, Smith dropped out of the eighth grade to work in the Fulton Fish Market to support his mother after his father had died.

Later, when Smith went to Albany—without a college or law degree—he became one of the state's most industrious assemblymen. He mastered the Byzantine workings of New York politics. He studied every paragraph of the bills that crossed his desk, and then, when he finally felt he could make a difference, he began pushing for laws that would ensure that women, children, and working men no longer would have to endure the indignities that he had suffered. Shortly after the Triangle Shirtwaist tragedy, Assemblyman Smith helped pass dozens of new labor and safety bills in just four years, covering wages, working conditions, workers' compensation, and factory safety. Sanita-

---

[5]The first unions were ineffectual and weak. If companies couldn't overpower labor in the courts—which they did easily in the early years—owners could break their hold by hiring nonunion workers who needed jobs.

tion and fire codes were established, and the seven-day workweek was abolished. Child labor was reformed.[6]

What we gained from Smith did not end with the laws he championed in the assembly. As governor—serving a total of eight years between 1919 and 1928—Smith was even more effective, prodding the New York State Legislature to increase funding for public schools and seeing to it that state monies went to poor schools in rural areas. He fought hard to get teachers much needed salary raises. He opened the civil service to women, signed rent laws that kept one hundred thousand New Yorkers from being evicted, set up children's courts, rebuilt state hospitals and created state parks, standing up to the wealthy landowners who opposed them.

But it took more than the loss of life, Governor Smith, or the union movement to create the consensus that government had to play an essential role in protecting the interests of working people—and thus the continued health of our free enterprise system. It took a much larger crisis: an economic collapse.

The Great Depression left nearly a third of the nation's wage earners unemployed. Bread lines filled city blocks. Soup kitchens opened while banks and factories shut down. Foreclosures and bankruptcies forced an army of the dispossessed onto the road, homeless, desperate, in search of bread, work, and a place to sleep. There was not enough food, medicine, or clothing. Thousands of children were struck down by tuberculosis, diphtheria, scarlet fever, or smallpox. Those who were strong enough and lucky enough found work peddling apples or shining shoes on the street corners—anything for a few pennies.

Out of these depths rose New York's governor, Franklin Delano Roosevelt. In March 1930 FDR formulated a plan for New York to cope with the economic disaster. Roosevelt's "five-point program called for a census of the unemployed, coordinated public and private relief agencies, local job initiatives, free employment agencies in every community of the state, and local

---

[6]In 1988, some eighty years after the enactment of this progressive legislation, I created a blue ribbon panel to study safety and health standards in the workplace and to offer recommendations. The law had been advanced since Al Smith's time, but in 1991 we adopted legislation implementing the most comprehensive revision of New York State's child labor law in three decades. These child labor reforms make our law among the strongest in the country. New York is the first state to require that children aged sixteen and seventeen secure permission from both their families and their schools in order to work at a job until midnight.

Three steelworkers atop a high floor of the Empire State Building symbolized the
spirit of New Yorkers at work during the height of the Great Depression.
Lewis W. Hine/NY Public Library

Lewis Hine called this 1905 picture "Mona Lisa Visits Ellis Island." This Russian family's faces hint of the hopes and dreams of millions of immigrants who followed them.
Lewis W. Hine/NY Public Library

Below: The great hall of Ellis Island is now a museum that attracts visitors of all backgrounds, especially those who want a glimpse of what their ancestors first saw when they came to America.
Don Pollard

New York Harbor is no longer the port of entry for immigrants, but Lady Liberty reminds us that America is still the world's greatest refuge for all those who are oppressed.

Mr. Kessler *(left)* gave the author's parents, Immaculata *(center)*, and Andrea *(right)*, the opportunity to own a grocery store. The author, then three years old, is in the foreground.

New York's dairy business is one of the state's most important industries. This young man's cow was the winner of the 1993 St. Lawrence County Holstein Club Show. *Don Pollard*

This is a typical rural landscape in upstate New York, some forty miles southeast of Cooperstown. *Don Pollard*

Niagara Falls is one of the most romantic places on earth and a unique destination, attracting hordes of tourists in every season. *Don Pollard*

The serenity of the Hudson Valley has been captured by William Clift in this photo of Constitution Marsh. *William Clift*

New York is home to nearly one million students pursuing degrees at more than 250 colleges and universities. *Bruce Davidson/Magnum*

Students like this young woman have become accustomed to doing their research electronically.
Don Pollard

A teacher works closely with a student at the Yeshiva in Borough Park, Brooklyn.
Harvey Wang

The State University of New York is the largest, most comprehensive state university system in the nation, serving 400,000 on 64 campuses.

The Erie Canal is often called the nation's first great infrastructure project. New York City Mayor De Witt Clinton envisioned a water and barge route that would make New York State the gateway to the Midwest.

When the canal was finished, travel time between New York City and Buffalo dropped from six weeks to ten days, and the economic results for the state were dramatic.

Today, the Erie Canal is no longer a major shipping lane, but it remains an active waterway for tourism and recreational boating.

The New York City subway
system is the fastest way to
navigate among four of the
city's boroughs. The
Number 7 line connects
Queens and Manhattan.
Harvey Wang

Below: The Brooklyn Bridge
is one of the world's most
photographed spans.
Bernard Gotfryd

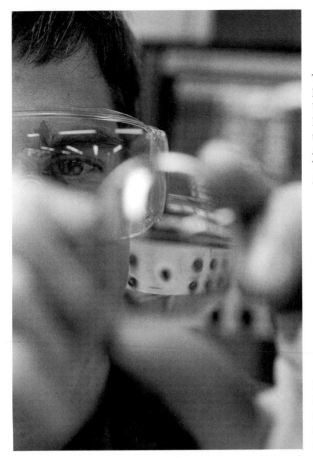

The Center for Optics Manufacturing at the University of Rochester is one of the state's Centers for Advanced Technology.
Don Pollard

Much of the state's high technology work must be performed in totally clean environments.

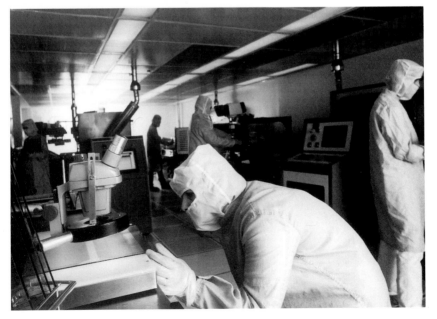

Already U.S. output in high-tech equipment exceeds the output of trucks and cars, so there is a constant emphasis on research and development.

A researcher at Regeneron in Westchester County is working to help solve the mysteries of degenerative diseases. Biotechnology is one of the state's emerging industries. *Don Pollard*

The contours of advanced technology will shape the economic destiny of virtually every business. New York State's partnership with academia and industry has been nourished for the past decade.

Board games are common scenes in New York City parks every spring.
David Lee

Cadets perform their daily rituals at the U.S. Military Academy. *Don Pollard*

New York City is the home of constant celebration, constant parades. This is the 1993 Dominican Day Parade in Manhattan. *Don Pollard*

New York's beaches are among the most beautiful in the world. The waves of summer entice children from Orchard Beach in the Bronx to Amagansett on the East End of Long Island.

The Capitol Building in Albany has been the home of some of our most inspiring leaders, including Theodore Roosevelt, Al Smith, Thomas Dewey, FDR, and Herbert Lehman. *New -York Historical Society*

Broadway at night is the epitome of neon advertising and also the home of the legitimate theater. *Santi Visalli*

This aerial shot of Levittown on Long Island
illustrates the dramatic emergence of
post–World War II suburban growth. The suburbs were virtually invented in New York.
Levittown Public Library

New York City's architecture spans every style,
from Frank Lloyd Wright's Guggenheim
Museum to the famous Art Deco–inspired
Chrysler Building. *Don Pollard*

With all its grandeur, New York City, like major cities everywhere, must cope with despair. Housing and economic opportunity for all remains a major challenge. *Don Pollard*

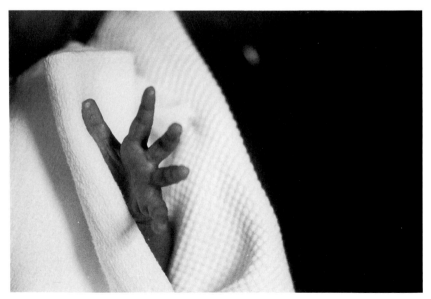

This is the hand of a baby named Tracy, who was born with the AIDS virus. Claire Yaffa's photo is all we need to remind us of our fundamental obligations to one another. *Claire Yaffa*

public works projects."[7] In 1931 he proclaimed in a special session of the legislature a governmental ethic that would help define the modern role of government in New York State: "When . . . a condition arises which calls for measures of relief over and beyond the ability of private and local assistance to meet—even with the usual aid added by the State—it is time for the State itself to do its additional share."[8]

When people lament the "modern welfare state," they ought to remember that before this governmental assistance existed, American citizens could starve to death. Roosevelt made a proposal to feed them. In 1931 cardboard cartons with food and clothing marked HOME RELIEF soon arrived on the doorsteps of dispossessed New Yorkers. New York's Temporary Emergency Relief Administration (TERA) offered those in need the first coordinated state aid anywhere in the country. The TERA was the forefather of FDR's national New Deal, distributing $48.6 million in relief during the first ten months of the Depression—helping some 1.5 million people in New York. When the relief load hit its peak, 17 percent of the state's population was on public assistance. Shortly thereafter, in 1935, the Federal Aid to Dependent Children program was established to care for widows and orphans.

Knowing that the people needed work as much as food, Roosevelt, who had been elected president in 1932, working with governors like New York's Herbert Lehman, put millions of Americans to work building public works projects throughout the nation.[9] In his first inaugural address, FDR said, "Our greatest primary task is to put people to work. This is no insolvable problem if we face it wisely and courageously. It can be accomplished in part by direct recruiting by the government itself, treating the task as we would treat the emergency of a war."

In the Depression, governments didn't view each other as adversaries, competing for tax dollars as they now do in the recessions of recent times. They saw each other as partners with a common ideal of helping those who needed help. It is a simple, wise concept, and it makes the most sense when the times are difficult. Of this period, New York Governor Herbert Lehman

---

[7]Ellis, Frost, Syrett, and Carman, *A Short History of New York State* (Ithaca, N.Y.: Cornell University Press, 1957), 417.

[8]*Public Papers of Governor Franklin D. Roosevelt,* 1931, p. 173.

[9]By 1943, Roosevelt's Works Projects Administration—WPA (originally called Works Progress Administration in 1935)—had spent $11 billion and employed at least 8.5 million Americans.

concluded, "In every one of these activities Federal and State cooperation of some kind was necessary."

It was Lehman who left perhaps the greatest reform legacy of that era. His "Little New Deal" exemplified the spirit of public service, of progressivism. *The Nation* magazine editorialized, "In his quiet and methodical way, this ex-banker achieved far more [in Albany] than was accomplished by either Smith or Roosevelt."[10]

New York benefited greatly from federal funding, much of which flowed through the Public Works Administration, the Civilian Conservation Corps, and the Works Progress Administration. Bridges went up from the Catskills to Buffalo. Health care and hospitals were expanded. Schools were constructed by the hundreds. Jobs were created in soil conservation, recreational facilities, reforestation. Over the course of the decade, hundreds of thousands of New Yorkers were put to work; many of whom built the infrastructure that continues to serve us to this day. It is hard to imagine how we could do without the projects built in that period: in 1935 construction began on the East River Drive; in 1936 the Triborough Bridge, linking Manhattan, the Bronx, and Queens, was completed; in 1937 the Lincoln Tunnel, which connects New York City with New Jersey, opened in midtown Manhattan; in 1939 both LaGuardia Airport (then named North Beach Airport) and the Whitestone Bridge opened, moving goods and people in and out of the New York region.

Upstate New York benefited, too. Governor Roosevelt saw that tourism was served with public money when he broke ground for the construction of the Whiteface Mountain Highway in the Adirondacks. Six years later he returned as president and dedicated the completed project to the veterans of World War I. Today, visitors can ascend the peak via an elevator that was built inside the mountain to accommodate people with disabilities.

Nearly a decade into the Depression, New Yorkers, having seen the carnage that impersonal market forces could wreak on individual workers, reached a consensus that government in New York would forever assume a special obligation to the needy. At the New York State Constitutional Convention in 1938, former Governor Al Smith, arguing that it was a disgrace that men and women and children still lived in tenement buildings, convinced the delegates that New York State should fund public housing for the poor.

---

[10]*The Nation*, January 13, 1940, pp. 30–31.

Even more important, New Yorkers used the occasion to carve into the state constitution a new provision, declaring that the "aid, care and support of the needy are public concerns"—the most expansive governmental obligation to the poor ever enunciated by any government in the United States. This distinguishes us from many other states in the nation, some of whom have recently dropped their state welfare programs.

That progressive impulse, which had been gathering momentum in New York ever since Teddy Roosevelt won the governor's office in 1898, was passed on to the rest of the nation through the national leadership of President Franklin Roosevelt, who used the federal government to provide a new measure of dignity and comfort to all Americans. In addition to creating the Tennessee Valley Authority, the Works Progress Administration, and the National Recovery Act, FDR signed two pieces of legislation in 1935 that were to shape the next fifty years: the Social Security Act and the Wagner Act. The Social Security Act became part of a peaceful revolution that transformed America, creating a national unemployment insurance program, bringing security to the old, assuring that a lifetime of hard work would be rewarded. The Wagner Act, which affected workers from coast to coast, established a "Magna Carta" for labor that allowed unions to flourish.[11]

With these two measures, the American union movement was able to link the interests of steel workers and mine workers and auto workers of every race, color, and creed. Once united, nothing could stop them—not the thugs, the armed guards, the scabs, or any of the other tools deployed by a heartless management. When American workers finally linked arms and put their small differences behind them, they began to take control of their own lives. With receptive ears in Washington, the union movement was able to ensure not just that American workers would be treated with dignity and paid a fair wage, but that they would be able to enjoy the fruits of the wealth they helped to create.[12] It was the union movement that gave us the benefits and the protections that

---

[11]The Wagner Act enabled the rank and file to organize unions and bargain collectively with employers. The law listed "unfair labor practices" by employers. It served notice to management that a refusal to bargain in good faith, blacklisting, the arbitrary dismissal of activists, or the use of industrial spies would not be tolerated—not by the unions and not by the nation.

[12]It took a crippled economy and a country that had fallen to its knees to create the intelligent recognition that business, government, and labor had to work together to create lasting American prosperity. Ironically, fifty years later we seemed to have forgotten this lesson. In the 1980s, as unions were being broken and union membership sagged, living standards declined for the majority of American workers. In the twenty-first century we will need unions again in this country. Whether we

we take for granted in the workplace today—and that have helped our government develop a special receptivity to progressivism.[13]

New York's Progressive Legacy

I came to politics relatively late in my life. As I began to develop my own political philosophy in the 1970s, I was not impressed by rigid ideological formulations. On the other hand, New York's history impressed me deeply. Much of what I came to believe was a natural outgrowth of a New York tradition that began in the streets of Union Square and extended to the chambers of the state Capitol in Albany and then to the highest offices in the land.

In 1983, when I was elected governor, I was as aware of the rich history behind us as I was of the plethora of new challenges before us. At the time, people advised me to select one area of public policy to concentrate on and make that the focus of my governance. Although such a strategy might have made it easier for historians to locate our administration in the continuing development of New York's history, I said at the time that doing so would be

---

use the term *management-labor relations, labor councils,* or *employee teams,* workers will once again have to be organized, motivated, and given a stake in their company's future. Call it "union" or something else, but without labor and management cooperating, we will not compete effectively in the twenty-first century. The management strategy preferred in the 1980s—skimming the hide off the working people to stay competitive around the world—is not fair or smart. We should not try to compete by reducing the living standards of American workers and their families in order to compete with standards from overseas that we declared were indecent one hundred years ago. Who will buy American products in the United States if real hourly wages continue to erode? Instead of reducing wages and benefits, we must find new ways to raise the living standards of our workers, through greater productivity, which means more intelligent and targeted private and public investments.

[13]It is not as easy today as it was in those times to point to flagrant violations of workers' rights, although our state labor department continues to do so. Today we take a different approach by calling attention to those businesses in which employees are recognized as valuable members of a successful enterprise. Our Excelsior Award program, created in 1991, became the first state quality award in the nation to emphasize labor-management cooperation and the workforce as drivers of quality in the workplace. Through the program, New York State highlights the activities of private firms, as well as those of public and educational institutions, that set an example of fairness, employee involvement, and productivity and demonstrate a standard of quality for others to emulate. This is not the kind of program that generally comes to mind when one considers the role of government, but it is the type of innovation that complements our attempt to do what is expected.

irresponsible in a state like New York, where all the problems and possibilities interconnect—and none will step aside to allow you the luxury of focusing on one or two.

My experience over the past decade has confirmed that. Rather than picking one area of public concern to highlight, we have tried to advance, in all areas of our public life, New York's historic governmental mission.

Constant reform has been the benchmark of New York's recent history, an effort to build on and refine the statutes that gave Americans many of their essential rights and protections. Other governors followed the lead of Smith, Roosevelt, and Lehman. Many left their mark on national politics as well: Dewey, Harriman, Rockefeller, Carey. All these governors continued, in their own ways, to use government actively to help push New York toward new levels of social and economic progress.

In 1945 Governor Thomas Dewey signed the Ives-Quinn Act, putting New York State in the forefront of civil rights legislation. The law, hailed at the time as the most significant piece of civil rights legislation since the post–Civil War Reconstruction amendments, outlawed discrimination in public-sector hiring and promotion based on one's religious affiliation or racial background, making such discrimination punishable by a fine or imprisonment.

Although Governor Dewey is most remembered for his efforts to build the New York State Thruway, the precursor to the Federal Interstate Highway system, he also proved to be a pioneer in the area of child care. During World War II, when women were called to work in New York's factories, Governor Dewey designed a $15 million program to help create child care centers so these working women could balance their work and family obligations. The expense was borne equally by the state, the localities, and the mothers themselves. In addition, Dewey was instrumental in establishing a system of junior colleges that returning war veterans or their orphaned children could attend.

In the 1950s Governor Harriman, understanding the special importance of higher education for the financially disadvantaged, increased the number of regents scholarship awards so more high school graduates could attend college. Governor Harriman concentrated his social agenda on difficulties faced by workers, consumers, and the elderly. He also laid the groundwork for antidiscrimination laws protecting senior citizens.

In the 1960s Governor Nelson Rockefeller left his mark in many areas, but particularly in public works construction and social programs that saved thousands of our neediest people from want and despair—in economic development, education, the environment, health care, and housing all across the state. He gave us the Empire State Plaza and made SUNY one of the nation's most expansive state university systems, bringing higher education within the reach of millions of young people. He was the architect of the Pure Waters Program, the first and largest of its kind in the nation. The practice of giving a portion of the tax dollars that flow to the state back to the local governments—"revenue sharing"—was a Rockefeller initiative, as was the creation of the Consumer Protection Board, numerous public benefit corporations, and the New York State Council on the Arts.[14]

Malcolm Wilson, Nelson Rockefeller's lieutenant governor from 1959 until 1973, served the state as governor briefly from 1973 to 1974. Though not given the opportunity to develop a legacy of his own, he continues to serve New York. Recently I asked him to lend his unique perspective and experience to our Temporary Commission on Constitutional Revision.[15]

Hugh Carey, whom I served as lieutenant governor, is most remembered for saving New York City from bankruptcy. But his efforts to reform New York State's health care system, one of his principal concerns while governing New York in the 1970s, have been just as important. In the 1970s he used the Moreland Act Commission to expose deplorable conditions and unscrupulous operators of nursing homes. Governor Carey averted a medical malpractice insurance crisis, and in 1977 he revamped the entire state Medicaid system— lowering the state's Medicaid costs for the first time in the history of our state. This has allowed New York to provide greater Medicaid coverage for more procedures than any other state. Carey managed to pass twenty-one progressive health care bills during his tenure as governor.

It is this kind of change that comes from the best instincts of New Yorkers, and this kind of change will continue to happen as long as there are New Yorkers.

---

[14]No doubt the cost of all this was high. As mentioned earlier, the state income tax, adopted in 1919, went to an all-time high of 15.375 percent under Governor Rockefeller. The state sales tax, adopted in 1965 at 2 percent, was increased to 4 percent in 1971, where it has remained.

[15]On July 26, 1993, I signed into law the bill that I introduced to redesignate the Tappan Zee Bridge as "the Governor Malcolm Wilson Tappan Zee Bridge."

Providing Protection to the Defenseless

Some periods of history are more interesting than others, more pivotal, more lasting in their impact on later years. Fifty or one hundred years from now, when some social historian sets out to describe the immensity of the human needs we faced as a society at the close of the twentieth century, that account will take into consideration several key trends. One will be that the nation's demographics changed dramatically: Americans are growing older and living longer. Another will be that the country produced a generation of children growing up more vulnerable than at any time in its history. The third, more familiar to accountants than demographers, is that in the last quarter of the twentieth century the nation's human needs converged with mounting fiscal pressures that threatened the ability of all levels of government to take care of those who without some help would not be able to take care of themselves.

Perhaps there is no area where government's role is more clear than in taking care of people afflicted with mental illness and developmental disabilities, an area of public responsibility in New York that formally began to adapt to the better wisdom and greater sensibilities of the modern era only in the last two decades.

In 1975, during the height of the state's fiscal crisis, Governor Carey signed the Willowbrook Consent Decree. That judgment concluded a civil rights action concerning the shameful treatment of mentally retarded persons living at the Willowbrook Development Center on Staten Island. More important, it was the catalyst for revolutionary changes on behalf of all New York State citizens with mental retardation and developmental disabilities, setting basic standards for state institutions. With the Willowbrook Decree, the state of New York recognized, legally and morally, a fact we had ignored for too long: everyone, regardless of degree of disability, is capable of physical, emotional, intellectual, and social growth. The decree reminded us that the thousands of New Yorkers with developmental disabilities share the same human ambitions: the desire to work, to learn, to grow, to participate, to choose, to love, and to be loved.

To our shame as a society, we had, before Willowbrook, forgotten those realities or chosen to ignore them. Smugly assuming that we were more enlightened than previous generations about human and civil rights, we were universally shocked when advocates for retarded persons and the media exposed conditions at Willowbrook in the mid-1970s. The image of the New York facility, typical of such institutions across the country, gave New York's image another blemish that would take years to correct. In those vermin-infested buildings, retarded children and adults were, as a matter of routine, stripped of their dignity, degraded, neglected, denied even a minimal level of participation in the community. They had done nothing wrong. They were "guilty" of only one thing: they were judged to be mentally retarded.

Had he achieved nothing else as governor, Hugh Carey would deserve the gratitude of New Yorkers because he faced the evil of Willowbrook and embraced a solution that would make amends for its sin and propel us into a more progressive age. Extending the spirit of the consent decree, Governor Carey went on to create a separate Office of Mental Retardation and Developmental Disabilities (OMRDD) in 1978. What followed was, simply stated, the largest commitment of resources ever made by any state to its citizens with developmental disabilities—one which continues to this day.[16]

With the state's response to the Willowbrook tragedy came a new recognition among professionals and the public that people with developmental disabilities need specialized care more than they need to be locked away from the rest of us. Since the dark days of Willowbrook, government, working in partnership with voluntary agencies, has transformed New York's system of services from a huge institutional monolith into one that is now multidimensional and, for the most part, community based.

We are still making steady progress toward the goal of closing all state institutions for persons with developmental disabilities—not because they are guilty of the sins of Willowbrook, but because we have found an infinitely better strategy for treatment. The truth is, no matter how hard the staffs work, no matter how much money is spent, an institution can never really be a home; nor can an institution furnish the same quality of life possible in a community.

During the past fifteen years, New York State's Office of Mental Retardation and Developmental Disabilities has expanded its residential and day programs, providing quality care for our developmentally disabled brothers and sisters in—not separate from—the mainstream of society. By 1992, *nation-*

---

[16]New York State's OMRDD budget is the largest in the nation. The overall budget comes to $1.7 billion.

ally, one out of every five persons moved from an institution into a community-based setting was a resident of New York State.[17] Likewise, community day programs have grown from serving about nineteen thousand people with mental illness in 1983 to some forty-five thousand today. Services range from counseling and medication monitoring to helping someone learn the skills to live more independently. As a result, New York is creating a service system that is more humane, less costly, more diverse, and more responsive to the needs of those served and their families.[18]

Although it serves a different population, the state Office of Mental Health has also pursued a policy of deinstitutionalization—taking people out of isolated "warehouses" and treating them in communities. Advances in the social sciences, the intervention of new drugs, and new legal precedents that said an individual cannot be institutionalized unless he or she is a danger to life—their own or someone else's—have all contributed to moving and keeping people out of state institutions. The state's goal has been to develop successful community alternatives for people with mental illness while reducing reliance on costly inpatient care. With the help of hundreds of volunteers and not-for-profit organizations, New York State has more than tripled its community residence beds (in community residences, supported housing such as apartments, residential care centers for adults, and single room occupancy buildings)—from just under 3,000 in 1983 to nearly 11,000 in July of 1993.[19] From 1986 to 1993 we increased spending for community mental health

---

[17]It is projected that by the end of 1993 fully half of our citizens with disabilities were being served solely in the community.

[18]We are still making steady progress on this issue. In fiscal year 1993–94, we took a new approach to budgeting that will allow for substantial growth in community-based treatment opportunities and improve the system even further. Breaking with recent tradition, our budget did not recommend development of a specific number of new beds or day program spaces. Instead it provided managers with a fixed-dollar amount to creatively purchase individualized service packages for persons with disabilities. When combined with the flexibility of the home and community-based services Medicaid waiver, the care at home Medicaid waiver, and expanded family support services, this new approach to budgeting focuses more than ever before on supporting individual needs rather than "brick and mortar" action. The new, annualized development budget approach will allow the creation of up to 3,000 residential and 2,800 day program opportunities by the end of the 1993–94 fiscal year as compared to previous goals of some 1,800 beds and 2,000 day slots. This increased development will be cost neutral. We will continue to close centers, but we will also enable OMRDD to address the needs of additional persons waiting to be placed in residential and day programs.

[19]Funding for these beds has risen from approximately $23 million in 1983 to nearly $153 million in 1993.

services by 163 percent and more than doubled the number of community beds. As a result, the number of adult inpatients has decreased from 22,000 to 10,500 in 1993. Admissions to state institutions also decreased from 24,188 in 1983 to 15,655 in 1993. In contrast, those being served in residential treatment community homes and apartments have increased from 6,000 to nearly 13,200 in the past decade.

One of the reasons we are able to treat people with mental illnesses in smaller, community-based settings is the great advances made in medical science in the past few decades. Today, many of the biological causes for the development of mental illnesses are known, and more are being discovered. New technologies are enabling scientists to observe the human brain in both health and disease, in ways that could only be dreamed of a decade ago. The extraordinary advances in molecular biology have also made it possible to detect differences in genetic structure that can distort or damage brain functions. Genes have been isolated for Alzheimer's disease, Huntington's disease, and perhaps even for schizophrenia. As further genetic underpinnings are found and understood, it seems likely that new treatments will also emerge. In the past, New York's research institutes, like the New York Psychiatric Institute and the Nathan Kline Institute for Psychiatric Research, have led the nation in developing drugs to treat mental illness—drugs like lithium, which controls severe depression and literally saves lives. New drugs and methods of treatment will not only allow us to treat more patients in the future, they will lower hospital bills, saving tax dollars as more New Yorkers are served on an outpatient basis.

Until science gives us a way to relieve and reverse all mental illness, government, working with the nonprofit sector, must do more to deal with the mentally ill who escape our care because they choose to live on the streets, as the law allows them to.

I am often asked, "Why are there so many more mentally ill homeless today than twenty years ago?" There are many reasons: the lack of affordable housing; the declining number of single room occupancy units in New York City; the increase in chronic unemployment among the poorest and least skilled workers.[20] Another central factor has been the darker side of deinstitutionalization—the shift in mental health policy, beginning in the late 1950s,

---

[20]As unemployment rates rise, so do hospital admissions for mental illness.

from institutional to community-based care, which in too many cases emptied public mental hospitals without providing enough follow-up as to where these people would go.[21]

Where the resources have been lacking to support these people in communities, the consequences have been devastating. Many of the people with mental illness who were let out of state institutions ended up in nursing homes. Others were consigned to adult board-and-care homes. Some wound up in prison. Still others were simply left to fend for themselves, distracted and disturbed, alone, on our streets. Today the plight of the homeless mentally ill is one of our greatest blights. Up to a third of the single, homeless adults living in New York City—with estimates ranging from eight thousand to twelve thousand people—are believed to have some kind of mental illness. Funding and delivering housing and social services to them is one of government's most fundamental responsibilities and challenges.

A variety of programs help these individuals. With state support, professionals assess people in public shelters to determine if they show signs of mental illness and refer them to special services tailored to that population. One of the ways the state and city of New York are trying to meet the needs of the homeless mentally ill is through a "New York/New York" housing agreement. Announced in 1990, this broad-based partnership unites city and state governments, as well as private and nonprofit sectors, to deal with the homeless crisis by pooling public and private resources. Instead of trying to solve many of the same problems separately, the state and city of New York are working in partnership to improve cooperation among all the agencies involved.[22]

Our first New York/New York initiative has reduced overcrowding in the city's emergency psychiatric wards and in its municipal hospitals. The second, the housing agreement, will provide housing and support services to over five thousand homeless individuals. Under the New York/New York agreement, the state and city are creating a comprehensive system of community care

---

[21]This population in New York fell from a peak of 93,000 in 1955 to approximately 10,500 in 1993.

[22]Initially we did not create as many bed slots as we originally planned. The reason involved not being able to attract the appropriate nonprofit agencies to sponsor the housing, as well as the usual problems associated with siting and construction. But the Office of Mental Health has solved many of the problems, and it is much closer to its original schedule. The New York/New York plan calls for housing 5,200 people. New York City will develop 1,400 beds, and the state will provide beds for another 1,900. The balance would be placed in other state-sponsored community residences and supported housing programs. The 1993–94 budget provided $25.4 million from the state.

with service-enriched single room occupancy housing for seriously ill individuals. This program not only gives people a roof over their heads, it will help reduce the use of public areas and shelters as housing and treatment sites for the mentally ill.

Just as problems with mentally ill homeless are not limited to New York City, progress has been made in other parts of the state. In October 1991 I traveled to Syracuse for a ceremonial ribbon cutting that officially opened a Salvation Army residence for sixteen homeless women recovering from mental illness or substance abuse. A $300,000 state grant was used to buy and renovate a three-story building that included eight rooms. The residence offers far more than shelter. It provides services that will help all of the women who stay there make the transition to independent living by teaching them skills they need to make a life of their own. Ongoing support from the Office of Mental Health and the New York State Department of Social Services represents a wise investment with long-term benefits for the individuals, government, and community.

The reality that the much larger percentage of the homeless population does *not* suffer from a severe mental illness suggests there are also other forces pushing people into the streets. Many of today's homeless have held jobs. Most have endured real hardship before becoming homeless. They are homeless because they are unemployed, in part because our economy no longer offers enough jobs for unskilled labor. They are homeless because of family breakdown, domestic violence, chronic poverty, or alcohol and drug addiction, or simply because of the nationwide shortage of affordable housing. Some people are shocked to learn that an increasing number of today's homeless are families, and that the fastest-growing group of homeless Americans is children.[23]

On a given night in June of 1991, as many as 28,300 persons, including over 11,000 children, were sheltered by local social service districts in emergency accommodations in New York State.[24] Estimating how many unsheltered homeless people exist outside the shelter system is far more difficult, but some estimates put that figure at approximately seventy thousand in New

---

[23]Some estimates report that three hundred thousand children are homeless in the United States.

[24]These accommodations included a variety of shelters provided by the state and by nonprofit agencies, churches, synagogues, and other private charities. *New York State Comprehensive Housing Affordability Strategy,* June 1992, p. 38.

York alone.[25] The more we learn about them—who they are, where they come from, and why they remain homeless—the more we understand that government must play a major role in helping them.

Recognizing this, New York State enacted the Homeless Housing Assistance Program (HHAP) in 1983, the nation's first capital grant program to offer housing and social services to homeless individuals and families. Within ten years the program provided grants to more than 275 projects across the state, assisting nearly twelve thousand homeless New Yorkers. Through HHAP, both permanent and transitional housing has been created for families, single persons, the mentally disabled, substance abusers, the elderly, youth, victims of domestic violence, and persons with AIDS.

Another approach we are taking in New York was developed by the innovative not-for-profit organization called HELP, founded in 1987 by my son, Andrew Cuomo. HELP works with state and local governments, with developers, bankers, architects, social workers, and volunteers, to build transitional housing and provide social services for homeless families—at roughly half the cost of the welfare hotels we all deplore.[26]

One story is all it takes to bring home the significance of HELP. Several years ago, a circus came to perform at Battery Park City. Andrew asked me to come because he had arranged for two groups of homeless children to attend: one came from HELP I in Brooklyn; the second came from the Martinique, a welfare hotel that was, at the time those children lived there, a screaming indictment of the society that had failed them. The Martinique was a grotesque scene out of Dickens, brought to life in midtown

---

[25]Ibid.

[26]The first project, called HELP I, built 190 units of transitional housing in the East Brownsville area of Brooklyn. The project contains 190 flexible two-room units that can be adapted to the needs of families of different sizes. Each unit has its own cooking facilities and bathroom. The environment is residential rather than institutional or commercial and embodies the best knowledge about how to help homeless families return to living on their own. The project was a model in public, private, and not-for-profit cooperation. The state provided tax-exempt mortgage financing of about $14 million through the Housing Finance Agency. The project was designed and built at cost by private-sector design and construction companies. HELP I is operated by the American Red Cross, which also provides social services to the families. The annual costs for one family have averaged about $20,500. That is considerably less than the estimated $36,500 it costs to house a homeless family in an unsafe, inadequate welfare hotel. Since its founding, HELP has not only brought over three thousand homeless families back into the mainstream, it has saved money and begun a whole new way of building the housing the people of our state so desperately need.

Manhattan: lead paint peeled from the walls; rats raced through the hallways. That day at the circus, when the announcer stepped to the micro-
phone and introduced the children from the Martinique, it seemed
everyone booed. The kids from the Martinique booed the Martinique, as
did the kids from HELP. Then the announcer said, "Now we have the
kids from HELP," and both groups let out a boisterous cheer. The kids
from HELP cheered because for the first time in many of their young lives
they had a good, safe, clean place to live. The kids from the Martinique
cheered because they loved the idea of HELP as much as they hated the
ugliness, the shame, and the cruelty of living in a welfare hotel.

On my way out, the kids from the Martinique rushed up to me. One boy
grabbed me by the leg, looked up, and said, "Can't you do something,
Governor? Can't you get Andrew to do something? Can't you get us out of
this place?"

They wanted to escape from the Martinique, to be cared for, to be looked
after, to be loved. That's what HELP and other programs like it can do. They
can rescue young lives by giving homeless families a chance to get back on
their feet—to find the transitional housing, the professional support, the
employment, and the *permanent* housing they need to get their lives back
together.

In virtually every state, housing finance agencies and departments of housing have forged links with developers, nonprofit organizations, and local
governments to ensure that we use our limited resources as effectively as
possible. But no state alone can adequately address this *national* problem. To
substantially reduce homelessness in our society, we must do a lot more,
because homelessness is the expression of a whole series of social failures: the
lack of affordable housing, unemployment, poverty, violence, drugs, illness.
What we need now is an all-out struggle against all these problems at the same
time. Social concern has to become fashionable again. So, too, must a renewed state and *federal* partnership.

As the federal government prepares an urban agenda for the rest of the
1990s, it should seek to address a broad array of social problems in an
integrated fashion, because we will not deal effectively with homelessness until
we deal with unemployment, job training, and drug and alcohol abuse.
Emergency food and shelter programs are short-term essentials to meet the
immediate, sometimes life-threatening needs of people with nowhere to go.
But our shelter programs must be designed as temporary stops on the way to

a more stable way of life for homeless individuals and families. Giving people the chance to recapture the dignity they're entitled to means more than simply providing a roof over one's head—as basic and important as that is. It means providing other social services where needed—child care, remedial education, job training, counseling, everything they need to step confidently onto the road to self-sufficiency. And that means we have to try harder.

Creating Affordable Housing

Today, too many New Yorkers, and too many Americans, still suffer from a lack of affordable housing. There is more than one cause, including the gradual withdrawal of the federal government from its commitment to housing assistance. During the 1980s, federal housing aid slowed to a trickle. New York alone lost nearly $20 billion in federal housing assistance between 1980 and 1992, a reduction that accelerated an increasingly inverse relationship between housing supply and demand. This came at a time when poor and low-income families were finding it harder to afford housing and when private home prices were skyrocketing, pushing them out of the reach of middle-class families. Adjusted for inflation, the median income for an individual American increased $64 from 1980 to 1990. By contrast, the median cost of a new home for that period, when adjusted for inflation, increased $16,170.[27] Every year since 1950, an increasing proportion of American families owned their own homes. By the beginning of the 1990s, that trend began to reverse itself—another warning sign that the American Dream seems to be slipping away.

To help keep the dream of home ownership within reach and to create affordable housing, New York State offers more than fifty housing programs that provide a wide range of services, including low-cost mortgage assistance, grants for low-income housing construction and neighborhood preservation, public housing modernization, and homeless housing assistance.

One of our most effective programs is the Nehemiah project, in East Brooklyn and the Bronx, where government, religious, and business communities have come together to build low-income and moderate-income housing.

---

[27]"The Decade by Numbers," *Harper's*, January 1990.

The Nehemiah homes are among the largest developments of their kind in the nation. So far, the State of New York Mortgage Agency (SONYMA) has provided more than two thousand loans to families to purchase these homes and has issued commitments for nearly three hundred more. Eventually 4,100 homes will be built for families who would otherwise be unable to afford their own homes. The unique combination of state, city, and private resources has enabled the Nehemiah planners to build homes at an average cost of $71,000 and sell them to low- and moderate-income families for as little as $56,000. People whose household income ranges between $15,000 and $25,000 and who have managed to save or borrow $5,000 for a down payment are able to live in this revitalized area of Brooklyn on monthly mortgage payments of about $400.

Another good example of the state's successful efforts is Carleton Park in Central Islip, Long Island. When I visited the area in April 1989, some families huddled into six-hundred-square-foot hovels, often without heat. Built forty years ago, Carleton Park was a deteriorating neighborhood that we helped revive and restore. The town of Islip, which joined with business leaders and New York State's Office of Economic Development, is working to make Carleton Park (now known as College Woods) a stronger, more stable, more racially integrated place to live, as well as a national model for suburban renewal.[28] In part, the plan calls for approximately 470 new and rehabilitated units of subsidized housing. Because state and local government helped finance the construction, homes that would have cost upward of $200,000 on the private market are being sold for as little as $98,000. The New York State Affordable Housing Corporation (AHC) has awarded more than $6.6 million to the College Woods project. And after the homes are constructed, SONYMA helps qualified first-time home buyers buy the units with loans at rates as much as two full percentage points below market. This intelligent partnership, which cuts the wholesale and retail costs of owning a home and has already helped 246 families buy a better life in Central Islip, has been replicated by New York's housing agencies from one end of the state to another.

---

[28]College Woods, located in one of the first economic development zones designated in New York State in 1987, is part of a larger plan to develop the entire Central Islip area. The redevelopment plan calls for a 120-acre industrial-technical park, the expansion of the New York Institute of Technology, the reuse of a major state mental health facility, approximately six hundred units of privately constructed housing, and a hotel-conference center with supporting commercial and retail services.

In the fall of 1986 I was in the North Country touring a twenty-four-unit housing project in Carthage that was made possible with funds from the state's Rural Rental Assistance Program. And on a cold winter morning in 1989 I officially opened the first of nineteen housing units to be renovated in downtown Albany under a private/public partnership financed in part with a $630,000 grant from the New York State Low-Income Housing Trust Fund. Two years later, shovel in hand, I was at the ground-breaking ceremony of the Cross Creek Townhouses in Spring Valley, an hour's ride from New York City. Assisted by a grant from AHC, this development has enabled forty-seven families with low and moderate incomes to purchase town houses. This project has been so successful that an additional forty-nine homes are being constructed with assistance from AHC.

These activities not only help improve the quality of life for thousands of New Yorkers, they also strengthen urban, suburban, and rural communities throughout the state.[29]

---

[29]Units assisted through the state's programs and through the federal programs that the state administers total approximately 280,000. This total includes units under contract or award and units under construction and units completed from January 1, 1983, through March 31, 1992. Working with not-for-profit organizations, local governments, and the private sector, we've moved aggressively on a number of fronts to help the homeless, low- and moderate-income tenants, and first-time home buyers. That record includes the following:

• The creation of the Homeless Housing Assistance Program—the first capital construction program in the nation to build emergency, transitional, and permanent housing for the homeless. So far, the $205 million in HHAP appropriations has provided funds for approximately 5,232 units.

• In April of 1985 I signed into law the Housing Trust Fund initiative, a $50 million-a-year commitment by New York State to provide the sound and affordable housing that is a key to our economic future. The first part of that bill created a $25 million low-income rehabilitation program. It created the Housing Trust Fund Corporation (HTFC) to make grants and loans to owners of buildings for constructing or reconstructing residential units in low-income areas. The bill also authorized HTFC to provide financial assistance to owner-occupied homesteading projects for the replacement or repair of heating, plumbing, and electrical systems. The homeownership program promotes reconstruction and rehabilitation of substandard areas through local public/private partnership initiatives, increasing and upgrading New York's stock of owner-occupied housing. The bill also created the Affordable Housing Corporation to provide $25 million in grants to not-for-profits and units of local government—or their designated agencies—so they can carry out the construction and rehabilitation of owner-occupied housing.

• In 1986 New York State, working with the city of New York, its financial community, and hundreds of community groups, reached an agreement with Battery Park City Authority, a public/private housing authority, to create affordable housing throughout New York City with the millions in commercial revenues the authority generates each year. Battery Park City, which is one

Health Care

Today, America has finally understood that it faces a confounding, even agonizing, paradox. The vagaries of the free enterprise economy, and the unevenness and insufficiency of our political and governmental system, have left us with daunting health care problems. In many places we have too few doctors and nurses; in most places we have too few trained for family and preventive care. In many instances we overuse or abuse our technology, while in a few places we don't have enough medical care. A few blocks from some of our leading medical research institutes lie people suffering, even dying, from diseases we thought we had conquered: drug-resistant tuberculosis, measles, congenital syphilis. Inside the neonatal units and the hospices lie the victims of our new plagues: babies the size of my hand strapped to respirators, clinging for life, born addicted to crack, or AIDS babies born to die. It is a shocking and humiliating truth that the United States ranks seventeenth in life expectancy and twenty-first in infant mortality rate among industrialized countries. According to the federal Centers for Disease Control and Prevention, only 3.4 percent of total health care expenditures are used for disease prevention and health promotion. Yet preventive health care could effectively

---

of the best examples in America of what can result when government and the private sector work together to achieve common goals, has assisted in the development of 1,140 units of affordable housing through mid-1993.

- In 1988 we created the single largest tax-supported housing program in New York's history— $326 million to finance affordable housing through the Infrastructure Trust Fund.
- The Affordable Housing Corporation, started in 1985, has provided $265 million in state appropriations to assist in the purchase, rehabilitation, or improvement of over twenty-two thousand homes.
- SONYMA has provided about $3 billion in loans to more than forty-nine thousand home buyers.
- The Housing Finance Agency has issued more than $587 million in bonds for the development of more than 8,450 units across the state.

As proud as we are of the resources we've committed to housing in New York since 1983, we are equally aware of the need to manage better the funds we allocate. New York's housing agencies are mindful of the need to find better ways to deliver social services to housing populations with special needs. We must find places for people to live when they come out of hospitals, prisons, and treatment centers. One way we've found to build essential social services into projects is through prudent use of low-income housing tax credits. County governments, whose powers to finance the construction of new housing have recently been affirmed by the state attorney general, must also become greater partners in our efforts to build and rehabilitate more low-income housing.

reduce deaths from cancer and heart disease and significantly lower the overall cost of health care in the long run.

People are dying because, lacking health insurance, they come to the hospital too late. Or they suffer more than they would have had to if we had only done the simple thing—provided the ounce of prevention called primary care: prenatal care; regular checkups; easy-to-understand instructions from a physician they could trust.

It's obvious to all of us that we must work harder to serve those who can't find or afford a family doctor or even a basic clinic visit; those who are most likely to let simple health problems fester—until an earache becomes a deafening infection or a little high blood pressure turns into a stroke. Again, we should be compelled by compassion but also by common sense. In addition to unnecessary and even tragic illness and disability, this neglect leads to overtaxed emergency rooms and expensive, preventable hospital admissions.

And the cost of it all is threatening to bankrupt the nation.

Until 1965 there was no successful national effort to make health care available to aging Americans. Lyndon Johnson's Medicare and Medicaid programs were the first great steps. But they are not enough to meet today's problems or to provide coverage for all our people. The United States now spends $900 billion a year on health care, roughly three times the entire defense budget. Yet some 38.9 million Americans—some two million in New York—have *no* coverage. Of all the Western industrialized nations, only South Africa and the United States do not guarantee affordable health care for their citizens. Private insurance for the middle class is so costly that employers are reducing and dropping coverage. Red tape is strangling the system, making it much more expensive than it need be, while our population grows older, frailer, and more demanding of health care.

For the past twenty-five years responsibility for expanding access and controlling costs has fallen primarily on the states. By 1993 Medicaid was the biggest expenditure for local governments, growing at a rate of approximately 13 percent in 1992 alone. According to some estimates, Medicaid costs are projected to grow as much as 25 percent a year by 1996 if no new reforms are implemented.[30] Most Americans now realize a solution can come about

---

[30]One of the most common complaints registered by local elected officials is that the growth in Medicaid spending is forcing them to reduce other services to their residents. Where this may be

only through leadership at the national level. In the end, the health care answer we're looking for is a question of balancing three issues: quality, cost, and access. As Washington debates a national plan to provide decent health care at a reasonable cost and make it available to all Americans, New York and the other states are engaged in their own domestic struggles.

In New York we believe that the pursuit of the highest-quality care must begin with prevention. We believe the rest of the nation can benefit from what we have learned in New York. Measles, syphilis, and tuberculosis have one thing in common—they are preventable. With proper and available public health measures in place, all of these illnesses could be eliminated. Yet despite our antibiotic arsenal, we have a resurgence of venereal disease and tuberculosis—some strains now resistant to the very drugs we thought had conquered them. Measles, which we thought we were on the verge of eliminating, is now stalking the children of our inner cities.

The results of failing to prevent are both tragic and unnecessary: for the 1,150 babies born with congenital syphilis in New York in 1990; for the 2,300 children who contracted measles in 1991; for the more than 4,500 people who were infected with tuberculosis in 1992—not to mention all the children needlessly poisoned by lead or stunted by poor nutrition and all the adults with illnesses and injuries that could have been prevented with intelligent exercise.

To halt the measles epidemic, the state has joined with local governments throughout New York. Working with New York City through another New York/New York agreement, the state has enlisted the help of community organizations to help us immunize fifty thousand preschool children in those neighborhoods with a high incidence of measles. Major initiatives are also under way to deal with the other current epidemics. Diagnostic services are being extended to reach the homeless, who are particularly susceptible to tuberculosis. Their treatment is being monitored carefully to assure that each patient completes the full course of antibiotic therapy. To combat syphilis, testing is being conducted in all hospitals, family planning clinics, in drug treatment units, and jails in the epidemic communities.

Prevention works—but it works best if we understand that the idea goes beyond vaccines and vitamins.

---

happening, New York taxpayers ought to be reminded that my administration has offered to assume the full costs of Medicaid now borne at the local level. Regrettably, that mandate relief proposal has not been accepted by the New York State Legislature.

Poverty and other persistent social problems offer fertile ground for virtually every type of illness. The epidemics that afflict us today are, in fact, concentrated in communities that are marked by poverty, inadequate health services, joblessness, overcrowding, substandard housing, and—most important—widespread use of illicit drugs. The relationship between illness, addiction, and physical frailty on the one hand and poverty on the other is not just a persistent coincidence. It is profoundly causal.

We might have predicted the statistics of ill health from the parallel statistics showing the growth of poverty in this nation and the widening gaps between the minority populations that are on the low end of the economic scale and the rest of America. Cardiovascular disease, chemical dependency, diabetes, infant mortality, and even homicide all affect the poor disproportionately. They are all expressions of the ravages and deprivations, the despair and the rage, of being poor in America.

To be intelligent, our approach to public health must be synergistic, applying *all* of our strengths to address all our vulnerabilities. In New York this has led us to enforce the first and strictest controls on acid rain because that relates to health; to pass exemplary laws to protect men, women, and children in the workplace; to promote the National Safe Kids Campaign, a nationwide effort to protect our children from preventable injuries—the largest killer of children under fourteen; to set up a program to help elderly people get the medication they need but cannot afford;[31] to pass a law that increased Social Security income to some 380,000 New Yorkers; to protect our citizens from having to impoverish themselves to pay for the care of their spouses in long-term care institutions;[32] to prohibit physicians from charging elderly patients above

---

[31]In 1986 New York State established the Elderly Pharmaceutical Insurance program (EPIC). EPIC was designed to help senior citizens meet the high costs of prescription drugs. However, because of the complexity of the program, by 1990 only eighty thousand seniors were using the program that was once projected to serve a quarter of a million. In 1990 New York State reformed the EPIC program to allow low-income elderly to join the program by paying a $10 "Life Time" fee to qualify. Higher-income participants will have to meet an annual deductible of only $150 in order to receive benefits. The complicated list of five different co-payments for drugs has been reduced to two co-payments, $6 for drugs costing up to $30 and $15 for drugs costing $30 or more. On average, the EPIC program pays for 62 percent of the costs of prescription drugs for seniors who qualify for benefits.

[32]In New York, where 85 percent of all nursing home costs are paid for by Medicaid, the state has entered into an innovative public/private partnership to help seniors secure and finance private, long-term care coverage without spending down all their assets.

the reasonable rate set by the federal government; to build new veterans nursing homes.

Thus, while we continue to research the causes and treat the symptoms of lung cancer and emphysema, we have also passed one of the nation's most effective and far-reaching antismoking statutes. And to help prevent chronic illnesses and disabilities—including cerebral palsy, retardation, autism, and learning disabilities—we've expanded access to prenatal care, especially for those women who previously fell between the cracks: those not poor enough to qualify for Medicaid but not able to afford private insurance.

Similarly, in an effort to prevent serious injuries and fatalities, we were the first state in the Union to mandate the use of seat belts in 1985; all the other states have since followed. Our Stop-DWI program was the first in the nation to set mandatory minimum fines and jail terms for drunk driving and the first to allow counties to use those fines to create alcohol education and highway safety programs. We set twenty-one as the minimum alcohol purchase age to protect older teenagers who were getting involved in a disproportionate number of alcohol-related accidents. And we *enforced* our new laws—an effort that established 1992 as the safest ever in terms of reducing the number of automobile fatalities on our state highway system and the fifth consecutive year in which we broke the record set the previous year.[33]

Expanding Access, Controlling Costs

Guided by these two principles—prevention and synergism—New York has actually been able to *expand access* to adequate health care, while implementing new procedures to control costs. In many ways we are far ahead of much of the country.

In 1988 New York expanded Medicaid coverage to ensure that all persons with income at or below the poverty level are eligible for health care.

---

[33]One of the ways we have discouraged drunken driving is through public service messages delivered by some of our finest professional and amateur athletes from New York and across the country. These credible and admired figures have attended training sessions on the subject and have volunteered their time to speak to high school students about the danger of mixing drinking and driving. In addition to reaching nearly a quarter of a million young people through the schools, they have also expanded their audience through radio and television messages distributed throughout the state. New York's Athletes Against Drunk Driving was the first statewide program of its kind in the nation, and we're encouraging other states to use it as a model, as is the National Highway Traffic Safety Administration.

That single piece of legislation was estimated to reach more than 200,000 New Yorkers, including almost 150,000 children who, at the time, were living in poverty but were not eligible for Medicaid because they were not considered to be *poor enough*. In 1989 New York State passed the Pre-Natal and Infant Care Act, which extended critical health care services to approximately seventy thousand poor women and their children. In addition, we have expanded medical coverage for children under thirteen through our Child Health Plus program; passed a Supplemental Nutrition Assistance Program, serving more than 30,000 elderly New Yorkers; and expanded in-home services for the elderly, providing personal care and chore services to some 26,000 home-bound senior citizens who might otherwise have no choice but a nursing home.

Perhaps the most important step in expanding access is to ensure that our public hospitals are able to serve our neediest citizens. Early during my first term as governor, I learned that one of the most serious problems we faced in health care was replacing the aging physical plants of our hospitals, and foremost among them were those serving the poor. We recognized that we had to make up the hospital's losses in caring for those most in need of health care and least able to pay for it. I declared a one-year moratorium on hospital construction, and during that year we developed what we hoped would be some good and practical ideas. With the help of the state legislature we created a bad-debt and charity care pool, an Emergency Hospital Reimbursement Program, and a Financially Distressed Hospital Program to empower hospitals to provide care that uninsured patients could not always afford. In effect, it is a kind of state health plan for the neediest part of our population, with hospitals as the main providers.

One of the innovations included in our ongoing hospital reform efforts made it possible for financially distressed hospitals to get the credit they needed to rebuild run-down, obsolete physical plants. Without this help no lending institution would consider their requests. So state government stepped in. We assembled the major payers for health care services and created a pool of money by using their funds as collateral for the issuance of special hospital project bonds. With these changes the state was able to rescue financially distressed public hospitals like Jamaica Hospital in Queens, Bronx-Lebanon Hospital in the Bronx, and North General Hospital in Manhattan. Saving them was essential because public hospitals embody the essential mission of our government—the even-handed pursuit of the common good. Public hospitals serve our neediest citizens with severe health problems.

At one time most Americans had a family doctor for routine care, one who knew their medical history, helped steer them to healthy habits, furnished inoculations and other preventive measures, and, when necessary, referred them elsewhere for specialized care. Many of us still enjoy that kind of personal attention. But if you are poor and on Medicaid, there's a good chance that's not the way it works. To get care for yourself and your children, you may have no choice but to go to a hospital emergency room, where instead of the kind of care you need, you may be subjected to redundant and unnecessary tests. All of that is very expensive for the taxpayers and not very good for you.

In New York we are providing better care *and* reducing costs by enrolling people eligible for Medicaid in "managed care" programs. Managed care can take different forms, but it essentially means giving poor people the chance to be treated the way most people are treated. As of June of 1993 there were already more than 225,000 Medicaid recipients enrolled in managed care programs in New York State. Our goal is to enroll 50 percent of Medicaid recipients—more than one million people—in such plans by the end of this decade.

The phrase *health care* usually evokes thoughts of the treatment process—all the marvelous technological and diagnostic resources of modern medicine. But intelligent reforms like managed care remind us that less glamorous advances can be just as important.[34] The quagmire of health care paperwork is itself a kind of disease. The symptoms are everywhere: too many forms, too many different rules and procedures, too many bills, too much delay in getting payments to providers. It's not simply inconvenient, inefficient, and wasteful; it's expensive. Nationally, dealing with this administrative nightmare accounts for *nearly two of every ten hospital operating dollars*—by some estimates as much as $167 billion a year.[35] It explains why, nationally, the number of health care administrators is growing three times as fast as the number of doctors. This

---

[34]We have been able to expand access, in part, because we control costs better than most states. We do it with first-in-the-nation innovations like our Certificate of Need System to ensure that capital expenditures are both necessary and affordable, and the Diagnosis Related Group (DRG) inpatient reimbursement system, which bases reimbursements on different case types as opposed to a per-day basis. We do it through certificates of need that protect against unnecessary duplication of costly services or facilities.

[35]"The National Health Care Phobia," Gregg Easterbrook, *Newsweek*, September 6, 1993.

translates inevitably into a needlessly higher national health care bill and a system so ponderous that it also gets in the way of delivering quality health care services.

One of New York State's cures for this bureaucratic illness is called the Single Payer Demonstration Project, funded jointly by the Robert Wood Johnson Foundation and the New York State Department of Health. The project creates a single electronic network—a clearinghouse—to automate and standardize the process of processing, billing for, and paying health care claims. This cost-cutting initiative, which simplifies the avalanche of complicated paperwork that has descended on the system, is the first statewide project of its kind in the nation. The system works a little like an automated teller machine, allowing many different banks to serve customers through a single electronic outlet. The dividends in increased efficiency are immediate: the clearinghouse verifies each patient's insurance coverage from a single source; the electronic network quickly tells whether a doctor must seek permission before certain procedures can be performed; the network helps hospital personnel file claim forms electronically, with no errors. By coordinating numerous elements, the Single Payer clearinghouse will speed the delivery of benefits to those covered by more than one insurance policy. It will simplify and accelerate payment to hospitals and doctors by transferring funds electronically on a routine, fixed schedule. It will permit us to test the use of a single health insurance card—much like the one President Clinton held up during his health care address to the nation in 1993—for all consumers. Like the automatic bank teller network, it will integrate all these functions into one comprehensive system. Best of all, when the system is eventually applied to all 260 hospitals in the state (by 1999), it could save taxpayers $200 million a year.

The fundamental and related challenges we face in health care involving access, cost, and quality will not be met simply by allowing health care providers to compete for consumers' dollars. Nor will our problems be solved through a command-and-control centralized bureaucracy. Competition has a role in our health care system. But that competition must be structured so that it does what competition should do: hold down costs and increase quality for consumers. The fact that we do not as yet have that kind of healthy competition has forced government to devise reforms that meet all our goals.

In the spring of 1993, while the nation awaited new health care reforms to take shape in Washington, I proposed in a Special Message to the Legislature a comprehensive reform of New York's health care system. The heart of my proposal involved shifting resources already invested in the system to increase preventive and primary care. If we do that, we will lower overall health care costs and improve our overall health.

How do we do that? By providing access to comprehensive care through health networks to more people, so patients go to a primary care provider for checkups because we know that in the long run preventive medicine saves millions of dollars in money not spent for the treatment of preventable illness.

Another way is to increase the number of physicians offering primary care. Only 30 percent of our physicians are primary care providers now, while 70 percent are specialists. In many other nations—nations whose citizens have greater life expectancy than Americans—the ratio is reversed. We need to increase our primary care capacity by giving financial incentives both to medical students to become primary care providers and to medical schools that emphasize primary care.

Specifically, I proposed that the state expand primary care and help to insure more children under age thirteen through the state's Child Health Plus program; that we increase the Medicaid payments to doctors serving patients on Medicaid so that more doctors will be encouraged to treat Medicaid patients in their offices. The plan I submitted would provide grants to doctors, hospitals, and health centers to set up primary care services; it would allocate grants to medical schools that recruit students to train for primary care positions; and it would forgive the loans of physicians who choose primary care training and who pledge to serve in underserved areas of the state. And to help rural regions where hospitals have closed or are in danger of closing, I recommended that the state invest new monies to encourage rural health networks.

Another important piece of New York's health care reform was passed in 1992. The community rating bill requires commercial health insurers to "community rate" the contracts they write. This law, which also requires that insurers allow for "open enrollment"—taking everyone who applies for coverage under a contract—prohibits insurers from "cherry picking" the healthiest candidates. In New York, no longer are commercial health insurers allowed to discriminate against individuals because of their preexisting medical conditions or presumptions about their health. This legislation, the first of its kind in the nation, has become a fundamental premise of the national health care plan proposed by President Clinton.

To control costs, I proposed that the state consider establishing a reimbursement system that will regulate fees charged by private physicians, while requiring doctors in private practice to gain prior approval before purchasing expensive technological equipment. Currently in New York, hospitals must submit a certificate of need in order to purchase expensive high-tech equipment. We should extend this policy to private practitioners. For example, the number of expensive magnetic resonance imaging systems—or MRIs—in a community should not exceed the number needed to serve that community. If only one or two of these useful million-dollar diagnostic tools are needed, it makes no sense for every provider in a community to have one. That just increases health care costs unnecessarily, as it did in western New York, where eight counties have as many MRIs as the entire province of Quebec, Canada.

The final aspect of the plan involves reorganizing the way health care systems function, giving greater power to business leaders, providers, and insurers to organize the way they manage the health care system they are a part of. Ultimately, by creating regional health care networks around the state, regional governing bodies could work together to control costs and manage their systems—a "managed collaboration" approach to health care that could have influence even beyond our borders.

For example, in Rochester, under a cooperative agreement between the region's major private employers and Rochester Blue Cross (the region's dominant insurer, which covers about 80 percent of the people), the people of Rochester have been able to hold their health care costs 34 percent below the national average—largely because a dominant insurer has enough leverage with hospitals and doctors to keep medical prices low. In Rochester people pay reasonable premiums, choose their own doctors, and receive excellent care. Rochester physicians still flourish in their private practices. A 1993 article in *Newsweek* described Rochester's program as a "guerrilla insurrection in health care reform," combining "the cost control of national health care with the best of market-driven medicine." Noting that Rochester's cost levels amounted to 9 percent of GDP, *Newsweek* estimated that if such levels were extended nationwide, "U.S. health care expenditures would decline by $285 billion per year."[36]

Health care coverage is a very complex issue, and it is obvious that the

---

[36]"The National Health Care Phobia," Gregg Easterbrook, *Newsweek*, September 6, 1993.

federal government must take the initiative to see that as many Americans as possible are provided with insurance. It is clear that President Clinton already has begun what will be a very long and arduous debate that may last well into 1994. It is critical that he forge a consensus that will lead to improvements in the system we have. The key question everyone is asking right now is, "Will President Clinton's basic health care plan work?"

Closer to home, the other questions we're asking are, "What kind of effect will it have on New Yorkers?" and "What will it mean for the 2.5 million uninsured citizens in our state?"

The president's proposal is designed to guarantee security for all Americans, and its emphasis on primary and preventive care has the potential to save thousands of lives lost to preventable disease and illnesses. Many of the poor who do not have access to anything but an emergency room should benefit from the plan. The model he would like to use—managed competition—attempts to provide services for those who do not have any, and this is a good thing.

But I'm worried about what will happen to our state budget if the original plan is enacted. There will not be any windfall for New York. Our initial analysis indicates that New York could lose up to $357 million in tax revenues. We could lose somewhere between $120 million and $900 million in increased Medicaid expenditures to sustain current benefit levels.

We must make sure that the health care plan eventually adopted by Congress does not contain these inequities. We have to work to ensure that the Medicaid matching formula is revised to reflect current realities. It is critical that we aren't penalized for offering more comprehensive health care services to our low-income families. And it must contain provisions that offer broad coverage on long-term care that adequately meets the needs of the elderly and chronically ill.

All this, I'm aware, is a lot to ask for. Yet we all agree that the system is in dire need of repair. We know that we must do something.

Facing Up to AIDS

Fifteen years ago an inspired public health expert might have been able to forecast the fact that health care was going to be an ugly mess by now. But that prediction would have lacked one immense factor that has made everything much worse than anyone had imagined: AIDS.

As the acronym for acquired immunodeficiency syndrome, *AIDS* was introduced into our language in the early 1980s, although by that time the virus that causes AIDS may have been undetected or unrecognized in the American bloodstream for as long as ten years. As physicians and scientists began to appreciate the tormenting complexity and terrible force of the syndrome, epidemiological patterns emerged. By 1983 AIDS had been diagnosed in people from thirty-six states, but most of the cases were found on the East and West coasts, with New York State reporting about half the total cases. At that time the people dying from AIDS were predominantly homosexual or bisexual men, although the syndrome was diagnosed in others as well: people who had been transfused—especially during treatment for hemophilia—and intravenous drug users who shared drug paraphernalia with other users. Later, AIDS was seen increasingly in women who had been sexual partners of IV drug users and even in the children they bore. Today, the AIDS infection is growing, alarmingly, among the teenage population. We even have found rare instances where people have been infected through the health care system, as in Florida where a dentist infected several patients.

In the past decade AIDS has caused immeasurable suffering. By 1993, 204,000 people across the United States had died of AIDS—45,000 of them New Yorkers. In New York City AIDS is now the leading cause of death for men and women aged twenty to thirty-five.[37]

We still have no cure for AIDS. We have no vaccine to keep people from getting it. We do not know, with any accuracy, how many people may be carrying the virus, all of whom, it must be assumed, are capable of passing it to others. Our best estimate at this time is that as many as seventy-five thousand more New Yorkers will die from AIDS in the next five years, while the number of women and children diagnosed with AIDS is expected to increase significantly.

Although nobody can honestly claim to have answers to all questions about AIDS, we know enough now to help people protect themselves against the virus if we can convince them to avoid the activities that can put them at risk. We know through the studies of epidemiologists and others that the AIDS virus has found only a limited number of ways to pass from person to person, principally through intimate sexual acts—both homosexual and heterosex-

---

[37]New York City, which has more HIV cases than the next four highest cities combined, and contains within its borders as many as 20 percent of the HIV-infected people in the country, is frequently referred to as the "epicenter" of the HIV epidemic in the United States.

ual—and through the practice of sharing needles among drug users. AIDS is not passed through a handshake or a mosquito bite or a shared glass of water.

New York State's course to combat the AIDS epidemic was laid out by a man who brought to this challenge, and all others, an unmatched capacity of mind and sensitivity, former New York State health commissioner Dr. David Axelrod. Dr. Axelrod understood that as dangerous as the virus was, perhaps our greatest enemies were fear, denial, ignorance, and intolerance. He is no longer serving with us because of a debilitating stroke, but in the early years of the AIDS assault he charted policies and practices that I believe are the most intelligent, realistic, and compassionate in the nation—and we continue to follow the course he set to this day. As a result, New York State is the national leader in creating and funding programs for HIV-infected people.

The state's effort to deal with the AIDS crisis began with the creation of the institutional structures necessary for an intelligent and effective response. In 1983 we established an AIDS Institute within the New York State Department of Health to work exclusively on AIDS-related problems and to coordinate the state's response. We were also the first state to appropriate tax dollars for AIDS research. In the ten-year period between 1983 and 1993, the state spent more than $1.5 billion on programs to prevent and treat AIDS. For 1993–94 alone, nearly $450 million was earmarked for the fight against AIDS. In part these funds will be used by the NYS Department of Health to implement AIDS Day Health Care programs at several new clinic sites that will complement work done at three hospitals formally designated as AIDS centers. Eventually twenty major medical centers will provide care for up to three-quarters of all the state's AIDS patients.

We believe we have the most progressive HIV-related Medicaid policy in the country. Reimbursement rates to hospitals, clinics, community organizations, long-term care and home care providers, foster parents, and, most recently, doctors have all been increased because of the huge burden they bear in dealing with this menace.[38] We have also passed legislation that allows

---

[38]We operate ten primary alternate counseling and testing sites in upstate New York, New York City, and Long Island that provide free and anonymous services. Satellite clinics in thirteen additional locations are staffed by regional HIV counselors. Counseling is also being offered through prenatal care and family planning clinics to women in high-risk categories, to prison inmates with AIDS who are preparing for release, to students at our SUNY colleges, and to recovering addicts in methadone maintenance and drug-free programs.

Medicaid coverage of health insurance premiums for persons with AIDS. And while we have taken aggressive steps to track the epidemic—becoming the first state in which infants were tested for exposure to the virus—we have also protected the rights of those infected, passing strong HIV antidiscrimination and confidentiality laws. New York State leads the nation in framing all major HIV policy issues, often setting guidelines in advance of federal pronouncements.[39] For example, when controversy arose about HIV-infected physicians and other health care workers, New York responded to scientific indicators instead of the political winds, refusing to embrace massive mandatory testing schemes that offered only false security.[40]

At the moment education remains our best hope for preventing the spread of AIDS. Our effort in that area has been massive, beginning with the distribution of more than five million pieces of AIDS literature.[41] We have established a toll-free AIDS hot line (1-800-541-AIDS); radio and TV public service announcements have been produced and broadcast; courses have been added to our community and high school curricula.

Despite the imperative to cut back on almost everything created by the most recent national recession, we have insisted that AIDS initiatives be exempted from our near universal budget cuts.

Have we done enough? Of course not. The obvious inadequacy of state resources is one reason. Another has been that the national government has not brought to the problem anything like the concern it warrants. For the past twelve years the national government has slighted the ill generally, and people

---

[39]New York's community rating bill prevents predatory underwriting practices by commercial health insurance companies who had previously discriminated against persons exposed to the HIV virus or assumed that they were at risk.

[40]The New York State Department of Health has a progressive policy on HIV-infected health care workers that is based on extensive scientific evidence. It promotes education and prevention through strict and universal infection control procedures in hospitals and recommends extending those procedures to other practice settings. It mandates infection control training and encourages *voluntary* testing. It calls for evaluations of HIV-infected workers who perform procedures that produce risk. However, it does not include mandatory testing or mandatory disclosure because those have been found not to be necessary and because the imposition of these mandates would be counterproductive.

[41]These include hundreds of thousands of copies of a New York State Health Department publication, *AIDS: 100 Questions and Answers;* transit ads in subway cars and buses; a brochure distributed with paychecks to every state worker entitled *10 Facts You Need to Know About AIDS;* copies of the same brochure provided for distribution to New York City municipal employees; special brochures directed at women; and bilingual brochures and posters aimed at intravenous drug users.

with AIDS in particular, in its allocation of resources, energy, and interest. We all hope that trend will be reversed with a new administration in Washington, which has promised to do more than its predecessor.

In the meantime, as we build our defenses and continue to search for a cure, we are mindful that AIDS has created another risk, the risk of confusing cause and effect, of forgetting that our common enemy here is a virus and not homosexuals or drug users or their sexual partners or their children. We're at risk of grasping for simplistic answers to complex questions, of believing, for example, that if everyone were simply tested for the virus, that in itself would stop it. We're at risk—especially the young—of behaving as if we are immortal, of believing that whatever we do, youth will protect us. We are at risk of forgetting that every person with AIDS is, like us, someone's grandchild, neighbor, co-worker, friend. We are at risk of allowing a virus to do what other forces, like racism, have threatened to do in the past: to dissolve the bonds that our common life depends on.

A successful struggle against this frightening and inexplicable killer requires more than money, programs, and research; it also requires our best instincts as a people.

The Current Toll of Social Pain

One of my hardest days as governor was a day a few years ago when I returned to the neighborhood in Queens where I grew up. I had feared that conditions might have deteriorated over so many years, but I was unprepared for so many dramatic changes. Instead of the faint hope of the 1930s—even amid the Great Depression—I saw the despair of the 1990s. Instead of people of diverse backgrounds working, striving to get ahead, I saw people in desperation, unemployed, without any purpose or prospects. The houses were crumbling; children loitered when they should have been in school. I watched people, many of them young, on drugs, a procession of the walking dead. Pimps and prostitutes patrolled the streets. I even saw a couple fornicating in the street. My part of South Jamaica, once a pocket of modest dreams and simple dignity, had become an area I barely recognized, ravaged by neglect, a vivid example of societal failure.

Worse, what I saw was not unique to the neighborhood I grew up in or to New York City or New York State. From Buffalo to Bedford-Stuyvesant, from

East St. Louis to East Los Angeles, from the Shaw district in Washington, D.C., to the South Side of Chicago, whole communities throughout the country are suffocating in drugs and AIDS and the social disorientation that poverty brings. It's the "other city" I talked about some years ago when President Reagan asked us to think of all of America as "the shining city on a hill."

Dr. Marc Miringoff, director of the Fordham Institute for Innovation in Social Policy, has made an independent study of sixteen different social problems—poverty, teen suicide, child abuse, drug abuse, infant mortality, school dropouts, crime rates, and others—covering the last two decades of life in the United States. His latest "Index of Social Health" revealed a disheartening picture: the nation's social well-being is at its lowest point since 1970.[42] Nine of the sixteen problems had grown worse. Child abuse and the gap between the rich and poor are problems that have become more acute almost every year between 1970 and 1990.[43] Miringoff concluded: "Of particular concern is the fact that America's social health has been at such a low level for so many years. . . . It seems clear that the worsening of so many social problems carries adverse implications for the social fabric of the country."[44]

What has made all this hardship infinitely worse has been the plague of drug abuse, which has taken on unprecedented dimensions over the past decade with the emergence of a highly toxic derivative of cocaine called crack. To the best of my knowledge, crack did not exist on the streets when I was sworn into office in 1983. But by the late 1980s crack cocaine had become the new business of the ghetto, causing violent struggles among drug gangs battling for turf and merchandise. In the neighborhoods where it has become a common presence, crack has wreaked havoc on a scale never seen with any other drug. There are at least four reasons: crack is viciously addictive but produces only a short, intense high; it is so cheap that virtually anyone can buy it, even a child with the money he steals out of his mother's purse; it is easier

---

[42]Miringoff's study is done annually. The latest study was published in 1992, covering statistics gathered in 1990, the last year all current figures were available.

[43]The major positive trend was a 50 percent reduction in poverty among the elderly.

[44]The ranks of the U.S. poor have reached 35.7 million, or roughly 14.2 percent of our population. One out of seven people, poor. This is the highest number in nearly three decades. Nearly half the poverty-stricken households have only one parent living in them. In New York State our figures reflect almost exactly the ratio of the nation at large. About 2.7 million are classified as poor, 15.3 percent of the state's population.

to use than other drugs because it can be smoked rather than injected; and it tends to promote desperate and irrational behavior in the user. In 1992, just before Thanksgiving, a Mastic, L.I., couple addicted to crack were indicted for trying to sell their *two children*—a four-month-old infant and a two-year-old— to their baby-sitter for $1,500. But the intensity of the physical addiction is only a piece of the problem.

Perhaps the worst consequence of all is the crime and violence spawned by drug use and the illicit drug trade. Ordinary cocaine and crack both have a high probable cause in relation to crime and violence, including homicide, especially in large cities like Los Angeles and New York. In Washington, D.C., the number of low-level teenage dealers shooting each other on the street has driven homicide statistics almost past the point of believability. Nationwide, homicide is now the leading cause of death for young African-Americans from eighteen until they reach middle age. The ripple effect of this madness is frightening: hospital emergency rooms and prisons overflowing; violent robbery, theft, domestic violence, and an especially desperate form of "sex for drugs" prostitution; more and more victims, many of them adolescents and even children. It is not uncommon to find children as young as eight or nine hired for $20, $50, even $100 a day to serve as lookouts or runners for local drug dealers—only to catch a bullet in the crossfire. When the stories make the headlines now, we hardly blink.

And the ripples don't stop at the city line.

Having grown up in New York City, I was amazed to learn when I first entered government that many of the classic "urban" problems are now commonplace in the countryside. Over the past decade it has become even more evident that, while cool forests and sleepy pastures may mask the social problems of our rural districts, they do not prevent them. Rural America, including rural New York, is not immune to teenage pregnancy, a high dropout rate, domestic violence, AIDS, or homelessness. The devastating drugs are there, the hardships are there. Poverty is surely there, too.

Forty-three of forty-four rural counties in New York have per capita incomes lower than the national average. In fact, over the past decade, the counties in New York with the lowest per capita income and highest average unemployment were all rural. And the obvious problems of individual poverty are exacerbated in rural areas by vast geography, sparse population, lack of transportation, and small tax bases: how useful is Medicaid if the nearest doctor is one hundred miles away?

In November 1991 I testified before the President's Council on Rural America in Binghamton, N.Y., to explain to federal representatives that in some areas federal actions and attitudes have made matters worse in rural America. For example, the Census Bureau has acknowledged that when it counted the homeless, it paid little attention to rural areas. According to the census, twenty-seven of New York's forty-four rural counties have no homeless at all, and a quarter of all the rural homeless in the entire state live in one jurisdiction, Fulton County.[45]

This kind of misinformation punishes rural areas by depriving them of their fair share of federal resources, after a decade in which federal cutbacks have made life more difficult at the state and local levels. For example, between 1975 and 1988 the federal share of total local government expenditures in New York's rural counties actually shrank from nearly 14 percent to less than 7 percent. If those rural governments received the same share of federal aid in 1988 as they did in 1975, they would have received nearly half a billion dollars extra. The impact in urban districts has been even more severe, forcing governments across our state—as I'm sure they were in other states—to scramble for stopgap answers rather than push for progressive solutions.

Nearly thirty years ago President Johnson saw the long-term effects that poverty can have on the well-being of a nation. After he had declared his War on Poverty, Johnson said, "If we stand passively by while the center of each city becomes a hive of deprivation, crime, and hopelessness . . . if we become two peoples, the suburban affluent and the urban poor, each filled with mistrust and fear for the other . . . then we shall effectively cripple each generation to come."[46]

This holds true today.

But the causes of all the pathologies we see—the broken homes, the poverty, the drugs, the crime, the violence, the murders, the teen pregnancies, the illiteracy, the sum total of all the despair—do not belong to the city alone, nor do their consequences. New York recognizes the problem and is dealing with it aggressively, if not adequately.[47] We know especially well that the effort to

---

[45]These statistics are based on 1990 Census Bureau data. By our own state estimates, these figures are conservative. They are most likely much higher.

[46]*Public Papers of President Lyndon B. Johnson*, 1966, p. 83.

[47]To help generate better communication between state government and rural New York, I proposed a Rural Assistance Information Network—RAIN—the nation's first computer service tar-

eradicate poverty and its destructive effects must begin with our children, nearly one in four of whom are growing up poor.

Decade of the Child

A few years ago the story of a little girl in Texas who fell down a well gripped the airwaves and the headlines of the whole country, for weeks. We worried together—all 250 million of us—prepared to help if we could. How could it be, then, that here, in the richest country the world has ever known, we continue to permit millions of children to succumb to the slow death of poverty, neglect, illness, illiteracy, addiction, and abuse?

Today, three million more American children live in poverty than in 1980. The number living in foster care homes, detention centers, and homeless shelters is rising dramatically and ominously, as are the numbers of crack-addicted mothers giving birth to addicted babies.

Each year in New York some quarter of a million babies are born. Nearly seven hundred times a day, all the hope and potential of the human condition are renewed here . . . and all its vulnerability as well. Currently some 2,700 infants born each year in New York do not survive the first year of life. In 1993, 10,000 New York babies will be born with, or will later develop, physical or mental problems that will hinder their growth and development, often because their mothers did not receive proper prenatal care.[48] And

---

geted at rural areas. It marked the first time that a comprehensive data base was developed to include all the financial and technical assistance that state government has to offer rural areas. Since 1989 this network has provided rural New Yorkers with computer access to more than 1,600 state and federal programs, census data, selected private funding sources, and comprehensive recycling information. With more than twelve thousand calls, RAIN has users in every New York county, twenty-two other states, Washington, D.C., and Canada. With RAIN and other programs, the New York State Office of Rural Affairs—the first cabinet-level office dedicated solely to rural concerns—helps to ensure that state government is as sensitive to Beekmantown, Batavia, and Bemus Point as it is to our metropolitan centers.

[48]Low-birthweight babies have continued to bring major hardships to our health care system. About one in fourteen babies born in the United States are dangerously low in weight (under 5.5 pounds). A low-weight baby is twenty times more likely to die in its first year of life than a normal-weight baby. And those who do survive are more susceptible to developing recurring illnesses, learning disabilities, behavior problems, and psychiatric disorders. The disadvantaged children who are born today are disadvantaged *before* they leave the womb.

although the effects on parents—particularly when they are themselves very young or raising a child alone—are not as easy to measure, they are not hard to imagine: emotional and financial stress; feelings of guilt, inadequacy, and resentment; tremendous burdens on people who, in some cases, are barely more than children themselves.

A few years ago, at a Christmas party for children in Albany, I was greeted by a beautiful child—I guess about four years old. She flashed a big smile and then kissed me on the cheek, saying, "Merry Christmas, Governor." A moment later the nun who was holding her told me the child was one of the dozen or so AIDS babies at their center and that in all likelihood the child would not live past the age of six. More like her are being born every week.

On another visit, this time to a clinic, I met a young girl named Mercedes. She was fifteen and having her second child. I asked if she knew about birth control methods. She scoffed at the suggestion that her child was an accident. She said firmly, "I wanted these babies. These babies are mine. I don't have anything else. No family, no job, nothing to look forward to. What else do I have?"

In the public arena, all of us have been telling each other for a long time that "children are our greatest resource," but as a society we have certainly not behaved as if we believed it. Clearly government does not have the first responsibility with regard to children. The primary duty should plainly fall to the family, preferably one in which the children can count on loving, stable parents. But we also know that today's reality is different. In the 1950s one in ten children returned from school to an empty house. Today two out of every three do. Nationally, parents average only fifteen minutes a day of one-to-one interaction with their children. One in two marriages ends in divorce. Over the past thirty years there has also been a sharp increase in single parenting. Sixty-two percent of African-American families with children are now headed by one parent. Between 1960 and 1989 the proportion of young, unwed white women giving birth to babies rose from 9 percent to 22 percent.[49] In such a world, government has a special role to play, not to supplant parental responsibility, but to support it.

These concerns and hopes motivated New York in 1988 to initiate a comprehensive set of children's programs that we call the Decade of the

---

[49]"Endangered Family," *Newsweek*, August 30, 1993.

Child, a ten-year commitment to see that New York's children are properly fed, housed, cared for, and educated. Through a "family network" of some 125 state programs, New York provides a continuum of care and services to children—from the womb, to the delivery room, through grade school and high school—helping them and their parents overcome the larger social forces that lead to the breakdown of families.[50]

We have expanded health care coverage and nutrition assistance to reach more pregnant women in need, supplementing the federal nutrition programs. Through the state's Pre- and Post-Natal Parent Education Hospital Program, every maternity unit in New York gives two free "parenting education" books to new mothers and fathers, some barely adults themselves. Through these materials, and through an initiative called New York Parent, which compiles all the state-funded programs into one accessible computer data base, we help parents take advantage of family and children's services near their homes. Through our Infant Health Assessment Program (IHAP), doctors access which newborn babies and mothers are at risk for future medical problems. Once released from the hospital, depending on their domestic situation or medical condition, mothers and children are eligible to receive up to three months of home care assistance from a social worker or a visiting nurse.

Because health and education are at the heart of our Decade of the Child, we have immunized more preschoolers and expanded our prekindergarten programs. Our efforts to preserve families take many forms. Sometimes the serious personal or behavioral problems of one member can destroy an entire family. To help deal with these pressures, family preservation workers go into troubled homes and give families advice and practical help to solve their problems so that children don't have to be removed from these homes and placed in foster care.

To help working parents, New York State provides child care facilities for many of its workers and flexible, progressive parental leave policies that go beyond the recently adopted federal policy. We also make a full range of start-up grants available for establishing not-for-profit, all-day and after-school child care programs. We have a Child Care Coordinating Council that helps parents find quality, licensed child care providers in their neighbor-

---

[50]The state has a toll-free number that informs New Yorkers about all the Decade of the Child programs on one computerized catalog. The number is 1-800-345-KIDS.

hoods. And in addition to educating the public about child abuse, New York State's Citizens Task Force on Child Abuse and Neglect has reached into the workplace, encouraging employers to be more "family friendly," to be mindful that their workers are also parents. To the extent employers can reduce some stress in the workplace—by making child care more available, by allowing for flexible time schedules, and by honoring workers when they need to take medical or family leave—we can reduce stress at home while raising productivity and reducing absenteeism on the job.

When children reach school age, we introduce them to good eating habits through our Nutrition for Life education program, teaching them that what they eat can affect how they feel and what they can achieve. Once they're in school, we work hard to keep them motivated so they'll stay and finish high school. One way to encourage this is through "community schools"—schools that are open before and after normal class hours, twelve months a year, with a full range of educational, recreational, and social functions. By 1992 the state had helped create forty-one community schools in twenty-two counties. By the end of the decade every local school district that wants such a school should have that capacity.

Perhaps the best way to keep young people on the right track, though, is through a one-on-one relationship with a role model interested in their future. Founded in 1987 by Matilda Cuomo, the New York State Mentoring Program fosters one-on-one relationships between adult role models and children, grades K–8. Today there are more than six thousand children and adult volunteers participating in the program through two hundred schools in thirty-three counties. The only statewide school-based early intervention program of its kind in the nation, the New York State Mentoring Program recruits mentors and receives support from 120 partner organizations, including major corporations, colleges, government agencies, and civic groups. In 1992 adult mentors contributed more than one hundred thousand volunteer hours to this public/private partnership.

Are the state's comprehensive antidropout programs having an effect? Recent trends are encouraging: from 1982–83 to 1990–91, the state's high school dropout rate decreased by 36.2 percent.

Keeping kids healthy and motivated is essential; so is teaching them to accept responsibility for their lives—and for the lives of others.

New York has a range of programs that help to prevent adolescent pregnancy, focusing on teenagers who are not pregnant but who seem to be at greatest risk of becoming parents before they are prepared to handle the responsibilities. Today New York has twenty-four comprehensive teen pregnancy prevention and service projects statewide. These programs help encourage young people to delay becoming sexually active, to promote the use of contraception and safe sexual practices, and to ensure that teens who do become sexually active have the support they need to give birth to healthy babies and become healthy parents. We have stressed the prevention of teen pregnancy through a model program called Alternative Avenues to Dignity, which provides educational support for teens. Recent trends indicate that these projects may be having a positive effect on the lives of single teenagers between fifteen and nineteen. After peaking in 1990, the pregnancy rates of fifteen- to nineteen-year-olds have begun to decline in New York.[51]

Also as part of our agenda, New York has made it easier for children to be adopted in New York through the Adoption Option, a 1991 initiative designed to improve the state's adoption practices and services. During its first year of operation, the Decade of the Child 1-800 "infoline" received nearly 25,000 calls, 11,000 of which dealt with adoption. With the help of New York's outreach programs—which include a *Family Album* publication that features the smiling faces of children waiting for new homes—the number of adoptions in New York increased by 26 percent from 1991 to 1992.[52]

Important new Decade of the Child initiatives were passed in 1992, including the Lead Screening Act, which identifies children at risk for lead poisoning; expansion of the Child Health Insurance Program (CHIP)—renamed Child Health Plus, which now provides state-subsidized medical coverage for children under age thirteen in low-income families. Today, outpatient coverage is available for nearly fifty thousand children. Other new programs include the Adolescent Tobacco Prevention Act, which will curb illegal cigarette sales to minors and cut down teen addiction, and the Early Care Bill, a progressive, community-based system of early intervention services for infants and toddlers with disabilities.

Inspired by the leadership of the honorary chairwoman of New York

---

[51]Since 1991 the birth and abortion rates have also been declining for teenagers fifteen to nineteen years of age.

[52]There are some one thousand children, from preschool to high school, waiting to be adopted in New York.

State's Council on Children and Families, Matilda Cuomo, we will continue adding initiatives each year, modifying, adapting, improving; learning from other states; testing our success; doing everything possible for our children, at least until the Decade of the Child concludes at the end of 1997. We look forward to making even more progress with the support of a presidentially led American Decade of the Child that will commit the entire nation to a comprehensive children's agenda for the next ten years.

We are spending a tremendous amount of wealth and effort in offices and agencies and homes across the state. Tens of thousands of people are devoting their lives to helping children save, improve, and enjoy theirs. We think we know the nature of their problems: the poverty; the drugs; the bad examples; the lack of hope.

But let's think about this some more. There is something more fundamental about the situation we need to address.

I remember speaking a few years ago to several hundred ninth- and tenth-graders in New York City. I spoke about the beauty of life, the many opportunities in their future, and the threat to all their hopes and dreams that drugs posed. After I'd finished, I asked them if what I'd said made sense. Most of them nodded. One didn't. A boy with a chipped front tooth looked at me with his head half-cocked to the side, his face impassive, but his skepticism showing through quite clearly.

"Didn't you agree with me?" I asked. "That your life is too precious to give away to drugs?"

"I'm not sure," he answered. "The stuff you said sounded good, but I don't really know. I'm not sure what my life is for, why we're here. I really don't understand it."

I was stunned by his answer, by its simplicity, by its staggering profundity. I told him he was awfully bright to be thinking about these kinds of questions and that a lot of what life was about was looking for answers. I said that if he did that with his whole mind and his heart, he'd never be sorry, and he'd discover all sorts of wonderful things as he searched, but that if he started looking for answers in three-minute drug highs, all he'd ever find was more emptiness.

I know I didn't reach him. And that boy's questioning and searching—and my failure to help him—has stayed with me ever since. He needs to be shown, and to somehow understand, that his life—and everyone's—is good, and precious, and full of purpose. For every child we can reach with that message, there will be thousands more who will not hear us, and if we do not find better answers to their questions, they will look for them in the only places they know—in a can of beer, in a vial of crack, in promiscuous sex, in violence, or in all of these things.[53]

We must find new and better ways to teach our children the values that we have most prized over the last two hundred years. Children who learn self-respect and self-esteem do not become drug addicts. Children who learn the value of hard work, honesty, and respect for the rights of others do not turn to crime and vandalism. Children who learn that tolerance and individual rights are essential to everyone's freedom do not embrace bigotry, racism, or sexism.

The novelist and screenwriter Richard Price put it more graphically: "This one drug dealer said to me, 'The scariest thing to a kid out here on the streets is not drugs, AIDS, guns, jail, death. It's words on a page. Because if a fifteen-year-old kid could handle words on a page, he'd be home doing his homework instead of selling dope with me.' "[54]

I remember talking to a teacher from upstate New York on a statewide radio show who called to share her anguish about what drugs were doing to our young New Yorkers. We talked for a while before I finally asked her what we should do. She paused for a moment and then said simply, "Governor Cuomo, make it everybody's problem." I've never gotten better advice—a modern echo of the African proverb "It takes a village to raise a child."

That was true in the 1930s and 1940s in the urban village called South Jamaica, Queens. My parents were at the center of it all. But there were others, many others in that community, who looked out for us children, guided us, taught us, loved us. Neighbors who felt a responsibility to all children, not just their own. Teachers with the skill and patience to help a young boy learn a new language—English. A quiet hero named Joe Austin, who with his own hands carved out a ball field for us to play on, got us off the streets, coached us, encouraged us, directed us; a man who with-

---

[53]I am not a psychiatrist, but it seems to me that most problems with drug abuse and addiction start with adolescent experimentation. Teenagers drink and drive because they feel they are invincible. They succumb to some aberrational form of magical thinking. They do not even begin to understand that they are mortal. One doctor who worked in a hospital in a tough, inner-city neighborhood recalled a youth coming into the emergency room with a gunshot wound. The youth expressed surprise that being shot actually *hurt*.

[54]Interview with Richard Price, *The New York Times*, September 6, 1992.

out ever preaching a sermon taught us teamwork, persistence, decency, tenacity, integrity.

Some neighborhoods have changed, but some things haven't. It's still true that people in the community know better than someone at a desk in Albany what the particular needs of their neighborhood are. Until recently we didn't acknowledge those community strengths enough, relying instead on a too often remote and bureaucratic system to decide what services were needed and how they would be organized and delivered. We've begun to change that by reclaiming the strengths of the community, changing the way government works with communities to provide services, dismantling bureaucratic mandates accumulated over the years that have in some cases become obstacles to progress.

One of the frustrations in government is the feeling that you can't make much progress for the people and the neighborhoods in greatest need because they are trapped in a complex web of social, economic, and medical problems—and the many programs we have to serve them go after only one strand of the web at a time. To fulfill our responsibility to our distressed communities—and to the taxpayers—we need some way of dealing with all the problems systemically and simultaneously.

In my 1993 message to the legislature, I proposed a concentrated, five-year initiative that will help us make a real difference where the need is the greatest—starting in fifteen high-poverty regions throughout the state. The program is called the Neighborhood-Based Alliance, and it grows directly out of the ideas that inspired the Neighborhood-Based Initiative in 1990. This program concentrates the power of a number of our best programs—our economic development zones, our GATEWAY training initiative, community policing, and community schools—to bring new hope to struggling neighborhoods.[55]

New York's Neighborhood-Based Alliance tailors services to specific community needs, as identified by the people in the area. It gives communities the

---

[55]Some of the goals of the Neighborhood-Based Alliance include expanding early childhood programs; initiating a comprehensive prevention program for teenage pregnancy; providing integrated employment and training services to economically disadvantaged adults; expanding apprenticeship programs for young people; and expanding the mentoring program. (We have six Neighborhood-Based Initiative sites, and we added eleven Neighborhood-Based Alliance sites in September 1993, bringing the total to seventeen areas.)

authority and resources to effect economic and social improvements for their residents. By providing services in one central location—ranging from mental health, alcoholism, and drug treatment to child care, training, education, parenting, and prenatal care—social workers and physicians can intervene early to help people in need avert avoidable disasters. Typically, people who need help from the state need help on three or four fronts at once—but until now, to get all the help they need they have often been Ping-Ponged across town and between phone banks in an impersonal, frustrating, and demeaning bureaucratic shuffle, forced to fill out duplicate forms in each place and tell their stories over and over to one agency worker after another. This takes energy and time that we would all rather see spent looking for a job or learning a new skill.

As we work to make our services more effective through initiatives like the Neighborhood-Based Alliance, we have also come to see that making headway against poverty in America will require deeper reform: a radical new approach to welfare.

Welfare Reform: The Path to Independence

After years of discussion and debate on the subject of social welfare policy and programs, one simple proposition has become the accepted central thesis: Work is better than welfare, and the welfare system should help people to become self-sufficient instead of encouraging dependency.

In 1986, former Harvard professor Mary Jo Bane[56] headed a New York State Task Force on Poverty and Welfare. After seven months the members of the task force devised a strategy to revamp the entire welfare system.[57] Their report called for a new social contract that encourages government's help in educating, training, and placing people in productive work, while encouraging recipients to bear their own responsibilities. Based on their proposals, New

---

[56]Mary Jo Bane became New York State's commissioner of social services in 1992 and in 1993 was nominated by President Clinton to serve as assistant secretary of the Administration on Children and Families in the federal Department of Health and Human Services.

[57]The work of the task force helped lay the foundation for national welfare reform legislation that was ultimately passed in 1988, led by two New Yorkers, Senator Pat Moynihan and former congressman Tom Downey.

York has pioneered ways to move people from welfare to work.

For years the most persistent criticism of the Aid to Families with Dependent Children (AFDC) program—which is what most people are talking about when they talk about welfare—was that the normal, commonsense incentives for working and getting ahead don't apply very well to the AFDC recipient.

That should come as no surprise. The welfare system, when it was created in the United States in the 1930s, was intended to rescue widows and vulnerable orphans from homelessness and starvation; it was designed to help families with no other means of support, in an era when women with children rarely worked outside the home. Over time, instead of encouraging mothers of young children to become independent, productive, and self-supporting, the present federal AFDC program did just the opposite. If you get a job, for every dollar you earn on your own, you lose a dollar in AFDC benefits. There are also strict limits on how much money you can save. If you earn too much—even if you and your family are still considerably below the official poverty line—you might lose all your benefits, including your family's medical coverage. You could end up worse off with a steady job than if you stayed on welfare.

That's not the way things ordinarily work for most of us. Usually, if you hustle, if you show some ambition and incentive, you do better. You're not punished for working. You are not taxed on what you earn at a 100 percent rate. Rather, you are rewarded. Wouldn't it make sense to have that same operating principle in our welfare programs, too? In New York we believe it does, so we have taken strides to create real, working alternatives to welfare.

One of the demonstration programs that emerged out of our effort to reform the welfare system is the Child Assistance Program (CAP), which has since been recognized as a national model for how government can help liberate single women and their children from dependency. The program, begun in the fall of 1988, is not just a concept; it is the first real alternative to the country's welfare system. It is also designed to match the circumstances of the majority of the current recipients of AFDC: single women and their children who are living apart from the children's father, who all too often fail to pay appropriate child support. The philosophy behind CAP is simple: By providing an alternative to welfare that enables people to support their family through work and guaranteed child support, we can help them get back on their feet and join the economic mainstream.

Under CAP, if you work, you benefit. CAP benefits are not reduced dollar for dollar against what you earn. Instead they are taxed at a rate that begins at 10 percent and rises gradually, until the point at which your income reaches about $17,300 for a family of three. And if you manage to save money, you are allowed to keep it—to build cash reserves for emergencies, for tuition, for the start of a little business, or for any of the things all the rest of us save for.

CAP also reduces the amount of bureaucratic intrusion. CAP participants get cash instead of coupons for their food subsidy so that they can shop for groceries like anyone else, without being stigmatized by having to use food stamps. They are also given greater freedom in managing their money.

The best testimony I've heard in support of the program came from a former AFDC mother who described CAP at an Albany press conference this way: "Welfare doesn't work. I am a single mother. I have four children. Several months ago I was introduced to the CAP program. The CAP program has given me positive things to look forward to in my future. I write now. I am an HIV educator. I work taking care of the elderly. I am going to continue my education. . . . Being on social services, there was a wall; and by that wall being there, I could not get over it. But now that I'm on the CAP program, I have gotten over the wall and am on the ladder to success."

Even though CAP enrolls a relatively small percentage of those currently on welfare in New York State, it holds the best promise for moving us toward the kind of welfare system we should have.[58] CAP does not promise to catapult its participants into the middle class. But it assures that their initiative won't be punished, as it too frequently is under the current system. CAP gives the taxpayers the assurance that the money they contribute is being used productively—to end dependency rather than to perpetuate it. Most important, the Child Assistance Program assists children, assuring that they get the support they deserve and that they have an opportunity to grow up in an environment where effort is rewarded and independence is possible.

The principles that work in CAP are easy to extend to the rest of the welfare system—for example, our insistence that noncustodial parents pay child support. New York was the first state to create a comprehensive, automated system for tracking and collecting child support. We were among the first to

---

[58]By 1992 CAP was working in seven counties in New York State. In a random assignment evaluation after the first year, independent evaluators found that the group that was assigned to CAP had on average 25 percent more work, earnings, and child support orders than the control group.

intercept the state income tax refunds and lottery winnings of delinquent parents. And we were among the first to notify credit agencies when more than $1,000 in child support is owed.

Another obvious emphasis of welfare reform is helping recipients find jobs. Because most of our welfare dollars go to single women and their children, we have made special efforts to target that population through a first-of-its-kind one-stop shopping concept—Comprehensive Employment Opportunity Support Centers, or CEOSCs. CEOSCs are places where we marshal in one setting all the education, training, and support services that poor women with children need to move off welfare and into jobs.[59]

In 1988 New York contracted with America Works, a privately owned company that recruits welfare recipients and trains them to become secretaries, health care workers, and mail clerks. Partially funded by the New York State Department of Social Services, America Works receives full payment only when they achieve a specific result—when an applicant can hold a permanent, full-time job for seven months. Seven out of ten people who go through the America Works program are employed a year later.

Through our current employment training activities, more than eighteen thousand Home Relief recipients—those who are able-bodied, single, and unemployed—are assigned to public works projects. In exchange for their grant, these people perform public service and gain work skills and habits in the process. To expand this effort in 1993, I announced the Working Toward Independence (WTI) program, which will put six thousand to ten thousand people currently on welfare to work within state agencies.

New York's efforts to give welfare clients the chance to earn their own way through enhanced day care, job training, and education were working miraculously well through the 1980s. By 1989 New York State had reduced its welfare rolls to their lowest level in twenty years. Regrettably, the recession and the accompanying unemployment that has rocked the region since 1990 erased those hard-won gains. In 1992 New York City's welfare caseloads alone exceeded one million people—the highest on record.

Understandably, as more people are out of work, and those who are working are asked to support those who aren't, the cry goes up to blame those

---

[59]Since the first CEOSC was opened in 1987, New York State has provided $12 million annually for their support. More than 15,000 people have been enrolled in training programs since 1987; 5,300 have been placed in jobs.

on welfare for shiftlessness at least, if not for weakness of the overall economy. Listening to talk radio hosts, one might conclude that unemployment and dependency could be solved if we simply "locked up" all those who have children out of wedlock or "sterilized" poor people who have too many kids. These are primitive, reactionary solutions—and the "facts" they are reacting to are usually false.

Few topics evoke more emotion than welfare and Medicaid, and few are discussed with as much misinformation. More than any other area of public policy, perhaps this is where New Yorkers most need to hear the facts. I can't count the times I've heard people assert, as if it were the gospel truth, ideas like this:

"Welfare is a lot of lazy, shiftless men standing around on street corners guzzling beer." The truth is, 87 percent of the welfare recipients in New York State are women and children.

"We're paying women on welfare to have lots of babies." Actually, the typical case in New York is a woman with two children.

"Anyone can get on welfare, and once they're on, those people stay living off us forever. It's a cinch to beat the system." On average, welfare cases are opened for two years or less. New York has stringent income tests, documentation requirements, and an extensive system to check and audit information provided by clients. Over 94 percent of benefits are paid out properly.

"New York is the Cadillac of welfare states." New York State is far from the most generous state when it comes to welfare. Way ahead of us are states like Alaska, California, Vermont, Connecticut, and Hawaii.

"People on welfare are making out pretty well." Actually, it's gotten harder to survive on welfare in New York. In 1975, even during the fiscal crisis, public assistance in New York put recipients at 117 percent of the federal poverty level. Now it's down to about 80 percent. A family of three in New York City gets $19 per day to cover all the necessities of life—including shelter.[60] In fact, the state's shelter allowance is so low, it has been challenged in court as unconstitutional. Imagine trying to find a heated apartment in New York City for a family of three for less than $300 a month. In Manhattan it costs that much just to park a car.

---

[60]The average monthly medical benefits were under $800 statewide ($850 in New York City). These were the highest individual expenditures. Total income maintenance averaged $209 statewide ($203 in New York City). Clearly these people are not getting wealthy on the dole.

This is not to say that the system cannot be improved or reformed intelligently. We understand that in New York and recognize our obligation to make sure that public assistance is being provided only to the truly needy. In 1989 the state legislature approved my Mandatory Job Search Initiative, which requires single, able-bodied Home Relief recipients to conduct a job search as a condition for applying for welfare benefits. Those who do not contact at least three employers per week can be disqualified from receiving benefits for a period of up to 180 days. Under state rules, those who are employable can be required to work or engage in training and may be sanctioned by the counties or the city of New York if they refuse.[61]

As a kid growing up in the city, as a lawyer, as a public official, I have been where welfare does its work. I was there when it was just "relief," the handout from government that kept families going during the Depression. I worked in the barrios and the ghettos. And one truth has persisted: Most of the people on welfare want to work. Compared with the rest of us, their desire to make their own way is at least as great and probably greater.

The poor and the powerless should not be blamed for the tough times we face. It would be wrong for New Yorkers to allow welfare and Medicaid to become scapegoats for the nation's broader economic ills. As of 1992, AFDC, Home Relief, and their share of Medicaid *combined* equaled only about seven cents out of every dollar spent by New York State.

In the final analysis, if New Yorkers want to change the welfare system—and most agree on the need—we should be talking about how we can help those now on welfare find work, not how we cut them off. First of all we need an economy that produces jobs. Then we have to help people on welfare avail themselves of these opportunities. We need to educate people and give them a chance to be more productive. Preaching family values is nice, and we all agree that our society would be better off with more families intact. But we must go beyond prayer or punitive measures that at best stigmatize, and at worst punish, children for choices made by their parents, who too often have

---

[61]There is an equal amount of misinformation concerning the Medicaid program. Medicaid provides basic health services to those who would not be insured by any other means. Those services are vital, not only to those who receive them directly, but to the rest of us as well, because they prevent the spread of disease and illness; they ensure that the working poor can continue to produce; that children delivered to poverty by accident of birth can receive the care they need for a healthy start in life. Once more, it is the elderly and the disabled who consume 65 percent of Medicaid expenditures. Home Relief clients, by comparison, consume only 12 percent; AFDC clients, 19 percent.

not yet reached adulthood. What we need now is intelligent welfare reform that gives people a chance to work their way out of poverty, instead of cutting new holes in the safety net that saves them from drowning in their despair.

We need to do that not just for the sake of the people on our rolls, but because we can afford neither the growing cost of welfare payments nor the loss of productivity it represents.

Toward a More Responsive Criminal Justice System

In the early evening of January 8, 1983, I was having dinner with my family in a small Mexican restaurant in New York City after a Georgetown–St. John's basketball game when I received an urgent phone call from my chief of staff. There was a crisis at the Ossining Correctional Facility, the prison in the Hudson Valley that was once known as Sing Sing. Inmates, some convicted of murder or other violent crimes, had taken over Cell Block B. They held nineteen prison guards hostage and had produced a long list of "requests." I had been governor for only eight days. It was a more violent baptism than I had expected.

My first impulse was to go directly to Ossining to take charge. My chief of staff, who had been in government much longer than I, and the commissioner in charge, Tom Coughlin, another seasoned professional, discouraged me. They had learned from long experience that the governor's presence would only increase the inmates' leverage. I deferred to their better judgment. Although I was uncomfortable being anywhere other than at the scene, I settled for setting up a command center at the World Trade Center in Manhattan from which I could stay in constant communication with Coughlin at the Ossining facility. On the way to the World Trade Center, it was impossible not to think about the uprising at Attica in upstate New York several years earlier. Indeed, I later discovered that at Ossining an inmate had hung out a bedsheet that read WE DON'T WANT ANOTHER ATTICA. I agreed that we had to do everything possible to avoid a recurrence of the tragedy that cost so many lives.[62]

---

[62]In September 1971, a prison uprising at Attica, in Wyoming County, New York, resulted in forty-three deaths—including inmates, prison guards, and four civilians.

The Ossining siege lasted nearly three days. We kept a phone line open constantly between the command center and Coughlin's headquarters, discussing every possibility and every decision. In the end, mostly because of the superb performance of Coughlin's Correction Department officials, there were no deaths, few serious injuries, and relatively little property damage.

Though the Ossining crisis ended peacefully, the incident only magnified the strain that had been placed on our criminal justice system. The arrests and convictions of drug offenders in unprecedented numbers had caused overcrowding in New York's prisons on a scale we had never seen before. Cocaine use, soon to lead to the crack epidemic, would begin to further overpopulate our prison cells with nonviolent felons. We were incarcerating offenders at such an unprecedented rate that it threatened our ability to house the prison population safely.

Immediately after the Ossining incident we moved to correct these conditions with the largest prison building program in the state's history. I knew that this would only be a beginning.

The truth was, however, that the problems in a single prison had a profound effect on how I viewed our entire criminal justice system.

We needed to reshape it immediately.

When I became governor, there was no single authority or mechanism that coordinated the efforts of local police and the state police, local sheriffs' departments, and the FBI, even when their efforts were part of one logical continuum, from local police arresting small-time drug dealers to federal authorities pursuing interstate and international traffickers.

One of my first official acts was to establish the cabinet post of Director of Criminal Justice. Now, the entire state's crime fighting apparatus reports to one individual who coordinates the efforts of all the different state agencies and shares information with federal and local authorities. Today there is better coordination and teamwork, and this has allowed us to introduce new methods and techniques and strengthen our law enforcement arsenal.

I viewed this arsenal in the broadest possible context. We had to better equip our law enforcement personnel. But we also had to build up every part of our state's criminal justice system. We had to put more police on the streets whenever our budget would allow it, and we had to hire more prosecutors and judges, too. (We created thirty-two new judgeships—seventeen in New York City alone.) We needed to unclog every bottleneck in the system to deal with lawbreakers swiftly and efficiently.

One place we made immediate headway was in our investigative methods. Since 1983, we have invested in the most advanced criminal technology in the nation. One example is the SAFIS, an acronym for "state-wide automated fingerprint identification system," which uses computer and telecommunications technology to make nearly instantaneous matches between fingerprints taken from the scene of a crime and fingerprints recorded in our criminal files.[63]

We've helped empower police forces across the state with more resources, both in the investigative units and on the street. In 1989, for example, we created a police accreditation program that was the first of its kind in the nation.[64] We made a strong commitment to the return of the neighborhood beat cop; community policing is now regular policy through most of the state. To make New York City's subways safer, we provided funding for more transit cops. They have had a good effect: in the spring of 1993, crime on the subways had decreased 28 percent in three years.[65]

We've also increased the troop strength of our state police to 4,000. Our state police force has become one of the premier police agencies in the nation. Its influence goes beyond our borders, as well. During 1992, the state police concluded a major six-year drug investigation that helped crush Colombia's Calí cartel—an international cocaine ring that rivaled the infamous Medellín cartel. Working with federal and local narcotics officials, state investigators helped to arrest 139 drug traffickers and seize more than six tons of cocaine and millions of dollars in illicit monies.

One effective tool for taking the profits out of the drug trade is the aggressive use of "assets forfeiture." Simply put, drug offenders can lose cars, boats, and other assets if they're involved in certain crimes. In 1990, I signed a bill

---

[63]Another new program, DNA "fingerprinting," can establish the guilt or innocence of the accused in certain crimes. A man convicted of rape was, in fact, freed in New York after serving part of a long sentence when a DNA specimen proved that he couldn't possibly have committed the crime. In that instance, DNA fingerprinting reminded us of how fragile our legal system can be.

[64]Through 1992, more than two hundred police departments had enrolled and begun to take advantage of the program's unique benefits: independent confirmation of compliance with professional standards; enhanced administrative and operational effectiveness; assurance that recruitment, selection, and promotional processes are fair and equitable; and diminished vulnerability to civil lawsuits and costly settlements.

[65]Felony crime in the New York City subway system had fallen almost continually during the twenty-eight months before July 1993, with felony crime down by over 25 percent since 1990.

that strengthened New York's forfeiture laws. The new law expanded forfeiture and established a more equitable distribution of the proceeds. The law has resulted in the collection of $21 million in 1993.

Most of the responsibility for drug enforcement, however, is borne by local governments. The growth in drug crime and violence has been most prolific in New York City. Between 1985 and 1989, the number of felony drug arrests climbed 132 percent. Arrests for violent offenses increased by 24 percent. It was clear that the city was in desperate need of state aid. Together, we created a comprehensive response called the Safe Streets, Safe City initiative. Legislation was enacted to provide financial support for the expansion of the police force to an all-time high of more than 38,000 officers. Community policing was adopted throughout the city. Security in and around schools was enhanced, crime and drug prevention programs were funded, and prosecution and correctional services were expanded.

Much more needs to be done, but Safe Streets, Safe City has provided a framework for progress. Since the inception of Safe Streets, Safe City, crime in the five boroughs has decreased. Between 1990 and 1993, the crime rate (known under the FBI line item as "total" crime) declined 15 percent and remains at the lowest level since 1985.

But December 7, 1993, brought a gruesome reminder of our continuing vulnerability when Colin Ferguson, a troubled man angry at the world, calmly strolled down the aisle of a Long Island Rail Road car during rush hour, shooting a semiautomatic pistol. He killed six people and wounded seventeen more.

From Miami to Tulsa, Denver to San Francisco, 1993 was studded with a grotesque array of brutal slayings—from teenagers robbing and killing foreign tourists to disgruntled employees going on shooting rampages. Capped by the murders on the LIRR, these incidents sparked a powerful fear, anger, and sense of urgency among the American people. The political system reacted.

Just weeks before the LIRR killings, President Clinton signed the Brady Bill, which requires a five-day waiting period before a citizen can buy a gun. Colin Ferguson, however, had bought his weapon in California, where the state stipulates a fifteen-day waiting period. When his application was cleared—Ferguson apparently had no history of mental instability—he purchased a pistol and returned to New York. Although the long-awaited Brady Bill marks an important milestone in the move toward serious gun control legislation, it is obviously not enough. What we really need are stronger federal laws to prevent felons from purchasing guns and to regulate federally-licensed firearms dealers more tightly.[66]

Meanwhile, to deal with the problem of illegal guns flowing into our state, New York created the nation's strictest state-level system of handgun control. Despite these laws, however, thousands of guns are already on the street and remain readily available. The vast majority come into New York from other states where licensing is less strict. In 1991, more than 90 percent of the illegal firearms seized by New York City police agencies were originally purchased in other states. Criminals and unscrupulous gun dealers have exploited the differences among state laws—while the Federal government has looked the other way.

New York State has forged agreements with criminal justice officials in those states from which most of New York's illegal guns flow—states like Virginia, Georgia, Florida, Ohio, and Texas—to share criminal intelligence, trace illegal guns to their source, and disrupt the business of illicit and disreputable dealers,[67] while public demand for gun limitations grew in states across the nation.

The powerful gun lobby, on the other hand, declares that the Constitution prevents restrictions on even military weapons like so-called assault rifles, and some Americans have decided that they need to arm themselves for their own protection. Gun sales increased dramatically at the end of 1993 all over the nation—despite the irrefutable evidence that a firearm in the house puts a member of that family at a far greater risk of being shot than those in households without guns. One gun lobbyist actually proposed that if there had been one licensed pistol holder on the LIRR, the slaughter might have been averted. That's frightening. We are indeed desperate when the argument

---

[66]Early in 1993, the Clinton Administration announced a new effort to cope with the crime epidemic. The House and Senate both have anti-crime bills that call for increased penalties for gun crimes, including new prohibitions on the sale and transfer of guns to juveniles, as well as the possession of guns by youths. The Senate's bill because is more comprehensive. In particular, it bans the sale, manufacture, and possession of nineteen specific types of semiautomatic weapons. In addition, President Clinton has asked the Justice Department to study the feasibility of a national gun registration and licensing system.

[67]Through our new "dedicated firearms-tracing units," New York and Virginia have begun sharing information on computerized data bases. We also have a new program called "Operation Gun Lock." It alerts New York City officials when an arrestee has a prior conviction involving a gun charge. In those cases, the accused are given priority for swift action by prosecutors.

descends to the point where people suggest that the answer to the gun problem is more guns. As this book was going to print, we were fighting with the Republican majority in our State Senate to move closer to sanity with our neighboring states. New Jersey and Connecticut have banned assault weapons, despite much lobbying from the NRA. I am hopeful our State Senate will finally respond by joining the New York State Assembly that has just passed my proposal.[68]

When it comes to gun violence and crime, we have no time to waste on whether we deal with only the penal aspects of crime or its root social causes. We should all know we need to do both right now. Indeed, we have to do everything we can: tough new laws, effective enforcement, tough love, more effective education of our children with respect to the drug menace, social programs, and economic opportunity for our children.

All of this is part of our agenda. All of this is expensive and difficult because violence has become embedded in our culture.[69]

One of the immediate challenges in addressing the problem of guns is how deeply rooted they are in the American psyche—not just as weapons of destruction, but also as the tools of heroes. The problem isn't new. Thirty years ago, I argued with my wife, Matilda, over whether we should allow our son, Andrew, to have toy guns. I believe as a people we are locked into a much larger debate over how we really feel about guns and violence. Guns have been routinely available for all of American history. And it's impossible to avoid the rain of bloodbaths and bullets on television, cable programming, and the movies. Surely this must contribute to the degradation and horror in our streets. The irony is that media owners and managers give people what they seem to want. If they are right, then the irony is that people are getting what they desire, and that is truly disgusting.

In many struggling neighborhoods, the sense of disorientation and nihilism

---

[68]An assault weapon ban was the first measure I mentioned during my annual Message to the Legislature on January 5, 1994. The Assembly passed the measure at a special session I called for on January 17, 1994, Dr. Martin Luther King, Jr.'s birthday.

[69]We have put crooks behinds bars in record numbers and still there is crime. One reason this course of action is not enough is that prison inmates constitute a small percentage of all those who commit crimes. A 1988 study of arrests in eight states found that only 12 percent of the 145,000 people arrested for violent crimes went to prison. And even the 145,000 probably constitute less than half of all those believed to have committed serious crimes in those states that year. So only about 6 percent of criminals go to prison—and still cells are overflowing everywhere.

is so pervasive that children have begun committing crimes we would have found inconceivable a few years ago. The perpetrators—and the victims—are getting younger. A seventeen-year-old in Brooklyn randomly killed a four-year-old boy waiting in a car to be taken to church. A fourteen-year-old boy burned a derelict for no reason other than curiosity. A pack of youths brutally raped and nearly killed a jogger in Central Park, teaching society a new word, *wilding*. A seventeen-year-old drug dealer is accused of murdering a beloved elementary school principal in Brooklyn who was searching for a distraught fourth-grader. Young people are committing more murders and other serious crimes than ever before.[70] And every year the caskets get smaller.

Elsewhere in this book, we describe the many strategies New York is pursuing to help repair the fabric of these troubled neighborhoods. But none is more important than tackling the epidemic of drug addiction. Drugs are crime's biggest commodity. We can see the residual effect every day in our prison cells—all across the nation.

The United States has more than one million people under lock and key, either in prison, in jail, awaiting trial or serving short sentences. In New York State, there are 65,000 inmates incarcerated at any given time—the size of a small city and two and a half times the number in prison in 1981.[71]

What is fueling this relentless increase in the prison population? Drugs. In our state alone, indictments, convictions, and prison sentences for felony drug crimes have tripled since 1983.[72] In 1992, 45 percent of those sent to prison in New York State were sent on a drug charge; nearly 80 percent were

---

[70]Delbert S. Elliott, a sociology professor and an expert in criminal violence, has argued that 50 to 60 percent of all crime is being committed by 5 to 7 percent of young people from the ages of 10 to 20 years old. Adolescents and teenagers are committing violent crimes like murder, aggravated assault and rape. Firearms among the youth are readily obtainable. Many of these kids will grow up and become adult fixtures in the criminal court system. The court system itself suffers from the same overload as the prisons. We do not have enough judges; we cannot process paperwork quickly enough. And the judges are forced to use triage when sentencing because they know that cell space is preciously scarce.

[71]One way to understand the problem is through a standard criminal justice statistic—the number of sentenced prisoners in state and Federal institutions for every 100,000 people. For New York, New Jersey, Connecticut, and the United States as a whole, that number has risen constantly in the last decade; in fact, during the last half of the 1980s, the relative figure for New York has surpassed that of the United States.

[72]Today, the only criminal offense that leads more certainly to prosecution than felony drug crimes in New York is homicide.

substance abusers. Inevitably, the cycle of arrests and re-arrests will continue until we can find a way to help these people overcome their addiction.

How, then, do you deal with the problem within the context of the criminal justice system?

First, we must retain the will to win the drug war, or at least to reverse the tide. Some say the best way to deal with the illicit drug plague is to legalize drugs. Those who favor legalization, as I understand them, argue that we have done all we can and have failed. Since we have never been able to beat this demon, "we ought to admit defeat," they say, "and save ourselves the cost of combating it." We ought to rely, instead, on the odds that addiction from newly legal drugs will strike someone else's family, but not ours.

I reject this idea as the abandonment of a whole generation of children—and adults—now caught in the web of addiction. I would not do it to my children. You would not do it to yours. We ought not allow the government to do it to our children. We can't give up just because the problem seems so hard to solve.[73]

Instead of resorting to legalization, we charted a comprehensive course of response, starting with the Statewide Anti–Drug Abuse Council in 1989. Under the leadership of Lieutenant Governor Stan Lundine, the council was charged with the duty of developing an integrated strategy to reduce drug abuse through law enforcement, prevention, and treatment. We explored every area that relates to the problem. Council members included experts in the areas of alcoholism and substance abuse, health, mental health, criminal justice, education, social services, and veterans' affairs.

In just a few years, the Anti–Drug Abuse Council has made dramatic progress in the attack against alcohol and drug abuse. It coordinates a drug and alcohol treatment system that serves more than 20,000 people on a daily basis. And it has helped to develop an expansive network of prevention programs in the schools and communities throughout the state. On the criminal justice front, the council has coordinated the treatment of addict offenders and assisted in the strengthening of drug enforcement.

Substance abuse treatment has also been extended to the prisons. With

---

[73]Legalizing drugs raises more questions than it answers. Who would get the drugs? How would you regulate it? How would it cut into the black market? Lotteries and legalized gambling have not sounded the death knell for bookmakers. What makes us think licit narcotics would eliminate illicit narcotics?

approximately 22,000 drug offenders in custody, we created an expansive prison-based drug treatment program that provides treatment to offenders even after their release. Upwards of 9,000 inmates are enrolled at sixty correctional facilities. Twenty-eight of the prison-based programs are operated as therapeutic communities. We have also expanded drug treatment opportunities in community corrections by securing dedicated treatment slots for probationers and developing prosecution-based diversion programs.

If we are to succeed in the fight against drugs, we will need to secure more federal support. Regrettably, the state and local governments have been forced to bear the burden of fighting the drug war, even though drug trafficking is primarily a national and international crime. Coca leaves do not grow in Duluth, nor opium poppies in Albany. Throughout the 1980s, the Federal government denounced drug addiction and the violence associated with it, but in allocating funds and resources, they treated the states as though we were still a confederation.

For example, President Reagan signed the Omnibus Drug Bill in 1986. But within three months, he gutted the bill by limiting most of the funding. President Bush subsequently promised to "stop this scourge," but his administration faltered in the area it supposedly believed was most important: enforcement. In 1992, while Federal drug charges were filed against some 23,000 defendants nationwide, New York State prosecutors indicted about one-third *more* drug defendants under state law. The U.S. attorneys for the Eastern and Southern districts filed fewer than 2,000 drug-related cases. And as of August 1990, the Federal Bureau of Prisons held just 2,200 inmates on drug-related offenses who had passed through the Federal district courts in New York, while our state courts alone incarcerated nearly nine times as many persons for drug crimes.

The traffic that brings drugs here illegally passes through the Army, the Navy, the Marines, the CIA, the Coast Guard, U.S. Customs, the Federal Drug Enforcement Administration—the whole national defense system.[74] And still the drugs pour in from places like Colombia, Bolivia, and East Asia. Once they get here it is virtually impossible to stop them from reaching

---

[74]The writer Richard Price, who in his last novel delved into the street drug trade in New York and New Jersey, put it cynically yet truthfully: "Once the drugs are on the street, there is no war on drugs except over who gets the best corners."

Queens, Utica, Rochester, and Buffalo. In 1992, New York State spent more than $2 billion fighting drugs, while the entire Federal government spent nearly $12 billion. Today, the states are the foot soldiers in the front line of the drug war—and the cavalry is nowhere in sight. State and local criminal justice authorities are apprehending, prosecuting, and incarcerating hundreds of thousands of criminals in drug cases that could fall under Federal jurisdiction.

The vast gap between Federal and state responsibilities in the drug war has created a huge law enforcement problem at the state and local level. Where are you going to put all these people you've arrested? How do you cope with overcrowding? What is the best way to deal with them, so they won't be re-arrested again for a similar drug crime?[75]

Until the Federal government becomes a more active partner, New York, like other states, must cope on its own. A crucial strategy is to keep the infection of drugs from spreading into new territory. For instance, through a new initiative called Operation Firebreak, special state police teams will attack outbreaks of drug dealing and violence in vulnerable communities upstate. Another approach we are stressing in New York is alternatives to incarceration—punishing *nonviolent* offenders in some place other than a cell that costs $100,000 to build and $25,000 a year to maintain.[76]

One of our most promising alternatives to a traditional prison sentence is New York's shock incarceration program, now the largest in the nation. Shock incarceration works something like military boot camp, using a regimen of structured, demanding physical activity and therapeutic counseling to help nonviolent felons to learn to respect themselves and the standards of society. Shock incarceration is also cheaper than prison. We estimate that we've saved $313 million so far, and 9,400 "graduates" have been released to parole supervision.[77] One former shock participant said, "I would like to start off by thanking you for a second chance at life because if I had sat in a prison I would

---

[75]The most obvious shortcoming in the Federal strategy has been its emphasis on enforcement, at the expense of prevention and treatment. There are encouraging signs that Lee Brown, the President's drug czar, will reverse those priorities and follow New York's lead in having a balanced strategy of enforcement, education, and treatment.

[76]On Riker's Island in New York City, we pay $58,000 a year to house a prisoner. This is double the cost of sending a student to our most expensive Ivy League schools.

[77]The recidivism rate for shock incarceration is no higher than for inmates released from prison.

have either wound up dead, or just rotted, and my mind and body would have gone to waste. . . ."[78]

There is no point locking up nonviolent, drug-addicted criminals who are likely to return to drugs and prison. Ultimately, we need to reform the sentencing laws so that drug felons are not automatically placed in prison. An alternative punishment that includes treatment makes a lot more sense. Regrettably, the New York State Legislature has not agreed to change the sentencing laws so this can happen, as I have proposed repeatedly over the years. Apparently, some legislators fear being labeled soft on crime and are afraid even to debate the matter. In the end this will change only when the people make clear to the reluctant legislators that they are neither as naive or unreasonable as the legislators suspect. The general public must make clear their awareness that we are not going to win this struggle just by locking away more and more of the people who supply street drugs. If there is any hope for large, long-term gains, it's on the demand side of the equation.

Increasingly, the public understands that the most important steps we can take now to fight this scourge are in expanding our education, prevention, and treatment capabilities. Because drug abuse is as much a public health problem as it is a law enforcement problem, rehabilitation must be a central component in our overall efforts.

Currently, in New York, we administer the largest alcohol and drug treatment system in the nation—and spend more than $1 billion to make it work. Our overall treatment capacity can serve more than 120,000. We are expanding both our outpatient and inpatient treatment centers to offer a full range of services, such as detoxification, counseling, relapse prevention, health services, and links with other human services agencies to plan care for patients after they are released.[79] Through the combined activities of the Anti–Drug

---

[78]As reported in an interview in *DOCS Today,* a publication of the New York State Department of Correctional Services, Summer 1992.

[79]A large number of substance-abuse providers throughout the state have started or expanded services for women and children. One-third of our 600 drug treatment programs provide special services for women. We are establishing more drug and alcohol services in temporary shelters for families. We have created a task force on integrated projects for youth and chemical dependency to ensure a coordinated approach among agencies to help high-risk, substance-abusing youth. So far, 21 treatment programs have received $4.8 million, and 62 prevention programs have been funded for $6.3 million. All of these programs are actively responding to the challenge posed by the drug epidemic.

Abuse Council, some 110 substance abusers now receive treatment on a daily basis. We have built an alcohol and substance abuse center in Livingston County, and as of this writing, four additional annexes have been provided in upstate New York.

Still, this effort is not enough. We have been woefully inadequate on the health side of the drug issue. For example, in New York City alone, there are approximately 600,000 heavy drug users. Yet there is severely limited bed space for rehabilitation. The need for more treatment facilities is even more critical because we know how much prisons cost. Clinics are expensive, too, but they are still cheaper than prison cells.[80]

I believe that we can at least agree that relief from the escalating real-life drama of guns and drug violence will require both tough laws and a whole-hearted commitment to giving our young people better alternatives than what is available on the street. But on many specifics, further agreement seems to elude us—almost to the point of paralyzing the public debate.

This last point brings up a much larger question: How does the citizenry exert its will if the Legislature can arrange to avoid sensitive or troubling issues? What can citizens do when they feel the democratic process is being held hostage by legislative gridlock?

The answer is contained in the state constitution, written over 200 years ago but still containing a mechanism for its own improvement. Every twenty years, the people of New York are given the option of holding a state constitutional convention to revisit the original document, to reform our laws and renew our democracy.

The time is now. The people will have the chance in 1997 to convene a constitutional convention where the people can shout the truths that some legislators have not yet heard.

---

[80]Ironically, right now, it is easier to provide drug treatment through the criminal justice system than the social service system because we don't have to fight local communities to site such treatment centers—a disturbing trend since it suggests that people have a better chance of getting help for their drug problem if they get arrested.

While many citizens applaud drug treatment facilities, too many will not tolerate even the most benign halfway house in their line of sight. Because of this phenomenon, "NIMBY," a now well-worn acronym for "not in my back yard," locating these new centers has not been easy. Turning the tide in the drug wars will require educating our children about the dangers of drugs, but also educating ourselves. To deal with this problem effectively, we must accept the fact that drug treatment facilities must be located somewhere.

Political Reform

Almost by definition, no democracy can ever be perfect. It is a continually evolving process, open to change and to the constant reaffirmation that "the people" can be trusted, that they are not the means to some greater end—Utopia, the millennium, or an electoral landslide—but an end in themselves.

I believe the best definition of democracy we've ever had doesn't go into great detail about the theory of democracy, the constitution it should possess, or the institutions it needs. It simply describes a living process: what Abraham Lincoln described as government of the people, by the people, and for the people.

The degree to which a people achieves democracy depends on how *open* this process is. It is not enough just to be ruled by those who keep the best interests of the majority in mind—government *for* the people. Nor is it enough for average citizens to play their own role in the selection of those representatives and in the entire enterprise of lawmaking—government *by* the people. Real democracy will endure only when all its people have the opportunity to use their government to help them share in the very sources of power itself: in education, in information, in wealth, in the material and intellectual advantages that throughout history the elite has sought to deny and arrogate to themselves. For democracy to survive, it must be, truly, a government *of* the people.

The evolution of democracy in our own country makes this point well. The principles first proclaimed in our Declaration of Independence were eloquently phrased and profoundly revolutionary. But the Constitution that translated those sentiments into a government permitted slavery and ignored women. And the individual states hedged the ability to vote with poll taxes, property qualifications, and literacy tests, so that the wealthiest part of the community—the privileged elite—would have a legislative weight out of proportion to their numbers. There are continuing debates over the extent to which the democracy's influence should be shared more inclusively—with African-Americans, women, immigrants, the poor, the illiterate, and the disadvantaged minorities. This question of access is vital: access to opportunity, access to power, and access to information. And access is promoted by government's *openness*.

The very basis of our political democracy—the silent compact that sustains the Constitution—is an understanding between our citizens and the people who represent them that the public business will be done *openly* and honestly, and according to the rule of law. "If men were angels," wrote James Madison, "no government would be necessary. And if angels were to govern men, neither external or internal controls on government would be necessary." Over the past two hundred years we have been reminded how right Madison was; the angels have not been running the show.

Sometimes dramatically, sometimes quietly, but always insidiously, waste and corruption have been with us, insinuating themselves into our public affairs, infecting the body politic with greed, venality, inefficiency. The infection has not been confined to any particular level of government, party, region, race, or creed. The impulse has been with us, pervasively, from the very beginning. The pages of our nation's history are full of examples: the "Black Friday" scandal in the Grant administration; Boss Tweed and Tammany Hall; Teapot Dome; Watergate; and Iran-Contra.

Abuse, waste, and scandal are with us today, as are the cumulative, corrosive effects they have on people's confidence in government itself. Many people have grown so disenchanted with government's apparent ineffectiveness and venality that they simply drop out of the process, becoming critics instead of contributors.

I understand the sentiment.

Before I got into government, I had developed an ardent disrespect for the way government worked . . . and didn't work. As a lawyer I chose to represent groups and individuals who I believed had been dealt with unfairly by government. The more I explored the abuses, the more I lost respect for the system. It seemed to me that corruption, both small and large, was commonplace in governments: building departments demanding bribes for permits; party bureaucrats doing favors for gifts; heavy-hitting political contributors getting special treatment; huge government contracts being arranged by government officials who later wound up working for the interested business entity; and all the while, the individuals without wealth, without connections, getting less than they were entitled to—or at least feeling that way because they knew so many who were not deserving got more. Then came Watergate, and my indignation—along with a lot of other people's—turned to anger. That finally prompted me to get into public life myself and left me with the lasting impression that integrity in government is vital to its very existence.

When government is tainted by official misconduct or the *appearance* of impropriety, the people are tempted to lose confidence in that government and the rule of law that it is supposed to foster. One of the worst effects of undetected and unprotected corruption is the impression left in the public's mind that all the powerful institutions of government—and even the body of the law itself—are corrupt. If that condition continues long enough and goes deep enough into the consciousness of the people, then the tacit compact between the people and their government will surely crumble. That is a recurring threat in any living democracy.

In the past decade, New Yorkers have been stunned and angered by a stream of allegations, malfeasance, and impropriety in politics and government in our nation's capital and in numerous states, including our own. However, the 1980s, which produced their share of scandal in New York City, also produced a new willingness in New York to root out abuses—and the appearance of abuses—in our government and in our political and electoral systems. Understanding the seriousness of official abuses of power, we have used the many good minds and strong hearts that make up the government in this state to transform moments of adversity into a catalyst for real change.[81]

In 1986 I signed an executive order that created the office of inspector general to investigate complaints of fraud, abuse, or corruption; to monitor day-to-day operations of agencies; and to prevent abuse by actively recommending ways to improve the management of state functions. New York State's inspector general has the legal power to conduct his own investigations and to gain access to records relevant to those investigations, whenever and wherever he sees fit. He has been given the power to subpoena witnesses and question them under oath, without the need for approval from the governor or prior permission from a court.[82] Since 1986 the office has opened more than 950 investigations, saving New York's taxpayers more than $4.5 million in state funds. A number of the cases involved criminal matters, which led to indictments and convictions; others were administrative mat-

---

[81]My first role in public life began that process. As secretary of state I was charged with the regulation of lobbyists. Under Governor Carey's leadership, we produced the first disclosure and conflict of interest policies for high-level public employees in the state's history. At the time, we had to do it by executive order because the legislature didn't want any part of ethics legislation.

[82]Today, New York's office of the inspector general has a staff of twenty-seven people and an office in three regions of the state. The office has the capability of accepting—and investigating—complaints from every level of our state government, from agency commissioners to entry-level employees, as well as from private citizens.

ters involving various agencies' deficiencies or employees' misconduct.

New York's first inspector general, a former FBI agent named Joseph Spinelli, has made a difference, but we don't pretend that his diligence is enough to fight waste, corruption, and abuse. The inspector general cannot assure accountability all by himself; he needs the full array of protective rules and legislation. So in addition to using executive authority, New York has also reinforced our accountability program with strong supporting legislation.

For the first time in our state's 210-year history, the New York State Legislature turned its attention in a serious and meaningful way to regulating the private interest of our public officials. The 1987 Ethics in Government Act, the most wide-ranging political reform in the history of our state government, extends to almost all government employees as well as to candidates for office. The law bars government officials from representing private clients before state agencies; it requires that all elected and appointed officials, including judges and state employees earning more than $53,000 or serving in policy-making positions, disclose their financial interests; and it restricts former state employees from dealing with the state after leaving government service. The law also created a New York State Ethics Commission with the power to receive complaints, conduct investigations, issue subpoenas, and refer matters for prosecution.

The same year, New York passed the Accountability, Audit and Internal Control Act. Although neither the public nor the editorial boards clamored for it, the audit bill is just as important as the ethics bill. For the first time, outside experts are reviewing and commenting publicly on the books, records, and internal control measures of the executive, the legislature, the judiciary, the comptroller, and the attorney general.[83]

These two laws were important first steps. But they only established a direction; they have not as yet delivered us to our final destination.[84] We still

---

[83]Specifically, the law provides for internal administrative and accounting control systems for all state governmental entities to safeguard assets, check the accuracy and reliability of accounting data, deter and detect fraud, waste, abuse, and error; the means to assure that personnel actually perform the services for which they are being paid; periodic state comptroller audits of the internal control systems of state agencies and major public authorities; external audits by independent accounting firms at least once every two years of the governor's office, division of the budget, the Department of Law, the Department of Audit and Control, and the legislature.

[84]For example, the ethics bill did not prohibit the holding of both public and party office. It did not prohibit party leaders from appearing before local agencies except in the city of New York. It did

have a great deal of political and electoral reform to complete before we can assert to the people of New York that we have restored honesty, integrity, and accountability in state government.

In recent years Albany has taken a few steps more toward the light. For example, we made voter registration easier and the forms more readily available; the NYS Tax Department and other state agencies can now help distribute and collect them. In addition, we took steps to encourage eligible high school and college students to register and vote. New laws also made it a bit easier for an outsider without vast resources to make it to the ballot against savvy incumbents. For many elections, it now takes fewer signatures to win a place on the ballot, and harmless mistakes on petition forms will no longer doom a campaign. This law, which also placed new limits on the size of campaign contributions, steers us toward intelligence and away from hypocrisy; but these changes, when compared with the magnitude of the remaining need, have been more symbolic than substantive.

Albany has much more to do on the issue of electoral reform. Our laws still do not include far broader reforms that would make the system more open to voters, more open to new candidates, and less vulnerable to the sway of big money.

In 1990 less than one-third of those eligible to vote in New York State did so. Five million potential voters in New York State are not registered. The Empire State ranks forty-second out of the fifty states in voter registration. Because our system rewards involvement and punishes aloofness, hurting those most who can't—or won't—get involved, we must all work harder to bring more people into the political process or risk further the vibrancy of our civic culture.

Both the state assembly and I have proposed that we go further to open up the process: by giving voters more time to register and limiting the purging of registration rolls; by dramatically reducing the amount of wealth that can be used to buy victories; and by giving the board of elections a new structure and real teeth. Behind closed doors, I have summed up the issue for Albany lawmakers this way: "Do you really want to make running for office and voting easier so more of the people actually get to participate, or

---

not prohibit state legislators from practicing before local agencies. And it conditioned prosecution on a vote of the entire ethics commission.

are you afraid too many of 'them' will show up and 'we' will lose?"

If everyone who is eligible voted, would it change the face of our politics? Would a lot of those who are in now be out? I think so. That's why some legislators want to keep the group of predictable voters as small as possible. If everyone could vote by absentee ballot for just one election, we would suddenly get what most of us say we want: "Change!" Those already in office are afraid of that change, so they argue that we shouldn't make voting too easy for people—it would somehow demean the significance of our democratic franchise. They continue to insist that prospective voters should be required to register weeks in advance, that everyone in the state needs to vote on the same day, that only those who are out of town on Election Day should use an absentee ballot. It's a sham.

What if New Yorkers could register when they actually went to the polls to vote? What if "Election Day" lasted a week? What if we encouraged people to vote absentee if they found ordinary voting inconvenient or just because they wanted to? Would it make things worse than they are, or might we just wind up with a stronger democracy? I trust the people enough to encourage them to speak, instead of setting up impediments to make sure we hear only from the same voters who put us in office.

Albany's failure to reform its campaign finance laws has meant that incumbents and wealthy political aspirants have an unfair advantage over others qualified to hold public office. The whole idea of having to beg for funds to run for office demeans the process. It creates at least the appearance of influence no matter how hard we try to avoid it. To correct this, I have proposed a campaign finance reform bill that would, for the first time in New York State, provide optional public funding of campaigns for statewide offices and state legislative offices, along with greatly reduced campaign contribution and expenditure limits, including political action committee contributions.

Another important area of reform I've advocated relates to the pension rights of public officials who are convicted of corruption. Many have argued that our existing laws are too lax; that deterrence and fairness are compromised when a person who has used public office to steal continues to benefit. I agree, and the people of New York would be better served if we closed this loophole.

New Yorkers would also be better served if we amended the state constitution to remove judges from the election campaign system and start selecting them on the basis of merit alone.[85] In order to restore public confidence in the judiciary, we must stop the charade of judicial nominating conventions where judicial temperament and legal knowledge are rarely considered and in which the true electors are political party bosses rather than the general public.[86]

A political reform agenda for the 1990s would not be complete without a proposal that would force the state legislature to consider controversial issues of significant interest to New York's voters. The limited initiative and referendum I've proposed requires the legislature to vote one way or another on a bill when 250,000 voters from around the state have signed petitions calling for a vote. This means that issues of importance will have to be debated openly on the floor of the legislature and voted upon by all the elected representatives. Even if a bill is voted down or vetoed, people will readily know whose failure to support it had contributed to its defeat.[87]

Why does New York need this device? The truth is that under our current processes, many bills of vital public importance—bills on key subjects like bias-related violence, the Bottle Bill,[88] life imprisonment without parole, campaign finance reform, and banning assault weapons—never even reach the floor of the legislature for a vote. All these issues are serious enough for members of the legislature to discuss in private, but for some inscrutable

---

[85]I have had the unique opportunity—one not available to any other governor in the modern history of this state—to appoint all the members of New York's highest court, the court of appeals. Those appointments, which were based on judicial merit and not political preferences, have helped to establish the New York State Court of Appeals as the finest top state court in the land.

[86]As the law grows and changes, there is much more we need to do in the area of judicial reform in New York State. We need to proceed with court merger, a simple and intelligent change that will make our judicial system contemporary, giving us what common sense and experience tell us we should have had a long time ago—a single, unified, comprehensive system of justice. I have submitted legislation to streamline criminal discovery and simplify misdemeanor trials as part of a long-needed reform of the criminal trial system, which has become overburdened, overintricate, and a source of frustration for victims and witnesses. I have proposed changes to the system of bail, strengthening it as a fundamental principle of law that gives real meaning to the phrase "innocent until proven guilty." And I have proposed streamlining procedures in the family court system to bring more expeditious justice to juvenile lawbreakers, while continuing to assure fairness for accused juveniles.

[87]It's important to stress what the initiative would not do. It would not allow the people to make laws directly. It does not call for expensive referenda that may be manipulated by special interests. It does not deprive members of the legislature of the right to initiate the legislative process, since the legislative initiative proposal would apply only to a bill that had been introduced in the legislature by an elected member.

[88]The Bottle Bill, discussed more fully in the "Beauty" section, has addressed the widespread need to recycle beverage cans and plastic bottles.

political reason, they are not serious enough to debate and vote on in public. I find that unacceptable; so would most New Yorkers if they knew about it.

Why won't the legislature deal with these issues? Because their extraordinary tenure has made them feel virtually immune in the current political process. The Republicans have controlled the state senate for fifty-five years with a single exception, and the Democrats have controlled the assembly for the last nineteen. Because they enjoy that immunity, they resist many beneficial changes that seem so urgently needed to so many citizens.

Isn't it absurd that the state senate can tell the press and the people that they have no right to see exactly how taxpayers' money—millions of it—was spent on campaign pamphlets sent to potential voters in the last election, because the "sunshine law" they passed, which opens other branches of the government, does not allow the light to reach their dark chamber?

Ultimately, "political reform" comes down to the issue of "change."

The 1992 presidential election produced an unprecedented expression of disapproval—not only of the prevailing economic conditions, but also of the way government conducts its business. That came as no surprise. Today the political system is not responsive to the will of the people.

Clearly, in New York the system has not been operating as intelligently, fairly, or efficiently as it should. The people have reason to be angered by the unconscionable delay that has become habitual in the legislative enactment of a state budget. They have reason to be vexed by the undue influence of well-financed agents of special interests, who—as it stands now—can attempt legally to use their power to sway lawmakers. They have a right to be outraged at an arcane political system, with Byzantine nomination, registration, and election laws that protect incumbents and the status quo while crushing potential challengers who lack sufficient wealth, political cunning, or connections.

Substantive change is needed to change the way things are done in Albany and at the local level across New York State. I don't have confidence that incumbents can make the changes that are necessary, because they are so entrenched in the ways of the past that it defies human experience for them to uproot themselves, in effect, to change the system that put them in power. What *will* change the system is a constitutional convention that gives real power back to the people of New York.

Our New York State Constitution was last extensively overhauled in 1938, but since then it has become increasingly outdated. That fact does not diminish the wisdom of the original drafters, nor of those who labored to amend and revise it more than fifty years ago. Much of it remains sage and workable, still a model for other states across the nation to follow. But evidence has been mounting for years, and mounting more rapidly over the last decade, so that important aspects of the New York State Constitution need to be fully reexamined. Reform is needed in the way we adopt a budget, in the system for choosing candidates and electing public officials, in the way we pay for the services all citizens need, in how we protect civil rights, and in how we maintain public health and safety.

A constitutional convention—a coming together of citizens chosen directly by the people for the purpose of reviewing and proposing changes to the state constitution—is the perfect tool for taking on these tasks. By law, we are scheduled to have the next chance to consider a convention in the 1997 elections. Given the people's eagerness for change, I believe they will vote positively. A convention will be held in 1998. We should have one even sooner, and we can, if the legislature will put it on the ballot before then. The process is simple: the legislature must pass a bill that places the question "Shall there be a convention to revise the New York State Constitution and amend the same?" before the voters of the state. If a simple majority of the people agree, then the voters choose convention delegates at the next general election, and those delegates must, as required by the constitution, "convene at the Capitol on the first Tuesday of April next ensuing after their election, and shall continue their session until the business of such convention shall have been completed." Any proposed new constitution that resulted from the convention's efforts would then be presented to all the voters for their approval. In one grand stroke of intelligent populism, we could make New York State the innovative incubator for democratic revival and change, a model for the entire nation, just as we did two centuries ago.[89]

---

[89]Currently, the New York State Constitution is silent on the manner of electing delegates to a constitutional convention. Just because we used an arcane, potentially unfair method in 1915, 1938, and 1967 doesn't mean we can't come up with a better system in 1997 or even sooner. The next convention should not be dominated by people of influence and political power or position but should reflect in its membership the mosaic of color, culture, and creed that is New York. I believe those delegates should be qualified to give voice to the grass-roots concerns of our people. While there is nothing in the state constitution prohibiting legislative or judicial representation at a convention, legislators and judges must compete for elective delegate slots along with everyone else. Each legislator

What could such a constitutional convention achieve?

A constitutional convention could empower people to pass an amendment that would compel the houses to vote on all important bills that never have made it to the floor. It could make it easier for people to run for public office; easier to register and vote. It could give us merit selection of judges. It could give new powers to local governments. It could ensure that Albany never again enters a new fiscal year without a budget. If the people want to limit the terms of their elected officials, they could do it.[90] If they want to put a ceiling on how much money elected and appointed officials can make, they could do that. If they want to completely overhaul the MTA, they could do that.[91]

When I suggest this or any other practical reform, people ask, "How do we accomplish this?"

Most of the time I say, "Call the politicians in Albany, call up your legislators and say, 'The governor is right; you should vote for these things.' " But New Yorkers, long accustomed to cynical posturing and the gridlock that has gripped the system, ache for a more tangible, tenable alternative. Now I have one: a constitutional convention. If they want to take back control of their government, they won't have a better chance in this generation to do so.

When I proposed this idea to the state legislature in my 1992 State of the State Address, I asked them, "Have we, the elected officials, performed our jobs so admirably and judiciously over the past few years that we are in any position to dismiss such an idea as mere folly?" Clearly the subject would likely

---

or judge selected as a delegate would receive his or her salary plus an assembly member's base salary—in effect, "double dipping" in a completely legal way. Further, state legislators would be deep into the regular legislative session in April, thereby diminishing the possibility of their full service as delegates. While I am not against elected officials serving as delegates per se, I am opposed to their receiving two salaries—legislative and delegate's pay—simultaneously. In my State of the State Address in 1992, I proposed that we also authorize public campaign financing for the election of delegates.

[90]The issue of setting term limits for New York City officials appeared on the ballot in the November 2, 1993, election, and it was passed with an overwhelming majority.

[91]Throughout my career I have argued that there should be no Metropolitan Transit Authority (MTA) because it insulates the politicians in Albany from responsibility and accountability for mass transit in New York City. I believe we should get rid of the MTA and make the elected politicians responsible. In 1983, in response to recommendations in a report by the special study panel on the MTA, I introduced legislation to change the organization and operation of the MTA. The new laws were designed to make the governor the principal bearer of responsibility and accountability for the MTA and strengthen the office of its inspector general.

impose a new discipline on how the legislature operates. They are right; it would. And it should, because the system is not working as well as it might, and only the people can make the fundamental changes that are now needed to fix it.

Is that too much trust to place back in the hands of the people?

Isn't that the way we started over two hundred years ago?

Beauty

Keeping New York Clean and Green

Whenever I fly over this state—and I do it frequently, by helicopter or small plane—I am reminded of how generous God has been to New York. We have been blessed with huge stretches of fertile land and wide-open spaces; abundant, virgin forests; the majestic Catskills and the Adirondacks; magnificent lakes, rivers, and streams. To the west sit the Great Lakes Erie and Ontario; upstate the diamond glory of the Finger Lakes; to the east the stately Hudson; southward the sparkling beaches of Long Island and the glittering edge of the Atlantic.[1]

As governor I have a sworn duty under our state constitution to "conserve and protect New York's natural resources and scenic beauty . . . its forests and wildlife." But in that call to stewardship is buried one of the most challenging contradictions we have to deal with in government: Should we be concerned with the earth as a purveyor of "natural resources" for human commerce and consumption? Or is it more important that we dedicate ourselves to guarding the fragile charms of its "scenic beauty" and ecological health? It would certainly be nice to do both, but doesn't one preclude the other?

It's possible to see our environmental challenges in such stark terms, but more and more, policy makers around the world are recognizing that these goals are not only not contradictory, but each is, indeed, indispensable to achieving the other. We can't afford to preserve our health and our wild places without the tax revenues and private contributions produced by a healthy economy—an economy that requires resources to run. At the same time, if we see the earth as ours to pillage for profit, we will desecrate much of the natural strength and beauty of the planet. Every component of our environment—land, water, air, and wildlife—is linked to every other. We can't expect to address any one of them in isolation from the rest. And because New York's piece of the planet represents just one living cell in a worldwide ecosystem, we can't expect to handle its problems unilaterally, without the help of other states and nations.

This recognition of interconnectedness and interdependence is more important today than it has been at any point in our history.

Around the world, whole species of life face extinction. Tropical rain forests

---

[1] For a full list of New York's regions and the places to see within them, see appendix A.

are menaced by the specter of deforestation. Greenhouse gases are building up in the atmosphere, distorting the familiar features of our climate. Cities everywhere weave their own shrouds of smog. The throwaway societies of the industrialized world produce so many millions of tons of solid waste each year that we're running out of places to put it. The oceans regurgitate the waste we choke them with, littering our beaches with debris. Even the sky has become an accomplice in our self-destruction, poisoning our lakes and forests with acid rain.

The sense of threat and pressure is real, but it isn't new. It has troubled us intermittently since the Industrial Revolution took root in America.

For the people of that period and for all the generations who came before, water had a magnetic attraction; people built their cities around it because of what it could *do*. But in New York in the late nineteenth century, at the peak of the period of industrial expansion known as the Gilded Age, we began to develop another idea: that water was part of a natural world worth preserving for its own sake—and for the sake of *all* the people.

The spur for this new speculation: the threat to Niagara Falls.

The enterprising merchants of the Empire State had seen the immense commercial potential of Niagara Falls and in their eagerness to develop it had tried to rearrange nature's design to their advantage. Over time, their tampering had endangered the survival of the falls themselves. Fierce political pressure was exerted by those who stood to gain personally through continued private use of the surrounding lands. Fortunately, New Yorkers saw what was happening and responded in a way that set a precedent for the nation: in 1885 the falls and the land around them were formally protected, and the "Niagara Reservation" became the nation's first state park.[2]

It was a milestone. For the first time, a state government had purchased land for the sole purpose of preserving a natural landmark. From there it was just a few short steps intellectually to another New York invention that emerged that same year: the first example of an untamed "wilderness park"— the Adirondack and Catskill Forest Preserve.

---

[2]Though Niagara is the first *state* park, it was not the first government-mandated park. That distinction belongs to Yellowstone, which became America's first national park in 1872, before Wyoming achieved statehood. In 1864 Yosemite was named a "reservation" by California. However, it was not officially designated a state park until 1890.

Once again, the impetus came from the feverish growth of industry. America was coming into its own. Factories and railroads were expanding. The demand for raw materials was increasing exponentially—and so, by extension, was the temptation to exploit the great forests of this state, including the immense northern region known as the Adirondacks. In fact, some regions had already been ravaged by the avarice of those who saw every available tree as board feet of lumber. In places, not only the forests but the surrounding systems of lakes, rivers, and streams—and the wildlife they supported—were being crippled and even destroyed.

When Governor David Hill signed the bill establishing the state forest preserve within the Adirondack and Catskill mountains, New York became the first government in the United States to recognize the special value of truly wild lands, and New Yorkers became the pioneers of a whole new attitude toward the environment.

They didn't call it the "environment" then. They didn't have our scientific understanding of the interdependence of nature's creation, the delicate balance of the food chain, what Rachel Carson called the "close-knit fabric of life." But the New Yorkers of 1885 knew that if they allowed the Adirondacks and Catskills to be stripped and mutilated, they risked the permanent loss of a beautiful and essential element of the natural world that surrounded them and which they were charged with guarding for the coming generations. It was a risk they weren't willing to take.

If the New Yorkers of that era had chosen to forget about those who would follow them, they could have had more for themselves: more exports, more raw materials, more land for development. Fortunately for generations to follow, they had a vision that reached beyond their own times. Whether they lived in cities or on farms, whether they were industrialists or immigrants, Democrats and Republicans joined together to set these lands aside, by law, for all time. And when that law didn't seem strong enough, they carved this direct and beautiful guarantee into the state's constitution: "The lands of the State, now owned or hereafter acquired, constituting the Forest Preserve as now fixed by law, shall be forever kept as wild forest lands." We remember that promise today with the signature phrase of the Adirondack and Catskill parks, "Forever Wild."

New York's foresight and idealism—and the successful precedents it produced, in the Adirondacks, the Catskills, and Niagara—inspired the whole nation. The influence of what the state had achieved helped support efforts from the creation of the National Park Service to the passage of the Federal Wilderness Act nearly eight decades later.

We were left with a fine park legacy. First and most obvious is our extraordinary inheritance of parks, especially our state park system. By 1924 New York had accumulated forty recreation areas, each one locally managed. But in that grab bag of individual parks, Robert Moses, New York's great public builder, saw the potential for a unified statewide system. With the backing of Governor Al Smith, he formed the New York State Council of Parks to guide park policy throughout New York.

Since that time the system has continued to grow, with the encouragement of governor after governor. By 1991 the New York State Forest Preserve, with its 150 state parks, 765 cabins, 76 developed beaches, 34 historic sites, 20 swimming pools, 116 campgrounds, 20 nature centers, 3 environmental education camps, and about 4,000 miles of assorted trails, was serving approximately 63 million annual visitors—more people than attended all the major league baseball games played that year and more than visited our national parks.[3] Park growth continues at a healthy rate: from 1983 to 1992, New York State acquired new parkland valued at well over $40 million. To preserve and enhance the system, in 1992 I proposed and the legislature passed the State Parks Infrastructure Fund, which will provide $300 million over a ten-year period to help repair and revitalize aging state park facilities, from Niagara to Nassau County.[4]

As the state parks have multiplied, they have reinforced an important perspective: that much of the idea behind preserving wild public land was that the richness of nature should be available to everyone—not just those rich enough to own an estate in the country. In 1929 Governor Franklin Roosevelt officially opened Jones Beach State Park—one of the world's great beaches

---

[3]More than eight million of those visitors frequented Jones Beach on Long Island, part of our Long Island State Park, which by itself is larger than the entire parks program of most states.

[4]The money, which comes directly from park user fees, provides stable, predictable, long-term funding. A short list of the parks that will benefit from the fund includes Fillmore Glen, Taghkanic Falls, Watkins Glen, and the Robert Treman state parks; the Allegany State Park in Cattaraugus County; Letchworth State Park in Livingston County; Chittenango Falls in Madison County; Chenango Valley State Park in central New York; Lake Taghkanic State Park in Dutchess County; and Heckscher, Hither Hills, and Montauk Point state parks on Long Island.

and a vital escape for the working people of the greater New York City region. The park owed its existence to the stubborn vision of Robert Moses and of Roosevelt's predecessor, Al Smith, who together pushed the project through despite the ferocious opposition of landowners who did not want Long Island's exclusive southern shores opened to the "teeming masses" of New York City. The beach we take for granted today was, in the end, made accessible to all New Yorkers in part by a state-backed investment that built a parkway to connect Jones Beach to the five boroughs of New York.[5]

The challenge of giving all our people reasonable access to natural lands is obviously toughest in the big cities, because in those close quarters the job requires so much more than buying up attractive acreage, hiring some rangers, and ordering the right picnic tables. In the cities you practically have to *invent* the land.

That's very much what we did with a state park in New York City called Riverbank, which opened in May 1993. Built above a wastewater treatment plant between 137th and 145th streets on the Hudson side of Harlem, it is the first-ever state park in Manhattan. Its exceptional site makes it unique in the United States. And its extraordinary facilities make it an oasis in a struggling neighborhood. For $129 million, the park's twenty-eight acres have been equipped with indoor and outdoor swimming pools; an auditorium that seats close to one thousand; a gymnasium for basketball, volleyball, or gymnastics; a two-hundred-foot ice- and roller-skating rink; two AstroTurf-

---

[5]Since then, hundreds of millions of people have come to Jones Beach, in good times and bad, to relax and revive their spirits and their bodies. In 1929 the Jones Beach Theater was the place to hear "music over the water and under the stars." But over the years, as the nature of public tastes in entertainment changed, seaside audiences dwindled and box office sales suffered. For years it had losses, and many lost faith in the theater as a viable medium to entertain the hundreds of thousands it had once reached.

One of the people who never gave up hope on the theater was commissioner of the state park system, Orin Lehman, who retired in 1993. Working with entertainment promoter Ron Delsener, Commissioner Lehman brought profitable entertainment back to the beach and, with it, $800,000 in annual revenues to New York State. The promoter invested $6 million in this state facility. Included in the improvements were replacing the folding chairs with new permanent seats, enlarging the seating area, providing better viewing areas for the physically challenged, installing larger, improved restrooms, and modernizing the food service area. The entire environment at the Jones Beach Theater is cleaner, safer, and more enjoyable than ever and now attracts every kind of music, from Barry Manilow, the Beach Boys, and Steely Dan to 10,000 Maniacs and the Spin Doctors.

covered fields for football, soccer, baseball, and softball; a four-hundred-meter track; basketball, handball, and tennis courts; a restaurant; and an amphitheater for cultural events. Open seventeen hours a day, it is easily accessible to tens of thousands of low-income residents who live in upper Manhattan.[6]

At the opposite end of the city, I had the privilege of inaugurating another "invented" green space, this one run by Battery Park City instead of the state parks agency. When I cut the opening ribbon in June 1992, Hudson River Park became New York's first waterfront park in forty years and the largest new public open space in Manhattan since the 1930s. It is one component of the original concept of the Battery Park City development, a scheme devised over a quarter century ago to transform ninety-two acres of vacant landfill into a place that would enhance city living. The park's many charms—its esplanade, its stonework, the Tom Otterness sculptures, the Demetri Porphyrios Pavilion—surely help fulfill that vision.

But Hudson River Park actually marks the start of a much larger effort to give the people of New York City better access to the consolations of nature. A few weeks before the park's opening, I signed a memorandum of understanding with the then mayor of New York, David Dinkins, to create a new waterfront park all along the city's Hudson shoreline. The plan will forge a continuous West Side esplanade, including open water areas and public recreation piers, that will link neighborhoods from Manhattan's southernmost tip to 59th Street, eventually joining with Riverbank Park in Harlem and reaching onward to Spuyten Duyvil in the Bronx.

As challenging as it may be to give city dwellers convenient opportunities to connect with nature, the reverse proves just as difficult: trying to preserve the Adirondack wilderness while giving the people who live there a reasonable chance to earn their own living and control their own lives. The Adirondack Park Forest Preserve, which began with 715,000 acres in 1885, today encompasses more than 2.7 million acres—the largest and most securely protected wilderness area east of the Mississippi. Just 200 miles north of New York City, the park offers ancient mountains and very old forests, the headwaters of the Hudson, countless lakes, and almost all of the 1,300 miles of New York's wild,

---

[6]"Creating Parks in a Crowded Metropolis," Mervyn Rothstein, *The New York Times*, April 4, 1993, Section 10, p. 1.

scenic, and recreational rivers. And it's growing. Since 1983 we have conducted the most aggressive program for public acquisition of scenic and
sensitive lands in a hundred years.[7]

But the park is also a unique patchwork of public and private lands, ranging
from colossal timber company holdings and vast private estates to clusters of
modest house plots. That unusual structure has its price.

The overarching questions we face as the Adirondack Park begins its
second century are these: "How do we make reasonable accommodations to
the demands of nature, the rights of a world of visitors, and the needs of the
130,000 individuals who live, work, raise their families, and do business in the
park? How do we preserve this magnificent heritage for the state as a whole,
forever wild, and still give residents of the park a fair and useful voice in
determining their own future?"

Certainly, finding a way to preserve the fabric of the park while allowing
careful economic development is one of the duties of the Adirondack Park
Agency. But the issues are so divisive and delicate that we need legislative
solutions, too.

I have met with people on all sides of the issue to consider their perspectives
and to remind them that no matter what we do or fail to do, something will
happen as a result: there is no freezing the status quo with respect to the
Adirondacks. If we do not protect the region, some of the largest and most
significant parcels will be subdivided, developed, and altered forever.

In October 1991 I offered proposals to avoid this kind of destructive passivity.
I asked the people of New York, both within and outside the Adirondacks, to
work with us in government to reconcile their disparate needs and desires. The
process taught us a great deal and is bringing us closer to the day when legislative
action will be possible. In April 1993 we offered the legislature a revised
Adirondack bill, designed specifically to preserve the rugged backcountry and
brilliant shorelines, especially those large tracts that define the very character of
the park. Some of them would be preserved by purchase for the public domain,
and development of pristine shorelines would be discouraged through tighter
land-use restrictions. I have also put forward a voluntary program that would
support long-term stewardship of forest lands by offering varying levels of tax

---

[7]Since 1983 the New York State Department of Environmental Conservation has acquired (in fee
and easements) 267,000 acres of land, 218,000 of which are in the Adirondack and Catskill preserves.

relief in return for a commitment not to develop a property and, in some cases, to allow public recreation.[8]

But New York's remarkable parks are only one side of the legacy we inherited from the early conservation achievements in the Niagara Gorge, the Catskills, and the Adirondacks. The other side was more abstract but has proven just as precious: an enlightened understanding of our broader responsibilities to nature.

In the century since those first steps to protect the natural world from our worst instincts, New York and New Yorkers have repeatedly lit the way in environmental thinking and policy. On the political scene alone the examples are impressive, starting with Theodore Roosevelt, a great New York Republican raised amid the beauty of Long Island, who went on as president of the United States to educate an entire country about the importance of conservation. From the White House he created the national forest system and the national wildlife refuge system. Years later, his cousin Franklin—inspired perhaps by his own upbringing along the Hudson—promoted the conservation of New York's natural resources first in the state senate, as chairman of the Senate Committee on Forests, Fish and Game, and later as governor. As president he created the Civilian Conservation Corps, whose workers restored and improved the nation's ravaged farm and forest lands during the Great Depression.

Our environmental tradition has grown stronger under each of our subsequent governors, especially Nelson Rockefeller—who spearheaded what became the national effort to purify the country's lakes, rivers, and streams—and Hugh Carey, who signed into law the state Environmental Quality Review Act, the Freshwater Wetlands Act, and the Returnable Container Law.[9] Over the past decade New York became the first state in the nation to adopt water quality standards for toxic chemicals, including some one hundred organic compounds. We were the first state to ban the use of chlordane, a dangerous pesticide. We were the first to establish an air toxins program that controls toxic emission standards for resource recovery plants and industries.

The state has also benefited from extraordinarily aggressive and effective

---

[8]I would offset these exemptions with payments to local governments from the Environmental Protection Fund enacted in 1993.

[9]The Pure Waters Program, initiated in New York in 1966 under Governor Nelson Rockefeller, formed the basis for the Federal Clean Water Act of 1972.

citizen action on behalf of the environment. For example, it would not be too much to say that the spirit of the modern environmental movement was spawned in the mid-Hudson valley in the 1960s and 1970s, through the insistence and imagination of groups like Scenic Hudson. Scenic Hudson rejected the idea that Con Edison, the proponent of a hydroelectric power plant, had the right to build whatever it pleased on the slopes of the Hudson's Storm King Mountain and sued the federal government to require that the environmental impact of the power plant be weighed by the Federal Power Commission. Scenic Hudson's victory eventually established both the legal and intellectual principle that not just government, but *individual citizens* had the right to act to protect the environment. This development led several years later to the passage of the National Environmental Policy Act and to the creation of the Environmental Protection Administration, pioneering progress for all Americans.

But like every other state, we have often had to learn the hard way— developing new measures to deal with emergencies and circumstances specific to New York.

Perhaps the most dramatic case in memory was the 1978 disaster at Love Canal in western New York, one of the country's first large-scale examples of the hazards created by dumping radioactive or chemical and other noxious wastes near residential communities. Through the physical, emotional, and economic suffering of the people of Love Canal, the nation began to learn just how costly and difficult it would be to undo the compound damage of environmental negligence, ignorance, and denial.

By the time I came to office, it was clear that Love Canal would not be an isolated incident unless we stepped up our efforts at both prevention and cure. Between 1983 and 1986 we expanded the enforcement staff at the Department of Environmental Conservation as never before. And as of April 1993 the state had secured commitments of nearly $1.5 billion for the inspection and cleanup of the conditions at approximately 550 hazardous waste sites, with the funds coming from the parties responsible for the waste.[10]

At the same time, the country was beginning to develop a new understanding about who might be held accountable for injuries sustained in such cases

---

[10]This is in addition to the $164 million spent to date from the 1986 Environmental Bond Act funds for the inspection and cleanup of 660 toxic waste sites. (*Executive Budget Briefing Book, New York State 1993–94*, p. 68.)

of insidious toxic exposure. This new consciousness eventually produced a landmark bill we adopted in 1986, known to lawyers as the toxic torts legislation. Previously, the tort law had been designed so that people who had been injured because of someone else's recklessness or negligence could sue for damages, but only within a few years of the time of the injury. Victims of a toxic exposure whose effects took years to emerge were left without legal recourse. The new law provides that where toxic substances are involved, New Yorkers may begin a suit for injury to themselves or their property either within three years of the *discovery of the injury and its cause* or three years from the date when they could, with reasonable diligence, have discovered it, whichever is earlier.[11]

As our environmental consciousness has grown over the last thirty years, New York has come to recognize more and more instances in which the cumulative catastrophe of our environmental abuses demands our attention and our dollars. Though less the stuff of national headlines than the crisis at Love Canal, our efforts to heal damaged ecosystems across the state have been vitally important to preserving the physical qualities that make the Empire State an attractive place to live and a productive place to do business.

The examples range from the romantic to the mundane. By banning DDT and importing young eagles from Alaska, we have been able in the past decade to restore the bald eagle to our landscape, from which it had literally disappeared. Less glamorous than eagles but more urgent for public health has been preserving the quality of our drinking water.

In the 1960s and 1970s New York devoted billions of dollars to creating sewage treatment facilities statewide that have markedly improved our water supplies. Since 1990 we have financed more than $1 billion to upgrade such plants and expect to provide $3 billion more by the turn of the century. We have instituted strict new regulations protecting the state's underwater lands (such as lake and river bottoms) and are recognized nationally for our groundwater protection efforts. On Long Island, where intensive development both strains and threatens to taint the supply of fresh water, we now have laws to phase out landfills that might lead to contamination. We took further steps in

---

[11]The toxic torts law also gave those whose claims were barred or dismissed under the old statute of limitations one year in which to commence an action. The immediate spur to create the law came from citizens who sought the right to sue for the eventual results of past exposure to DES, asbestos, tungsten carbide, polyvinyl chloride, and chlordane.

1990 and 1993, passing laws to protect the Long Island Pine Barrens, which stand guard over the largest source of pure groundwater in the state.

But for sheer scale of effort and accomplishment, no case in New York rivals the restoration of the Hudson River. By 1970, the year of the first Earth Day, the Hudson was encumbered by the waste, debris, and poisons of more than a century of expanding populations and aggressive industrial development. The river had everything in it but clean water. Rescuing it required enormous amounts of money and years of persistence, but federal and state programs eventually provided the resources, and now the Hudson is dramatically cleaner.[12]

To extend the vision of a healthy Hudson beyond the water itself, in 1991 we established the Hudson River Greenway—a linear district extending up both sides of the Hudson from New York City to Albany and Rensselaer counties. The greenway includes both public and private lands, ranging from existing parks to industrial facilities. But all of these properties are now united under the guiding eye of the Hudson River Greenway Council and Conservancy. The essential goal is to protect the habitats, scenic places, and historic sites of the river and at the same time make it more accessible for recreation. But rather than relying on the vagaries of litigation or piecemeal zoning battles to do the job, the greenway orchestrates the *cooperative* efforts of all the towns, villages, groups, businesses, individuals, and government entities with an interest in the property on or near the river's banks. Since 1972 the state has bought more than 1,500 acres of spectacular Hudson landscapes; now, as part of the greenway effort, we have worked with local conservation groups to acquire other exceptional sites in the region, including Nutten Hook, which offers a panoramic view of both the river and the Catskills, and Esopus Meadows Point, a diverse waterfowl and fish habitat near the Esopus Meadows Lighthouse.

Efforts like these help rescue and preserve valuable resources. But, ultimately, if we want our relationship with nature to do more than lurch perpetually between crisis and cleanup, we have to change the way we live, adapting our familiar habits and technologies to the limitations of a natural world that can no longer afford to forgive our mistakes.

An obvious place to start is with the automobile, that great incremental

---

[12]Once again, citizen action was essential. For example, the Hudson River Fishermen's Association successfully sued Exxon and other companies for polluting the river.

polluter. Today, like every state in the country, we are busy trying to assess and respond to the standards specified in the 1990 Federal Clean Air Act and its recent amendments. But many of its provisions were old news to us: over the past two decades, nearly all industrial, residential, and municipal sources of air pollution in New York State have come under control, and air quality has improved significantly enough that other states and even the federal government have begun to use our methods as a model.[13]

But none of it means very much if we can't put a dent in the pollutants that escape from our cars and other motor vehicles—the single biggest cause of air pollution in our state. Recently we toughened the state's auto emission standards by adopting the California Low Emission Vehicle (LEV) program, which will greatly reduce allowable emissions from all cars sold after 1995 and by the year 2003 will require that 10 percent of all cars sold in New York State be totally nonpolluting. Although the LEV program has been challenged in the courts by automobile dealers and manufacturers and in the legislature by other groups, we're determined to press ahead with this and other programs to improve the air we breathe.

Gaining ground in the battle against air pollution hinges on an aggressive assault armed with equal parts of common sense and advanced technology, from carpools to catalytic converters. Parallel strategies apply to our solid waste problem, but that is a fight we are only just beginning because it has taken so long to persuade the people that there was a "garbage problem" at all.

We know that solid waste has been an urban nuisance for at least 2,500 years—ever since the Athenian city council passed history's first ordinance prohibiting people from throwing garbage into the street. But the awesome arithmetic of solid waste seemed to have little shock value with the public until the infamous garbage barge *Mobro* began its journey from New York Harbor across our television screens in the summer of 1987, hunting desperately for a place to unload. Before the *Mobro,* too few of us cared that New Yorkers were generating about twenty-two million tons of garbage a year, more than

---

[13]Our air pollution control program includes a computerized air emissions inventory and a statewide air monitoring network, as well as air operating certificates regulating environmental limits for some 65,000 sources. Toxic pollutants are monitored at 185 different stations to measure New York's air quality.

a ton for every state resident—and we were running out of room for it.[14] Capacity wasn't the only problem: most of the garbage went to old, unlined dumps that we sweetened with the euphemism *landfills*. As these primitive facilities began to leak the toxins they contained, they were contaminating our lakes, rivers, and groundwater supplies. Many had to be closed even before they reached capacity.

The *Mobro*'s grim Atlantic odyssey made it temporarily embarrassing to admit that you were from New York, but it also served as a crucial goad to public action.

In 1988 New Yorkers of every stripe—Democrats and Republicans, upstaters and downstaters, environmentalists and industrialists—joined together to develop environmentally sound and fiscally prudent programs to deal more comprehensively with the state's garbage problem. The result was passage of the Solid Waste Management Act, which established responsibility for waste reduction, reuse, recycling, incineration, and landfilling. The act also mandated municipal waste separation and recycling. In response, New York City recently adopted the most ambitious recycling program of any major city in the world.[15]

The scale of the solid waste problem demands as many solutions as we can devise. Since packaging materials make up about a third of what we throw away, we are working with manufacturers to cut down on unnecessary packaging.[16] Part of the answer also lies in more ambitious municipal recycling programs, since New Yorkers recycle only about 23 percent of the solid waste they generate each year. And to make the recycling process economically viable, we also need to develop markets for goods made from recycled materials. Through New York State's Office of Economic Development, we are giving businesses and communities financial and tech-

---

[14]Figures given are for 1990.

[15]In New York, as in many states, solid waste management is primarily a local government responsibility. Yet most municipalities simply do not have the resources to bear the financial burden of managing their waste alone.

[16]New York State is part of the Source Reduction Task Force of the Coalition of Northeastern Governors, a cooperative venture of industry, government, and public interest groups to reduce volume, weight, and toxicity of packaging. Of the nine northeast states, seven, including New York, have passed legislation that will dramatically reduce the use and presence of mercury, lead, cadmium, and hexavalent chromium in all packaging.

nical assistance to help increase the use of recycled and recyclable materials.

No matter how systematic or imaginative our solutions in New York, a number of our most troubling problems are beyond our power to fix on our own—as when we share a major resource with another state or suffer the environmental consequences of behavior beyond our borders.

In 1984 New York became the first state to regulate the emissions that cause acid rain, and our sulfur-in-coal and oil limits are still the strictest in the country. For years we had calculated the dimensions of the acid rain threat and experienced its fallout—the dying lakes and forests and fish, the decaying public monuments. Real progress, however, was beyond our grasp, because the key sources lay beyond our jurisdiction, in the factory smokestacks of the industrial Midwest. It was obvious and well documented that the scope of the problem was national, but for years federal intransigence blocked any movement toward a national solution. As we saw the mounting damage in New York, we decided to reach out to the state with which we were most fiercely at odds—Ohio, one of the nation's large emitters of sulfur dioxide. Through extensive negotiations with Governor Richard Celeste of Ohio, we broke the logjam and created a framework for a workable plan to reduce the sulfurous emissions that turn rain into acid rain.[17] Working with New York's Senator Moynihan, we also developed amendments to the 1990 Federal Clean Air Act that will eventually reduce the nation's harmful emissions of sulfur dioxide by at least ten million tons annually and nitrogen oxide by more than three million tons over a ten- to fifteen-year period.[18] As Congress gradually began to approach the acid rain issue, these ideas, along with the spirit of equity and partnership behind our 1988 Ohio–New York agreement, offered an innovative strategy for handling a complex environmental and economic threat.

Naturally that spirit is a little easier to establish when two states share the pleasure and responsibility of a precious natural resource. New York's northern reaches are linked to Vermont by a beautiful sliver of water called Lake Champlain. Though its reputation depends mostly on its physical glories, it

---

[17]Under the Cuomo-Celeste Acid Rain Agreement, acid deposits would be slashed by 50 percent over fifteen years through a reduction in emission of sulfur dioxide of ten million tons per year and a reduction in nitrogen oxides of at least three million tons annually over the next decade.

[18]To help achieve an equitable sharing of costs, we also proposed mechanisms to help finance the capital costs of controlling such emissions. These suggestions included subsidizing some of the capital costs of compliance and of introducing new technologies.

also serves as a busy corridor for recreational boat traffic on the route between New York City and Montreal. In the 1980s we recognized that decades of development on both states' shores were threatening the lake's vitality and especially its fish. Pairing up with Vermont to solve the problem seemed an obvious step, and in 1977 the two states together created the Lake Champlain Salmonid Restoration Program and agreed to regulate wastewater discharges and agricultural waste. In 1988 we carried the idea to its logical extension, reaching across the international border and creating a three-way Canada–Vermont–New York agreement to improve water quality and to protect fish, wildlife, and environmentally sensitive areas around the lake.

On our northwestern borders, New York, with the second largest shoreline on the Great Lakes, has a stake in some other troubled waters—Lake Erie and Lake Ontario. Over the years they have been assaulted from every direction: factories, cities, homes; tons of waste products dumped directly into the lakes, legally or illegally, as well as into the streams and rivers that feed them. Toxic chemicals have accumulated in the sediment and poisoned the food chain. It's been a long time since you could eat its fish without health warnings about not eating them too frequently.

The balm for these wounded waters will be another collaborative interstate effort—but even with the prospect of help, the scale of the problem is daunting. Erie and Ontario are integrally linked to the entire Great Lakes system. Taken together, the Great Lakes form the world's largest freshwater source and contain 95 percent of the freshwater in the United States. Today the whole system is taxed beyond its ability to clean itself. But New York depends on the Great Lakes far too much to sit idly by and watch them decay. More than three million New Yorkers rely on the lakes for potable water. Nearly 90 percent of the hydroelectric power developed from the Great Lakes provides power to New York. Fourteen percent of the population of the Great Lakes basin and 15 percent of its agricultural land are in New York State. We own more than four thousand square miles of the lakes themselves—second only to Michigan—and we have more than one thousand miles of shoreline in the Great Lakes–St. Lawrence region.

The threats to the lakes today are so great, so pressing, that they demand collective action by every adjacent state. That's why the Council of Great Lakes Governors—representing Michigan, Indiana, Illinois, Ohio, Wisconsin, Minnesota, and New York—created the Great Lakes Protection Fund, a nonprofit corporation that will administer a $100 million environmental endowment for the lakes. The fund, the first of its kind, is expected to generate between $7 million and $10 million in interest each year to help clean up toxic hot spots, monitor water quality, study the effects of contamination on wildlife, and identify and reduce risks to human health.

The $12 million New York contributed to the fund is in keeping with our size and our shoreline, but it is only a fraction of what we'll have to spend in the coming decades on a range of environmental fronts. Though we have done a good job in controlling or eliminating most new sources of traumatic environmental damage, the bill for reversing decades of carelessness is only going to rise.

One revenue stream I believe we should be using to support our environmental initiatives is the unclaimed deposits on bottles and cans. New York's "Bottle Bill," which requires merchants to charge a returnable deposit of five cents on beer and soda cans and bottles, was designed to achieve a few specific environmental goals. By giving people an incentive to return their empties, the bill aimed to reduce litter, bolster recycling, and save scarce space in landfills—and it's working. A side benefit is that collecting and cashing in discarded bottles has become a helpful source of extra income for people of limited means.

What some might see as the bill's most dramatic effect was completely unintended: the vast majority of unclaimed deposits have become a windfall for the beverage industry. Whenever a bottle or can goes unreturned, its nickel deposit stays in the pocket of the beverage distributors. Since the law was passed in 1983 they have already retained roughly *three-quarters of a billion dollars* in deposits no one has claimed.

I believe it's time that the people of New York, who, after all, supply the deposit money, finally claim those billions of nickels and use them to strengthen our environmental cleanup and enforcement programs instead. Though the legislature is apparently content to let the bottlers hold on to these funds, I will continue to push for legislation that would divert this money to the cause of the earth.[19]

---

[19]It's an important question, yet the state legislature has refused even to consider it, preferring instead to let the beer distributors and soda bottlers keep sixteen billion nickels that the state could be sharing with local governments to deal with pressing environmental problems, including the solid waste problem and the need to protect other priceless open spaces. Eventually, if I keep up the effort and the public is finally made aware, public pressure may force them to do the right thing.

Without such dependable income, we have had to turn to other sources of funding to meet our massive environmental needs in the last decade. In 1986 New York's voters passed the $1.45 billion Environmental Quality Bond Act, the ninth environmental bond act approved in New York since 1910. That money has allowed us to clean up hundreds of toxic waste sites, clean and protect the air and water, protect our historic resources, and preserve and acquire sensitive lands.

A few years later, as our needs in these areas continued to grow and outpace our resources, I proposed the 1990 Environmental Bond Act, which was narrowly turned down by the voters. This suggested another tack, to make sure we would have adequate funds for environmental projects through the end of the decade: a dedicated fund for the environment. (In general, as a principle of governance, I dislike locking up funds for a particular purpose, because it limits your ability to respond constructively to all the changing needs in the state. On the other hand, I have seen over and over that the budget process often slights the environment. Until evergreens get the vote, a dedicated fund appears to be the best solution.)

In 1993, after several years of hard negotiations, New York passed the Environmental Protection Fund, a dedicated revenue stream projected to generate nearly $100 million a year by 1996. This fund will help us answer our many environmental responsibilities, from closing local landfills to encouraging recycling, from preserving the state's open spaces to enhancing our magnificent parks.

The National and International Environmental Challenge

Around budget time in Albany, it's easy to start thinking that our biggest environmental hurdle is finding enough funding. But the real boulders blocking the path to intelligent action on these issues—here and around the world—are a good deal less tangible. One arises from the special nature of politicians, the other from the general nature of human beings. Politicians tend to be different from scientists, who—as C. P. Snow once observed—have to think of one thing, deeply and obsessively, for a long time. Between the ten thousand competing concerns of governance and the intense pressures of election seasons, politicians rarely have time to "study" any problem in a way that a scientist would recognize. Given the bewildering high science it now takes to measure and express our ecological circumstances, elected officials without a special inclination for study will simply go looking for problems with easier answers.

This becomes a real impediment to serious, sustained environmental progress only when it encounters in the voters a concomitant feature of human nature—the tendency to resist contemplating unpleasant possibilities as long as it is possible they may not occur. That reluctance could become for us one of the deadly sins.

Though we can't be sure, it seems increasingly likely that a century or so from now, historians will look back on this era as one when biospheric changes of a magnitude never before experienced perceptibly threatened the balances that sustain life on this planet. And they will be able to judge, by then, whether we who saw the warning signs responded to them with wisdom and strength. In New York we have written too much of this nation's environmental history to travel forward blindly now, indifferent to history's judgment. But as thoughtful and ambitious as we make our state's environmental strategies, they can only be one brick in what must be an international fortress against ecological degradation.

The 1992 Rio Summit in Brazil began the process of building such a global coalition for intelligent action. In fact, that the summit took place at all was hopeful in itself. One hundred and seventy-eight nations sent delegates to Rio—men and women representing every region, religion, race, and ethnic group and every political and economic point of view. This convergence of cultures and philosophies confirmed that the impulse to protect the earth and repair the damage we've done transcends flags and borders, springing from the very heart of human existence.

The agreement represented by the Rio Declaration of Environment and Development—Agenda 21—and the two treaties signed on climate change and biological diversity were all encouraging.[20] Those documents detailed consensus on hundreds of issues, recommending changes and new programs that will guide us into the coming century.

One concept stood at the center of the Earth Summit agreements: "sustainable development," the principle that human survival depends on develop-

---

[20]I was particularly heartened by the Climate Change agreement, since four years earlier in 1988 Governor Madeleine Kunin of Vermont and I convened a Global Climate Change conference that made many of the same recommendations for stabilizing and reducing greenhouse gases.

ment of resources, but that continued development depends on a healthy planet. In essence, our future hinges on our ability to move forward economically without cutting a swath of ecological destruction. We cannot assure safe, healthy, and productive lives for our children and our children's children unless we stop fighting, stop polluting, and start conserving our natural resources.

The realization of this principle may be a long way off, but its wisdom is unimpeachable. It calls for all to take responsibility, some more than others because some have more influence and greater means. The citizens of the developed countries—especially we Americans who enjoy a higher standard of living and who consume a disproportionate share of nature's resources—should bear a greater share of the burden. As a nation and as a species, we must learn to avoid waste. Given our technological power and potential, we must remain conscious of the way that it can alter the fundamental biological, chemical, and physical processes that sustain life on earth. Where we know we are already doing harm—even if we don't know with exact scientific certitude what the consequence will be—we should begin to change our habits and our technologies.

If we live by these principles, we can follow the path to a future where conservation and recycling are part of everyday life, where fuel efficiency and pollution control are the priorities in transportation and production; a future that invests in, and reaps the benefits of, new, nonwasteful technologies that will improve the quality of human life whether you live in New York or New Delhi.

If these principles seem too demanding, however, we can simply "stay the course," with the industrialized North—Europe, Japan, and North America—consuming the lion's share of the world's resources and pumping out tremendous pollution, while the developing nations of the South expend their precious natural wealth in a frantic effort to lift their populations out of poverty. But we should remember the warning of President Gaviria of Colombia: "Sooner or later, the planet will send all of us the bill, rich and poor alike."

The Clinton administration has already demonstrated that progress can be made—both in negotiations with the logging communities of the Pacific Northwest and in terms of international agreements.[21] The appointment of

---

[21]On April 21, 1993, the Clinton administration indicated that the United States would sign the international treaty protecting rare and endangered species, as well as follow a specific timetable to

Secretary of the Interior Bruce Babbitt is encouraging on its own. But there is much more we can do. We need a basic policy for preserving biodiversity beyond the slender reed of the Endangered Species Act; we need a national strategy for promoting biotechnology; we need a national policy that fully integrates our environmental, energy, transportation, and agricultural policies to support sustainable growth.

Perhaps the biggest challenge is education.[22] If more of our people understood the scope and the implications of the environmental issues we face—from ozone depletion to global warming—I believe they would work startling changes on the social and political landscape. I believe they would be prepared to change their habits and attitudes. And I believe they would be pushing their leaders to respond more aggressively across the board.

I think they would respond to the fundamental morality in the goals of the environmental movement—a direct appeal to our need for mutuality. Our commitment to preserve the environment for future generations—as distinguished from ourselves—is an act of selflessness, a true contribution to the common good. Some will try to obscure this truth, labeling environmentalism a special interest and portraying it as an impediment to progress and prosperity. But, in fact, the care and protection of nature is the highest kind of *common interest*—for every one of us on earth.

That is why caring for the environment is, for me, a uniquely beautiful part of our governmental endeavor. Our democratic governments are not allowed to promote any formal theology in this country. What, then, do we say to our children about our ultimate values? What do we say to human beings about the way they ought to behave? The environment is one area in which we seem to be willing to allow the assertion of what could only be called a moral value.

When you are concerned about the lakes in the Adirondacks or the health

---

reduce the threat of global warming. ("Clinton Supports Two Major Steps for Environment," *The New York Times*, April 22, 1993, p. 1.)

[22]In New York City the board of education has created a special "environmental high school" that will serve as a model—a testing ground—to teach our young people about developing, preserving, and improving the world they will inherit. The students take required courses in addition to their standard studies in environmental science, and they also have to intern four hours a week with state or local agencies directly involved with environmental matters to graduate. The school, to my knowledge, is the only one of its kind in the United States. It opened in September 1992 and will be expanding its classes and size in the years to come, providing a fresh and renewable source of environmental activists for New York State.

of New York Harbor or the greenhouse effect, you are not talking about yourself or even your own family. You are talking about generations that you will never know—generations of children who will never even know your name. That sustained concern is the ultimate selfless act. It is a magnificent statement about our human obligation to one another.

In our approach to the environment—in both philosophy and our practice—we manifest more than an intelligent instinct for survival. We manifest our deepest values: our reverence for the life that surrounds us and for the generations before us who planted and preserved the earth; our concern for the generations to come and for all the magnificent links of creation, reaching forward beyond us, to places and to dreams we ourselves will never reach.

Hope

———————————————

Toward an Investment-Led Recovery

One of the great attributes of the American people is their ability to remain optimistic in hard times. We have proved this in the past, when wars have dampened our spirit, or when the Depression threatened to put us out of business. Still, we see the need to work hard, to better ourselves, to improve the nation as a whole. Despite the staggering amount of bad economic news New York—and the nation—has endured in the past few years, we have tried to move forward. In a way, we're being tested again.

As a governor, I am forced to confront the often considerable gap between what I would like to achieve and what is possible. Much of this gap is defined by how much money the state can afford to spend. Every year around tax time, I'm confronted with the stark reality of governance. It's much the same thing typical American families face when they look in their checkbooks and never seem to have enough. Although I frequently confront a treasury with less than I expect, I still remain hopeful. There are things I can do.

We need to keep making sound and substantial investments in the kinds of public building programs that create immediate jobs—while we streamline in-state travel and make New York a more inviting place to live and do business; we must strengthen the high-tech infrastructure that will help us stay competitive in the years ahead; and we need to help New York firms realize the rich opportunities of markets around the world.

Reforming Our Approach to Borrowing

To move with confidence on any of these measures, however, we need to make sure our fiscal house is in order, especially when it comes to financing major capital projects.

When elected officials want to build for the people—a road, a bridge, a tunnel, a hospital, a school—the money may come from any of three principal sources, often in combination: taxes, borrowing, or federal funding. All three are problematic in these days of fiscal strain. Governors all over the United States have been facing budget shortfalls. Voters have adopted a universal disdain for both borrowing and taxes, and the huge federal deficit and debt make Washington a shaky source of support.

In 1990 New York State placed a proposal on the ballot to borrow

$1.98 billion for protecting and preserving the environment. It was defeated. In 1992 we again asked New Yorkers for approval to borrow $800 million for infrastructure projects that would have created both temporary and long-term jobs. This bond act, too, was rejected by the voters.

In context, these results seem to reflect not so much a dismissal of our immediate environmental and economic goals as a double dissatisfaction with how the state makes the decision to take on debt and with how much of it New York has incurred over the years. We are responding now with dramatic proposals to reform the way we borrow.

In our drive to impose more responsible borrowing practices, we need to acknowledge that debt is not inherently bad. The ability to borrow is indispensable to running a modern state, just as taking out a mortgage is the only way most people could ever buy their own home. A strategy of "No More Debt, Ever" would be as destructive to the state in the long run as the most profligate spending spree. But as we place stricter controls on how we borrow, we must be careful to avoid the mistakes many states—including New York— have made in the past: deferring key investments in public works, only to pay the price in lost jobs, inadequate or inefficient services, and costly efforts to catch up later on. In our state that means correcting some recent errors as well as a pattern of borrowing that reaches as far back as the 1950s.

Most of all, we need debt reform that helps us escape from a cycle in which our rising need for funds is matched by sinking rating for our bonds. A few years ago the financial community lowered New York State's bond ratings, despite our record as a perfect credit risk.[1] Low ratings force us to accept higher interest rates when we borrow, and we are fighting to have our high ratings restored. We're making progress. In fiscal 1992–93 we ended the year with a surplus and were raised to the highest rating available for short-term borrowing. And in the 1993–94 budget we put away more than $100 million in a reserve fund to help cushion against financial risks.

We need to continue this positive direction to get our long-term rating lifted. At the same time, we are working with the legislature to put together a more efficient long-term approach to funding our capital needs. Following

---

[1]Fourteen states had their bond ratings reduced by one or both of the major ratings agencies between 1987 and 1991, and only three state ratings (as of this writing) have been upgraded since then. Across the country, 1991 was the worst single year for ratings downgrades in three decades— indicating the widespread fiscal problems resulting from the national recession.

my proposal, the legislature has given first passage to a constitutional amendment that will usher in a new beginning in the fiscal management of New York State government. These changes would cap overall debt, ensure fuller opportunity for the people to approve or disapprove borrowings, reduce the debt-service cost of our borrowings, and reduce the chance of profligate use of debt.

I have also proposed statutory changes that would institute a new, centralized process for planning all the state's capital investments. Each year the state would release a single, unified plan that would outline the capital projects we need to finance, explain how we propose to pay for them, evaluate our capacity to incur additional debt, and establish specific debt limits for our various capital programs.

Although this kind of strategic planning has become essential, it won't be easy because real precision isn't possible in predicting future obligations. For example, government officials making decisions about debt in the 1970s could never have known that in not much more than a decade crack cocaine would send so many more people into the criminal justice system that we would have to build new prisons to hold them. Yet the fact that we must pay for those prisons certainly makes it harder to cover the debt we inherited from the past.

Despite these inherent difficulties, however, a better capital planning process is the only way to give the voters the information they deserve about state borrowing. This aggressive new regime for reforming our approach to debt represents a major step forward in our continuing effort to improve our fiscal position as we restore New York's economic muscle.

Building a New, New York

An important part of this effort is an ongoing initiative unveiled in the fall of 1991 to help stimulate the economy with $30 billion of infrastructure investment called "the New, New York." Its projects range from local highway improvements costing a few million dollars, to midsize university research centers, to billion-dollar multibuilding complexes that will eventually house new retail outlets, offices, apartments, parks, and schools. While they lay the groundwork for future economic development, these projects are expected to produce more than three hundred thousand construction-related and permanent private-sector jobs over the next four years—jobs New York desperately needs.

A key focus is transportation. The caricature of New York City as one big traffic jam does reflect one truth about our state: we have to move an awful lot of people and products every day. Keeping our transportation system intact and up-to-date requires that we build almost constantly. Through the New, New York, we are pursuing a variety of projects that will give us faster, more efficient, and less ecologically damaging ways to move freight, tourists, business travelers, commuters, and just plain New Yorkers where they need to go. Across the state, we are investing hundreds of millions of dollars in making our roads work better—from building the state-of-the-art Corning Bypass in the Southern Tier to adding a crucial fourth lane to the Long Island Expressway.

Some of the work is designed to open a whole new era of enhanced transportation capacity in the Empire State.

At the moment, the predominant way to get freight to the huge population centers of Brooklyn, Queens, and Long Island is through the streets of Manhattan—one of the busiest places in the world. This is made difficult by a daily infusion of tractor-trailers, many of which shouldn't have to be in the city at all. Other states have solved similar problems by diverting some or all of their freight traffic to rail lines: nationally, 25 percent of freight moves by train. But in the New York City–Long Island region, that number falls to only 3.5 percent. A big part of the reason is that our existing rail system can't accommodate the height of certain railcars currently in use. Our solution, called Freight Link America (also known as the "Oak Point" link), will provide a new route for much of our freight traffic, but it will require building only about two miles of new track along the Harlem River shore exclusively for cargo trains.[2] The benefits of this simple idea spill over in every direction. Shippers will save time, money, and fuel. City drivers won't have to compete for road space with so many trucks. The roads themselves will suffer less wear and tear. And New York City's air—especially on the Long Island Expressway in Queens—will be easier to breathe. The New York State Department of Transportation estimates that the Oak Point rail link project will reduce shipping costs by $100 million a year and save $500 million in future road improvements.[3]

Another major improvement in New York City transport involves a better

---

[2]The project is being funded by the Port Authority, the city, and the state.

[3]The Oak Point rail link is expected to produce two thousand construction-related jobs and protect an additional five thousand permanent jobs.

way to move people: the tens of millions of people who need to get to and from—and between—Kennedy and LaGuardia airports each year. Unfortunately, and to the astonishment of visitors from other leading cities—Tokyo, Paris, London—there is currently no train or subway that leads to either of these airports from New York City. And getting between the two by public transportation is even more difficult. To relieve New York of this competitive handicap and end this frustration for all our travelers, we are now developing a fixed-guideway "automated people mover," or APM—in essence, a light-rail system dedicated to airport travel. The APM will also connect travelers to the Long Island Railroad and the city's subway system.[4] The project will be financed through a federally imposed $3 departure fee paid by everyone flying out of JFK and LaGuardia. The fee should generate $100 million a year and is already being used to pay for the initial planning process.

New York City is not alone in needing modernization of its rail technology. For New Yorkers who need to travel between any of the state's major cities, the problem is a familiar one: in-state air travel can be prohibitively expensive, but our urban centers are spread too far apart to make driving an inviting routine. The railroad is the standard compromise, in terms of both money and time. But for the most part—here and across the country—the rail systems haven't benefited from substantial technological improvement in many years.

That's starting to change. In September 1993 New York was selected to receive $3 million from the federal government for an advanced high-speed rail project, thanks in large part to the efforts of our lieutenant governor, Stan Lundine, a highly respected former congressman. We'll use the money to develop and test experimental turbine-powered locomotives that could reach speeds of 125 miles per hour.

By far our most ambitious train-related project involves an extraordinary new technology: magnetic levitation, or "maglev." Using powerful electromagnets, maglev trains travel in suspension above a special guideway, eliminating the kind of steel-on-steel friction that limits the speed of traditional trains. As a result, these special trains are quieter, more energy-efficient, and much faster. At their top speeds of 300 mph, they will travel 100 mph faster than the most advanced trains currently running in France and Germany and

---

[4]New York tried to establish a "train to the plane" subway line once before, which failed, essentially because it was really a "train plus a bus to the plane." The streamlined APM system avoids that miscalculation.

significantly faster than the bullet trains operating in Japan. Imagine cutting the commuting time between Albany and New York (140 miles) to less than an hour. Imagine, too, a similar run between Boston and Albany; New York and Massachusetts are currently studying the feasibility of such a maglev project.

Although it will never approach the miraculous speed of maglev, another initiative will make it easier for thousands of people to get to work in and around New York City: the high-speed ferry. We have already chosen the companies we will negotiate with to set up several routes on the East River, the Hudson, and throughout New York Harbor. Operations are scheduled to begin in 1994. One day Manhattan's midtown docks will see a daily flood of commuters who used to drive to the city from the Hudson Valley, Staten Island, and Queens. Every one of them will represent a gain for the city's air quality and traffic flow. Long Island presents another possibility for water transport: the site of the decommissioned Shoreham nuclear power facility may present an opportunity for high-speed ferries to and from Connecticut.[5]

No matter how many ferry routes and futuristic trains we offer, however, there will still be New Yorkers across the state who need to drive, so we're working to make our highways smarter as well as smoother. New York was one of the leaders in "smart" signage; many of our highways already have overhead variable-message readouts to warn motorists of traffic jams, accidents, and dangerous road conditions. On the Tappan Zee Bridge and the Port Authority Trans-Hudson crossings, we've also had success with electronic toll collection. The system should eventually put an end to the rush-hour routine of waiting at the tollbooth in an acre of traffic. Soon we will also make our highways safer with a variety of special sensors, some installed in our cars, which will be able to "see" road hazards and help navigate in inclement weather, and others embedded in bridges and tunnels to track their structural integrity.

Beyond these advances in transportation technology, our vision for the New, New York includes special plans for aging urban waterfront areas across

---

[5]We're attacking the transportation problem in the streets of our urban centers as well. New York State is providing the Bus Industries of America, located in Oriskany in the Mohawk Valley, with a $2.3 million grant (matching an equal federal grant) to develop a low-floor, low-emission transit vehicle. This environment-friendly, handicapped-accessible bus could set the standard for large-city public transportation across the nation.

the state. We hope to redeem these classic examples of industrial decay by transforming them into attractive, economically productive pieces of the metropolitan landscape.

We will use as a model the spectacularly successful Battery Park City in Manhattan, a flagship of waterfront revitalization in this country. From a landscape of broken bottles and rotting wharves, we have built a ninety-two-acre complex of offices, apartments, and open space cited by *Time* magazine as one of the best designs of the 1980s. *The New York Times*'s architecture critic, Paul Goldberger, described the Battery Park development as "the finest grouping of skyscrapers since Rockefeller Center."[6] From concept to completion the project took a very long time, but in the process we learned how to make such endeavors work.

Perhaps our most ambitious new waterfront plan is "Queens West," a residential and commercial complex that will crown seventy-four acres on Hunter's Point, across the East River from the United Nations. A century ago this slice of Queens was an industrial eyesore, sending the reek of processed glue, varnish, soap, and petroleum wafting across the river to some of the toniest districts in Manhattan. An 1881 issue of *Harper's* magazine reported that "Hunter's Point has become a great center of terror and disgust to the people of New York. For many years it has breathed out offensive odors such as were never tolerated in any Christian land."[7] Even the statement's arrogance can't diminish the power of the sentiment it captures.

Today, after several different bouts of industrial evolution, the site smells fine again, though it's sadly underused: a bottling plant, a tennis bubble, a bunch of dormant factories. In the New, New York, Hunter's Point will show the way to the future of the proud borough of Queens. By the turn of the century, Queens West will offer 2.1 million square feet of office space and a 350-room hotel. The site will also boast fifteen apartment buildings—home to 6,400 families—along with 274,000 square feet for retail and community use and a place designated for an elementary school. The project will be beautiful, too: nineteen of its acres will be designated as open space, including a mile-and-a-quarter esplanade along the East River.[8]

---

[6]Neal R. Pierce and Jerry Hagstrom, *The Book of America: Inside Fifty States Today* (New York: Norton, 1983), 47.

[7]*Harper's*, August 13, 1881.

[8]With start-up financing coming from the state, the city, and the Port Authority and the rest from the private sector, Queens West will cost $2.3 billion. In the short term, the investment will trans-

On the Hudson side of Manhattan, a similar development called Riverside South is already under way. It will make use of long dormant railroad yards, replacing them with graceful housing for some 5,700 families and a twenty-three-acre waterfront park. Located in a politically vocal West Side neighborhood, this immense project suffered considerable criticism in its planning stages, largely because of its scale and concerns as to whether current sewage treatment facilities could accommodate it. In response, Riverside South has been redesigned intelligently, and the New York City Council has approved the plan.[9]

Two hundred fifty miles to the northwest, in Syracuse, we have our eye on sixty-seven acres around Lake Onondaga and on the banks of the Inner Harbor Canal, including a stretch of canal-front real estate whose charmless storage tanks have won it the name "Oil City." With the proper mixed-use development, the area seems bound to rise from the ashes of industrial decline to become a rich boon for tourism. In preparation, we will consolidate the state's barge terminal operation into a smaller area, and the first phase of redevelopment could be finished by the mid-1990s. The Inner Harbor project will feature a promenade of restaurants, art galleries, and retail outlets—a shopping mall with a view. A marina that will harbor up to two hundred pleasure boats will also be designed to accommodate larger vessels offering dinner cruises and entertainment. There are plans for waterfront housing, including both rental apartments and modestly priced condominiums. A major park is on the drawing board, too, complete with an amphitheater for concerts, a family ice-skating rink, and a winter garden.[10]

---

late into an estimated fourteen thousand construction-related jobs, representing $428 million in wages and salaries. When complete, Queens West is expected to provide nearly ten thousand full-time jobs and almost $100 million in sales, income, corporate, and business tax revenues for the city and state.

[9]Beginning with seed money from the city and the state, private-sector firms will foot most of the bill for the $2.5 billion project. It's expected to produce fifteen thousand construction-related jobs, and the developer has agreed to contract at least 20 percent of the work with minority- and women-owned firms.

[10]This joint public/private investment will cost around $1 billion. Roughly 20 percent of the funding will come from government, the remainder from the private sector. We expect 2,000 construction jobs to be created, with another 535 permanent jobs when the Inner Harbor project is completed. East of Syracuse, along the state barge canal system, is a smaller city, Utica, which has many of the same characteristics and problems caused by an urban economic slowdown. We are currently studying the

We have another grand opportunity in Buffalo. At one time Buffalo was New York's gateway to the West: a huge proportion of all the goods headed for the middle and western parts of the country had to travel up the Hudson River, across the Erie Canal, and right through Buffalo. The prosperity of the position lasted for well over a century. Then, suddenly, in 1959, the opening of the St. Lawrence Seaway made it possible to transport goods in big ships directly from the Atlantic, without passing through New York at all. Buffalo's fortunes began to dim. Simultaneously, its heavy industries started their decline. Today, in Buffalo, we see the artifacts of change: empty factories, crumbling buildings, unused oil refineries and storage tanks; in some places, even the remains of hazardous waste and environmental neglect.

Recently, the region's economy has begun to stabilize, in part thanks to the U.S.-Canadian Free Trade Agreement signed in 1988. Now we are making the most of this economic boost by proposing a massive economic and recreational development program, embracing ninety-two miles of the Lake Erie shore, including a good deal of pristine land. The project will offer a rich blend of piers, plazas, promenades, restaurants, and marinas: the proposal includes land dedicated to parks, a beach, and a marine science research and education center. There will be places for fishing and hiking, along with several miles of bikeways. Greenways will connect public shorefront areas to inland sections of the project. One important component of the development, the Buffalo Harbor Center, is being designed by the same architect who revitalized both Battery Park City and Baltimore's Inner Harbor East.

Laying the Tracks for High Technology

In the summer of 1992 the American economy was languishing, enfeebled by a prolonged recession that was technically over but didn't seem to be. But in July of that year, *The New York Times* observed that "technologically advanced, service-oriented companies were already experiencing growth." We could hardly claim to be surprised. Some of us who remember the vacuum tube may have a little trouble warming up to the microchip, but no one doubts

---

idea of developing Utica's Harbor Point section for a mixed-use complex that could attract tourists and new industry.

that high tech is the key to the future. The contours of advancing technology will shape economic destiny in virtually every business, every stage of education, agriculture, medicine, communications, environmental protection—even music and art.

The national economy is adjusting to this reality slowly. Already U.S. output in high-tech equipment exceeds the output of trucks and cars. All of us, not just our manufacturers, have a stake in how well our society prepares to meet the high-tech future—and government has a special role to play.

A key part of our responsibility in building a New, New York is to make sure we are investing adequately in the right kind of high-tech infrastructure. The infrastructure that will matter most won't be made of pipes and paving. Some of its avenues will be made of materials whose names we are just learning to say with confidence—like fiber-optic cable. Mostly, however, the infrastructure of the twenty-first century will be made of the gossamer webbing of human expertise—imaginative public-private-academic research alliances, colleges whose students are getting the right training, institutions that can help us get the fastest access to the best information. As with all infrastructure, we will value these things for the power they give us to move ahead.

Earlier I described a number of our key high-tech initiatives, like our Centers for Advanced Technology. Others bear mentioning here. For example, in the space of a few decades we will all come to rely on a national fiber-optic cable network that will translate and transmit images and sounds with even more dazzling speed and clarity. Government can help coordinate all the competing players with an interest in how the network is designed. Government can also make a useful contribution by advancing the technological infrastructure.

We already have the framework of a modern communications highway called NYSERNET, an acronym of the New York State Education and Research Network.

NYSERNET is a precursor to the electronic information superhighway of the future, a concept that has been lauded by the Clinton administration. NYSERNET has immediate benefits in medicine; perhaps it even will save lives some day. For example, New York has been keeping a registry of the yearly incidences of cancer since 1940, one of the oldest such data bases in the nation. By placing the statistics of breast cancer on the NYSERNET, doctors, researchers, and health planners can have instantaneous access to the county-by-county demographics of the disease. The information can then be used in early-detection and preventive medicine programs.

So far, however, most of NYSERNET's capabilities are limited in scope, confined largely to a handful of university research centers. When NYSER-NET and networks like it are fully realized, they will involve all of us in new kinds of communities that will depend much more on common interests than on shared geography. A doctor in Elmira will be able to make an X ray or an MRI scan and transmit it in a moment across the Atlantic to confer with a specialist in Europe. Schoolchildren in Jamestown or Staten Island will be able to benefit from the special expertise of a teacher in Voorheesville or Scarsdale. An engineer in Rochester and a scientist on Long Island would have instantaneous access to each other's work. An architect in New York City will be able to revise plans for a government building with the project manager in Buffalo, without either of them even leaving their offices. Many of these operations will depend on the capabilities of high-speed "massively parallel" computers—one of many advanced technologies under development here in New York. It is no surprise that the forty-mile stretch between Syracuse and Cornell has earned the local nickname the "Supercomputing Corridor."

The implacable pressures of the marketplace and of an increasingly competitive scientific community have made research speed more important than ever. On Long Island, three prestigious institutions—SUNY Stony Brook, the Brookhaven National Laboratory, and Cold Spring Harbor Laboratory—have joined forces to create the Long Island Research Institute. By pooling the technological and intellectual resources of the three institutions involved, this unique federal, state, and private effort is speeding the development of a number of technologies, including a kidney preservation apparatus for transplants and a new device that will make it easier to close the breastbone after open-heart surgery.

Another unique collaboration among government, industry, and academia—the Center for Integrated Manufacturing Studies (CIMS) at the Rochester Institute of Technology—is helping New York companies become more efficient, more competitive, and more creative in solving problems—all through the use of the latest manufacturing technologies. The idea was born in 1989 when RIT officials set out to help stop the flow of manufacturing jobs from New York State. Working closely with production-line employees, the CIMS has already helped one company find the best way to computerize its manufacturing and has developed a special electronic communications system that serves several local firms. The CIMS's early success has led to growth. In June 1993 we broke ground on the construction of a 165,000-square-foot building that will house twenty-two new laboratories, with the help of $9.5 million from the state. The biggest boon will be to small and midsize businesses that couldn't afford to sustain such specialized expertise in-house.

As a state, our ability to keep up in the high-tech marketplace will depend on having people who are up to the task, so part of our job as a government is making sure we are training enough engineers and scientists to staff places like the CIMS in Rochester and the member labs of the Long Island Research Institute. In 1993, through the Higher Education Applied Technology Program, the state authorized up to $75 million for additional research centers at six independent and three public university campuses.

With New York's remarkable record of invention and entrepreneurial success, one could argue that our state is a living library of scientific and business expertise, housing more sheer talent for the marketplace, more ingenuity, and more experience than any community anywhere in history. To make sure we can capitalize on this cumulative expertise, we are creating a dramatic new, fully computerized, super-high-tech storehouse of information: a science, industry, and business library inside the imposing French limestone shell of the old B. Altman's department store in midtown Manhattan. Work has already begun on the conversion. As part of our New, New York agenda, this "library without walls" will ultimately serve as the world's largest source of business and scientific information, containing two and a half million volumes. The project will cost nearly $100 million.

In different ways, all our high-tech investments will be good for our economic prospects. Some will help produce or sustain good, stable jobs for New Yorkers, now and in the future. Others will help prepare our people and our businesses to enter a demanding marketplace with confidence. And all of them will make it a little easier to face the global contest ahead.

The International State in the Twenty-first Century

Not long ago a reporter asked if I believed the end of the Cold War had left the nation without a central, unifying challenge. I told him that it might seem that way, and it might even be nice if we could relax in the luxury of our affluence, replaying the victory of a Cold War that engaged our energies for decades. But we can't because the United States is locked in a new struggle: the global competition for markets, jobs, technology, and wealth.

How well we live at home will, increasingly, be affected by how well we compete abroad, against rising nations that have leaped over a century of industrial evolution to become economic Goliaths. It will depend on how well we compete with the European Economic Community, which is gradually fusing together into the world's largest economy, equipped with the world's largest consumer market; and with competitors in Third World countries that can pay their workers a fraction of the wages and offer none of the benefits that we provide here. As a nation, for two decades we have been coasting, and that's no way to embark on an uphill battle.

Certainly a great deal of our attention must go to making all the practical, sometimes painful changes that fall under the heading "Improving Competitiveness." But a crucial step beyond streamlining operations is making sure that potential buyers and investors overseas know what we have to offer.

No one doubts that New York is already a player in the global marketplace. We are the tenth largest economy in the world. California is the seventh. The others are nations. The largest and most prominent financial institutions are headquartered here. We are home to over four hundred thousand businesses, including more of the Fortune 500 industrial and service firms than any other state. By 1990 New York led the nation in the dollar value of exported medical and measuring instruments, in products for the printing and publishing industries, and in electric and electronic equipment.

Our exports achieved steady growth in the 1980s, reaching a record high of $31.4 billion in 1990. And they are on the rise again: by 1993 our sales to foreign countries, and their investments here, were growing faster than the national average. Western Europe continues to be the major port of entry for our goods; with $13 billion in annual sales, it accounts for 35 percent of our total exports, sustaining one hundred thousand jobs in New York State each year. As developing countries expand, a unified trading bloc emerges in Europe, and some resolution is reached on North American Trade, the Empire State is poised to take off.

Global New York

To help New York firms get linked into this global economic network, in 1990 we launched the "Global New York" initiative. The program gives us a way to help small- and medium-size businesses assess the risks and benefits of going into the export trade. If their prospects look good, we can help them identify appropriate markets and buyers and coach them on selling their goods and services overseas. Crucial to the success of our efforts have been our seven economic development offices abroad, one each in Germany, Hong Kong, Italy, Japan, and the United Kingdom, and two in Canada.

An example helps illustrate the value of these overseas offices. When Confindustria, the national industrial association of Italy, gets requests for U.S. products from Italian distributors—or when Italian companies seeking to locate in America approach the United States' commerce office at the American embassy in Rome—they are referred to *our* Milan office because it's the only American state office in Italy that handles these issues.[11]

Through our international offices and trade consultants spread across New York, we offer a team of "export experts" who understand the nuances of foreign markets, foreign customs, and foreign trade restrictions. They represent New York at international trade shows, provide sales leads, refer buyers directly to New York exporters, and extend technical assistance to New York firms. And they help businesses match their product lines and market interests with potential buyers abroad. New York's Export Marketing Assistance program, which has already helped five hundred New York firms to find agents or distributors overseas, is one of the most sophisticated of its kind in the United States.[12]

The state continues to analyze the implications of European economic

---

[11]While in Italy, I signed an agreement with the president of the National Italian Research Council to share technology and open markets worldwide for New York and Italian high-tech industries. The initial focus will be on biotechnology, advanced materials, optics and imaging, computers and information systems, and telecommunications.

[12]The Global New York program is not limited to exports alone. We also teach New York companies how to sell to federal and state agencies, how to obtain subcontracts, and how to win federal research and development grants. Our Global Export Market Services (GEMS) provides matching grants to companies to secure the expertise necessary to get them involved in international markets. One of the most innovative export programs in the United States, it has already provided $1.5 million in grants to more than two hundred firms around the state.

integration, identifying the best targets for trade and investment. We are building on the agreements we already have with Canada, our largest trading partner, in the hope that new markets will open as our northern neighbor emerges from its national recession. We are also searching for new markets in Eastern Europe and the former Soviet Union, in Mexico and Brazil, in Hong Kong, Taiwan, South Korea, and Japan. In Africa we are working toward an International Partnership Program with South Africa, which will assist in the orderly political transition there and enable New York State businesses to take advantage of the economic expansion that is expected to follow the new elections.

At a time when Americans are growing disturbingly resigned to reports of United States jobs slipping away overseas, we are scoring some small victories in the other direction. One of the most satisfying is the story of General Railway Signal in Rochester. With the assistance of New York State, they signed a $103 million contract to supply signaling equipment to the Taipei subway system in Taiwan—exporting high-quality American products instead of high-quality American jobs.

Attracting Foreign Investment

During my first two terms as governor, I did not travel abroad to promote New York's business interests. That was a mistake. Thereafter I made trade missions to Japan, Israel, Italy, and Argentina to improve our economic and cultural relations.[13] My wife, Matilda, and Vincent Tese, the state's director of economic development, as co-chairs of our International Partnership Task Force, have traveled more extensively.

The trips have produced a new energy in our trading relations. Israel imported nearly a billion dollars of New York goods and services in 1992. (We are also the single largest importer of Israeli goods and services.) New York has more Italian businesses operating within its borders than any other state. And Japan accounts for more than a third of the trade we do with Asia.[14]

---

[13]New York's International Partnership Program builds long-term relationships among governments, academic institutions, businesses, and trade groups. So far, New York has made pacts with Israel, Italy, Poland, Japan, Lithuania, and Jiangsu, a province in China.

[14]Despite the problems and differences our nation has had with the Japanese over trade practices, Japan is New York's second leading export market, and direct investments in New York by the

As we reach out to such business partners overseas, we have a great deal to build on, in part because of the diversity that defines New York. What other state can boast that one in six of its people—three million New Yorkers— claim family ties to Italy?[15] In what other state can you watch half a million people march in a West Indian–American Day Carnival? What other state is home to the St. Patrick, Columbus, Pulaski, Steuben, Puerto Rican, or Greek Independence Day parades? The feasts, festivals, and convocations through which we celebrate the traditions of the Old Country—wherever it may be—are a hallmark of New York culture. I believe we can build on that pride, affection, and cultural understanding to promote new *economic* ties between our state and all the countries that have provided us with new New Yorkers over the centuries.

As we focus on rebuilding the job base in New York, we are making aggressive efforts to encourage foreign firms to set up manufacturing opera- tions here. Through carefully targeted letters, promotional pieces, and questionnaires, we ask them, in effect: "What are your goals? If you are in- terested in expanding into the United States, have you considered head-

---

Japanese totaled $13 billion in 1991, the last year for which statistics are available. About fifty thousand New Yorkers are working because of this involvement. We also share our technology. In just one example, Hitachi donated to the state's Science and Technology Foundation a $100,000 spectro- photometer, a machine that is critical in cancer research and pollution control.

However, not all our efforts to locate foreign businesses in New York go smoothly. In 1992–93, Olympus, the Japanese camera and optics company based in Lake Success and Woodbury, was embroiled in controversy as it sought to expand and build a new office building on Long Island. When a suitable site was finally found in Huntington, there was an uproar from some citizens who felt that the company's employees would add unacceptable amounts of traffic to their neighbor- hoods. Olympus decided to withdraw its proposal and is currently looking for a new site on Long Island.

[15]Because we share such deep and abiding ties, in 1987 New York started the first *Due Case, Una Tradizione* program with Italy, forging cooperative ties in trade and investment, science and technol- ogy, the environment, health, education, and culture, to explore further the singular tradition we share. Today, more than nine hundred New York firms have business activities in the Italian market. The relationship is reciprocal—197 Italian enterprises do business in New York, employing nearly six thousand. New York was the *first* and *only* state in America to open an economic development office in Italy—courtesy of the Milan Chamber of Commerce. In recent years we have formalized an accord with Consiglio Nazionale Ricerche (CNR)—the equivalent of America's National Institutes of Health—to provide for technology transfer, information exchange, and collaboration on scientific and research projects in a number of public health areas. They will work with the New York Science and Technology Foundation to match scientists and private industry, developing workshops on both sides of the Atlantic.

quartering your operation in New York State? How can we help?"

The results have been encouraging.

In June 1990, ABB Traction, Inc., a subsidiary of the Swiss firm ASEA Brown Boveri, Ltd., began to manufacture railroad equipment in Elmira Heights, creating an estimated 368 jobs in the Southern Tier.[16] Along with other firms like Morrison Knudsen, which opened a New York plant in 1983, ABB Traction has become part of a new industry with the potential to provide every new train car that we need. The Elmira Heights plant of ABB is also producing cars for other transit systems; in 1993, we helped them secure a contract for the city of Philadelphia. Also in 1993, state assistance enabled Bus Industries of America, a wholly-owned subsidiary of a Canadian firm that first established operations in Oriskany in 1983, to begin fulfilling back orders for urban transit buses for sites across North America—including New York City.

There are more examples of efforts to encourage foreign investment in other industries as well. In 1991, Consolidated Westway Group, a subsidiary of Suc de Kerry from France, opened its commodity brokerage operations in Manhattan's World Financial Center, employing 140.

Working with the city of New York, our London trade office began a campaign to encourage the British conglomerate Trusthouse Forte to establish an airline catering facility in Jamaica, Queens. By 1992 the British company was employing 350 people in New York and was making plans for a $5 million, twenty-five-thousand-square-foot expansion.

In the fall of 1993, the New York State Job Development Authority persuaded LUCK GmbH, a highly respected German firm, to manufacture its high-quality upholstery fabric in Keeseville, New York, about fifty miles south of Plattsburgh. The operation will start with thirty employees and expects to expand to one hundred.

---

[16]We have provided assistance to various companies since 1983, helping to build a base of transportation-related equipment manufacturing firms. For several years, this meant that as we rebuilt New York's transportation infrastructure, New York firms were at least in the competition for billions of dollars worth of work. In fact, on the same day in December 1992, I visited two New York firms to congratulate them on separate contract awards: Morrison Knudsen Corporation received $100 million from Amtrak to design and manufacture 50 new-generation railcars; and Bus Industries of America was given $41 million to build 200 buses for the NYC Transit Authority.

Before 1983, we purchased all of our subway cars outside of New York because we had no train makers in this state. Today, New York is home to three of the largest manufacturers of railcars in the United States. And we have the country's largest bus manufacturers.

Executives at A. G. Electronics, a small high-tech company headquartered in Bologna, Italy, were planning to locate in Florida, until they began talking to us. Now they have filed papers to incorporate in New York State.

Hundreds of other foreign companies, big and small, are setting up operations throughout the state.[17] In New York City alone, some 2,500 foreign-based companies employ 200,000 people. As European and Asian firms seek new inroads into the North American market, we must continue to capitalize on our reputation as the international capital of culture and commerce by promoting our strengths aggressively to foreign industrialists, government officials, and financiers.[18]

On my trip to Italy, we forged a joint marketing agreement between New York State and Alitalia Airlines to promote New York as a tourism destination. Under this two-year pact, Alitalia will benefit from increased ticket sales and New York will improve its ability to attract Italian tourists. The agreement was the first between Alitalia and any American state, and it's similar to a joint program we set up with Japan Air Lines. We're currently trying to negotiate a similar deal with El Al, the Israeli national airline.

When Banca Di Roma buys a $12 million, ten-story building to conduct their banking operations here in New York City; when Galeries Lafayette, one of France's largest retailers, opens a department store on Fifth Avenue; when Minolta opens a plant in Goshen; when Toshiba invests $115 million to refurbish an old Westinghouse plant in Horseheads so that it can manufacture thirty-five-inch TV picture tubes—the result is thousands of precious new jobs for New Yorkers.

We expect more jobs to be created in New York in the next few years thanks to foreign investment in our energy base. Ansaldo Industries of America, the subsidiary of a Rome, Italy, firm, plans to build four new electric

---

[17]In the past few years, Palfinger, Inc., from Austria opened an eleven-thousand-square-foot office and warehouse facility in North Tonawanda to make and distribute industrial cranes; Jakko Poyry Consulting, a Finnish firm that consults for the paper industry, opened an office in Tarrytown; and fellow Finns who manufacture sheet metal roofing, Scandanaving Profiling Systems, located in twenty thousand square feet of space in Lackawanna.

[18]Harry Cipriani's restaurant, located both in New York City and in Venice, recently decided to manufacture egg pasta in New York for the U.S. market. By making pasta in New York—thereby cutting down on shipping and exporting costs—Cipriani believes he can reduce the selling price by 40 percent. If we can convince other European firms that this is a sound idea, our economy will reap the benefits.

power and steam cogeneration plants in the state. Sithe Energies, a company partially owned by a French conglomerate, has announced plans to build a 1,000-megawatt natural gas electric plant in Oswego County.

The possibilities for future gains seem just as promising.

They are as alive as they were for the immigrants who rejected their meager prospects in southern Europe a century ago and set out for the promise of America. Today we stand on the brink of a new era of international *business migration* to this country. We want New York, the International State, to become home for as many of these immigrant businesses as we can get.

Why not? If the 1980s were known as the Decade of the Pacific, why can't New York help turn the 1990s into the Decade of the Atlantic? With our resources, our location, our waterways, our workforce, our proximity to the richest market in the Western Hemisphere—with our strong ties to the culture, blood, and history of practically every country on earth—who can match our uniquely fertile soil for growing a foreign business in North America? With our seven foreign economic development offices, our "export-expert" consultants, our International Partnership Program, why shouldn't New York lead the country in international trade? Certainly progress toward a lasting national recovery demands a willingness to aim that high.

Renewing the Partnership for National Economic Growth

The direction President Clinton seeks for the nation is the road to enduring recovery. To close the federal budget deficit, the government must reduce spending, increase revenues, and slow the growth in health care costs by reforming the health care system. To stimulate economic growth, government must help keep interest rates low while making the kinds of targeted investments in the nation's future that were so scorned in the 1980s.

The quality of our future together depends on decisive action from Washington now. The economic policy of the last twelve years failed because it created a crippling debt and annual deficits and because it neglected all the components of a successful economic formula other than capital. It failed to deal adequately with roads and bridges and transportation; high technology; clean, dependable energy; a healthy environment; free and fair trade policies; and, most of all, human resources—healthy, educated, skilled, motivated human beings.

For the past twelve years investments in these crucial areas were, to a great extent, left in the hands of state and local governments—at exactly the time that these governments faced cutbacks in federal aid and huge increases in the needs of their people.

With states and cities engaged in a primitive struggle for their fiscal survival, they cannot make all the important investments that need to be made. In order for our economy to grow in the future, we need *all* parts of our country, all cities, all states, all regions—all Americans—to grow, to prosper, to reach their full potential. If we expect to restore the strength of the national economy—and revive the hopes of the people—Washington will have to participate. That's why the nation was invented: out of many, one.

CONCLUSION

"Above all, try something." The words belong to Franklin Roosevelt, but the idea belongs to New York, an ongoing experiment in action, a test of what a people can produce with natural resources, an advantageous location, talent, vision, and a clear and constructive recollection of their mistakes and missed opportunities.

We know all we have achieved, but we are painfully aware of how far we remain from our full potential as a people. Like the whole nation, New York has not begun to realize all its promise and possibility. We are still struggling to include all New Yorkers in the circle of opportunity: too many are out of work; too few young people believe they'll have the chance to succeed; drugs and violence still threaten us all.

Because New York is a microcosm of America, we believe both our shortcomings and our accomplishments can be instructive beyond our borders. This book has been an effort to share that experience and its instruction.

The American Dream was perfected in New York. For two hundred years New York has helped build futures for generations of seekers, constantly moving in and moving up. Our history is a treatise on the rewards of outrageous aspiration, personal initiative, and hard work in a robust free enterprise economy.

But if all we had been was a showcase for personal ambition, we would not have become all that we are. Together, the people of the Empire State, in our finer moments, have built an extraordinary history of enlightened action and community of purpose. There surely have been dark hours—all-too-visible examples of painful setbacks that have temporarily halted our progress along the way. But, clearly, we continue to move forward and upward as a people and a state.

The soul of the state seems to me to reflect a kind of progressive pragmatism. Pragmatic, because it understands that some problems are beyond our power to solve, that we can't do all we'd like to for everyone, that achieving the greatest good means weighing some needs over others. Progressive, because New Yorkers have always tried—preferring the inconvenient struggle for human progress over the seductive comfort of complacency. We have taught ourselves—but must be reminded repeatedly—that the spirit of inclusion makes us richer and wiser as a people; that we have an obligation to help the vulnerable; that none among us has the right to exploit the labor of another; that our legal liberties are rare in human history; that the earth is ours to work with but not to waste; that there are obligations that bind us to coming generations.

Just as important, New Yorkers have learned that as a work always in progress, democracy requires a constant reaffirmation of commitment, of the patience to struggle with disagreement, of the wisdom to be grateful for incremental progress and the alertness to seize large gains. The period of New York's history most familiar to me should remind us that such gains are possible.

During my tenure as governor we've invested more than $50 billion in building and rehabilitating our brick, mortar, stone, and glass infrastructure. This helped make our roads and bridges safer than at any time in our recorded history. In the next few years, our New, New York program will add $30 billion more of this kind of investment—spanning everything from high-speed ferries to waterfront developments around the state—generating at least three hundred thousand more jobs.

In preparing for the complex global economy of the twenty-first century, we know we must excel in all kinds of high technology. In the last ten years we have built a high-tech capacity that is now unsurpassed in the nation. We are the communications capital of the world—and will remain so. Our Centers for Advanced Technology are searching for tomorrow's products, medicines, and engineering applications. Our exports to foreign nations (and their investments in New York), already among the fastest growing in the country, will continue to grow as we take advantage of new markets opening up in the East as well as in Europe. In the next century, an increasing tonnage of "Empire-made" goods will find their way to our overseas customers.

Above all, we will continue to invest intelligently in our people, taking care of the old, the infirm, the disadvantaged, and the developmentally disabled. More children will benefit from our Decade of the Child programs—intended to nourish them, give them more medical care, more early education, and more mentoring. Tomorrow's workforce will be better prepared than ever before, helped in part by our state university system, which provides exceptional value in today's higher-education marketplace. The twenty-first century will be a happier and healthier environment for the next generation of our youth.

In all our efforts, we will continue the process of change, helping to set the national pace on a number of fronts, as we have throughout our history.

Our seat belt law, the first of its kind and now almost a decade old, began saving hundreds of lives immediately. We had the first acid rain law, and we passed environmental legislation that not only cleaned our lakes and rivers, but protected huge tracts of public land from future development. We produced the first energy plan that is fully integrated with environmental concerns. We were the first administration in our state's history to coordinate all criminal justice services, which led to innovative approaches in fighting crime: community narcotics enforcement teams, a statewide automated fingerprint identification system, a shock incarceration program to ease overcrowding in the prisons. We integrated our state economic development programs under one agency and became the first state to establish an assistance program to house the homeless. Our Child Assistance Program is another national first— an alternative to welfare that encourages work instead of penalizing it. We have made great gains in our health care system. I have proposed further changes and reforms, all of which, I am hopeful, will be adopted.

Our court system has already undergone dramatic improvement. We now have a high court that is regarded as one of the best common-law courts in the country, with the first woman, the first female chief judge, and the first African-American ever appointed to a full term. In the next century we will be closer than ever to bringing justice and fairness to all New Yorkers.

We're working cooperatively with businesses—more closely than ever—to strengthen our economy. We're listening to the concerns of companies, big and small, so we can provide a better climate for commerce throughout New York State.

We will maintain our strong support for agriculture, protecting our family farms and enhancing them with the power of high technology. We'll work to strengthen tourism by marketing our natural and manmade treasures, by cutting the hotel tax, and by investing further in our "Gateway" visitors centers.

We must continue a sound policy of fiscal austerity, restraining our spending so that we can invest in things we need. There must be no new entitlements, no excessive legislative member items, no unbalanced budgets.

We must continue to help local governments control taxes and spending. We should not create any more unfunded mandates, and we should get rid of or reduce the impact of many existing mandates, especially Medicaid. We should provide local governments with an option to substitute a local income tax for their real property tax, at least on a limited basis.

We must make other fundamental changes that the legislature has declined to deal with. The Republicans, who have controlled the senate, and the Democrats, who have controlled the assembly for longer than most of us can remember, need to be reminded that a constitutional convention would reform our political process and make it more expedient and more equitable.

In all our efforts, we must adhere to a philosophy that values work as our objective and the measure of our success—a philosophy that insists upon individual, corporate, and governmental responsibility; that protects our people's right to make their own meaningful choices; and that encourages, always, the idea of family.

That's what I have advocated and implemented for all the time I've been in the state's service, which is the whole of my public career. I believe this philosophy will help us overcome the national recession and create a new, vibrant business atmosphere in our state—where our technology centers and our factories outproduce and outsell overseas competitors, putting our own people to work instead of on the unemployment lines; where many of those who now wind up in treatment centers or prisons are instead working in laboratories or offices or in the trades—using their skills productively—helping themselves and the rest of us; where every neighborhood school is a good one—where children can be children, where they can grow up the way we did, with a chance to go to college, to get a good job, and to one day own their own home; where all New Yorkers have affordable, quality health care; where people are excited about voting again, because they have seen their government consider its own weaknesses and transform itself into a vital and active representative of all their interests.

I am optimistic about our ability to do all these things because at their very best, the people of New York have understood what seems to be the most difficult truth of all in this land tamed by the rugged individualist. It is the simple truth of Jeremiah: You will find your own good in the good of the whole society.

One terrible episode became an unforgettable reminder of the eternal truth of that powerful principle. On a shattering day in February 1993, a terrorist's bomb exploded underneath the World Trade Center in Manhattan, an outrageous act resulting in six deaths. In no more than minutes, fifty-five thousand people were forced into a hell of smoke and darkness and fear and uncertainty. Yet they responded with a miracle of intelligence and bravery and calm—fifty-five thousand people of every race and culture, mostly strangers to one another, who all understood that they had to depend on one another to survive. They did, and they survived magnificently. In the intensity of our pain, we saw—in a flash—what we were made of as a people. It was a demonstration of strength, a demonstration of cohesion, a demonstration of intelligence . . . an *antidote* to the stories of routine violence and disorder, of bitterness between races, of hostility and intolerance.

If New York holds a lesson for the nation, it is this: Now—before we become so fragmented that we cannot be made whole—we need to develop a sense of national community, sharing benefits and burdens for the good of all.

Without an intelligent commitment to one another, we will grow defenseless against politicians who offer wedges instead of solutions, who seek to divide us against one another for their momentary gain.

Without an articulate sense of our common interest, we may forfeit the wealth and the strength of our nation to those infinitely articulate voices called the special interests.

Without the willingness to see our own good in the good of the whole community, we will not achieve all we should. We cannot afford to lose the next generation to drugs, or AIDS, or inadequate education—even if they're not your children, or mine, they are our children. There can be no separate city. No man is an island. No woman. No race. No neighborhood. No town. No state. No nation. Our future will be determined by how well we bring together all the parts.

From our uncertain origins, through billions of years of evolution that still remain largely a mystery, a chain of life has connected the countless fragments of the universe, reconciling apparent contradictions. From water came vegetation, evolving into new and more complex forms, eventually into living organisms, the higher forms of life, and finally to human beings—with minds, souls, the capacity to think and then to think better. Out of a struggle for survival, human beings, understanding their need for one another, came together, creating clans, tribes, villages, then nations and whole civilizations, progressing in fits and starts, inexorably toward the light.

Today, as the world continues to evolve materially and technologically, we must help forge connections that bind human beings together, so that we can realize more fully our potential as a species. People to people. Parent to child. Worker to owner. The individual to the community. Black to white. Arab to Jew. Bosnian to Serb to Muslim. Nation to nation. Continent to continent. We must join philosophy and practicality, the spiritual to the material, compassion to common sense.

Ultimately, a better future, whether it be for New York City, our state, this nation, or the planet, will depend on our willingness to believe that even if we can't perfect the world, we can certainly do more to lessen its pain and to realize its promise. That constant struggle to push us, inch by inch, up the mountain is portrayed here in New York as well as it ever has been.

For too long—I think—we have dismissed our strengths, shrugged off our achievements, and allowed the headline writers to concoct the whole image of New York. Sometimes we have even been made to doubt ourselves. We should imagine instead all we might achieve if we cast our lot a different way, if we chose rather to live by the sweet wisdom that E. B. White offered us years ago: "New York is to the nation what the white church spire is to the village—the visible symbol of aspiration and faith, the white plume saying the way is up."

Excelsior!

REGIONS OF NEW YORK

Capital-Saratoga

New York's Capital-Saratoga region offers an exciting mix of history, culture, and sports adventures. This upstate region is a series of urban centers and rural settings, city living and farm experiences. It is the state's capital and is home to a unique blend of architecture, art collections of the rich and famous, the historic Capitol Building, and the futuristic Empire State Plaza. (The oddly designed theater at the plaza had novelist Isaac Bashevis Singer wondering if it was shaped like an egg or a blintz.) Boat tours cruise up and down the Hudson and Mohawk rivers, stopping in Albany, Schenectady, and Troy. In Schenectady, visitors enjoy exploring the historic Stockade area, shopping in the Canal Square shopping district, roaming the Rose Gardens in Central Park, and attending concerts at Proctor's Theatre, where off-Broadway meets upstate.

From the Saratoga Battlefield to the music and dance at the Saratoga Performing Arts Center—summer home of the New York City Ballet, the New York City Opera, and the Philadelphia Orchestra—visitors can experience the American Revolution and new revolutions in music and dance in America. When patrons of Saratoga's famous racetrack are not placing their bets during the August meeting, they can also find a relaxing retreat at the National Museum of Dance, the National Museum of Racing, and the Thoroughbred Hall of Fame—all just a few miles from the track. In Rensselaer and Cohoes, tourists can discover the first remnants of early Dutch settlers and great bargains at the region's many factory outlets. In Washington County, the landscape and people made famous in paintings by Grandma Moses are also worth seeing.

The Catskills

New York's rolling Catskill Mountains and the Catskill State Park are the perfect settings for a unique blend of exciting tour adventures: invigorating mountain activities and exciting self-contained vacation resorts. The heyday of the "Borscht Belt" and its long line of comedians is now part of our heritage, but many top hotels still attract good-size trade shows and people on holiday. The "Monster" golf course at the Concord Hotel is as challenging as any in the United States.

The Catskills present an upstate experience with an occasional flair of New York's urban atmosphere. From a historically re-created industrial complex at Hanford Mills to the friendly old communities of Windham, Roxbury, Phoenicia, Roscoe, and Woodstock, tourists can visit and join in a variety of ethnic musical festivals and ride the range at dude ranches. Sports enthusiasts find excitement in canoeing and rafting (or tubing) on the Delaware River. The Catskill Game Farm, Zoom Flume, and Carson City are all major stops for children. And there is plenty of downhill and cross-country skiing at the more popular hotels and resorts.

Central-Leatherstocking

Often called the heartland of New York State, the Central-Leatherstocking region literally has a very deep "heart." It is formed nearly two hundred feet below the surface at exciting Howe Caverns, the largest underground chambers in the northeastern United States. The leatherstockings, which gave this part of New York State its curious nickname, were actually protective leather leggings worn by frontiersmen as they blazed trails in the wilderness between the Mohawk and Susquehanna rivers. Cooperstown (named for the father of the American novelist James Fenimore Cooper, author of the popular Leatherstocking series), on Lake Otsego, is also famed as the site where Abner Doubleday is said to have laid out the first baseball field and is home to the National Baseball Hall of Fame. Here groups also stroll the wooden sidewalks at the nineteenth-century Farmers' Museum and see more than 250 pieces of America's finest folk art at the Fenimore House.

A popular stop in nearby Oneonta is the National Soccer Hall of Fame.

Canastota is the home of the International Boxing Hall of Fame, where famous pugilists hung up their last pair of gloves. In Utica, F. X. Matt Brewery and the Munson-Williams-Proctor Art Institute and Fountain Elms are scenic stopovers. History buffs relive the past at the reconstructed eighteenth-century Fort Stanwix and ride packet boats at the restored Erie Canal Village in Rome. Music lovers marvel at the eighteen rooms of antique pipe organs, nickelodeons, and music boxes at the unique "hands-on" Musical Museum in Deansboro. Theater and the arts both thrive at the Glimmerglass Opera in Cooperstown and the Cidermill Playhouse in Binghamton. Tours cruise the historic Mohawk River/Erie Canal and enjoy the many festivals throughout the region. Broome County takes particular pride in its collection of historic carousels, a free exhibition.

Chautauqua-Allegheny

Bordered by Lake Erie, one of the Great Lakes, the Chautauqua-Allegheny region is the gateway to New York State from Ohio and western Pennsylvania. Tours and tastings are abundant along the Chautauqua wine trail, with such tastes as fruity native Labruscas, exquisite French-American wines, and European-style Chardonnay and Riesling. Quiet vineyard activities contrast with the exciting harbor life of Dunkirk and Barcelona Harbor, near Westfield. Collectors shop for fun and profit along the popular "antique trails" from Ripley to Silver Creek.

Jamestown, birthplace and hometown of the late star of the "I Love Lucy" show, hosts the annual Lucille Ball Festival of New Comedy, with plays, short films, and a stand-up comedy showcase. The century-old Chautauqua Institution is an internationally recognized cultural and learning center, on Chautauqua Lake, that continues to teach and entertain. Nearby is New York's Amish community, home to the homemade quilts, tinware, and other crafts of the Amish people. On the twenty-two-mile-long Lake Chautauqua, visitors can ride the waters on a replica of a Mississippi River paddle wheeler, the *Chautauqua Belle*, and an authentic sixteenth-century English merchant ship—the *Sea Lion*. The sixty-five-thousand-acre Allegany State Park provides plenty of outdoor opportunities.

Southwest is Salamanca, the only city in the United States located on a Native American reservation, site of the Seneca Iroquois National Museum and Salamanca Rail Museum. Discover geological treasures at Rock City Park, in Olean. Tour the village of Fredonia to learn about the birth of the first U.S. Grange and Women's Christian Temperance Union or stop at Lily Dale, a community that has been the center for spiritualism in America for more than one hundred years.

The Finger Lakes

Lake country and wine country, the Finger Lakes is one of the most beautiful regions in the northeastern United States. Home to the Corning Glass Center, a popular group tour stop in the Northeast, the region boasts more than thirty wineries and a 150-year tradition of wine making. Sample wine making at the Taylor Winery Visitor Center in Hammondsport, at Widmer's, in Naples, or at the Canandaigua Wine-Tasting Room. Travel scenic routes along Keuka, Seneca, and Cayuga lakes. Cruise along the Erie Canal or on the lakes from bases in Canandaigua, Geneva, Skaneateles, Ithaca, Watkins Glen, Hammondsport, and Syracuse. Ride the rails north of Owego. Visit the National Soaring Museum in Elmira or try the sport first-hand at Harris Hill and soar high over the valleys around Elmira, summer home of Mark Twain.

The performing arts await you at Canandaigua's Finger Lakes Performing Arts Center; the majestic Hill Cumorah Pageant near Palmyra; the new Mark Twain Musical Drama at Elmira. Heritage and history tours must include the Genesee Country Village's authentic fifty-five-building complex in Mumford; the National Landmark Seward House in Auburn; the National Women's Hall of Fame in Seneca Falls; the fifty-acre Sonnenberg Gardens and Mansion in Canandaigua; and the 1890 House-Museum and Center for Victorian Art in Cortland.

Waterfalls by the hundreds fill the region. The most famous are found in Letchworth State Park—world-famous Watkins Glen Gorge, and the 215-foot straight-drop cascade at Taughannock Falls.

The contrast between metropolitan and rural living makes the region a haven for all sorts of shopping interests. Tours of Syracuse, Rochester, and Elmira can include entire shopping complexes and factory outlets, as well as downtown boutiques and modern suburban shopping malls.

The Hudson Valley

Relive America's early years amid the scenic backdrop of the majestic Hudson River valley. The heritage of the Old Dutch and English stands beside purely American institutions: President Martin Van Buren's home in Kinderhook; Franklin Delano Roosevelt's home, library, and museum in Hyde Park; the U.S. Military Academy at West Point; George Washington's headquarters in Newburgh. There are winery tours and tastings and many nineteenth-century homes and great mansions to explore: the lovely Boscobel Mansion in Cold Springs, the Gothic Lyndhurst Mansion in Tarrytown, and many sites overlooking the Hudson River.

The valley's history has earned it a reputation as an antique collector's paradise, and it's an area for appreciating art and architecture. This is a stop for museum goers in all forms, from the Trotting Horse Museum in Goshen to the American Museum of Fire Fighting in Hudson. Fascinating theme festivals and county fairs focusing on New York State's history abound throughout the region and its surrounding communities. Visit Mountainville's Storm King Art Center; Katonah's Caramoor Center for Music and the Arts; Tarrytown's Philipsburg Manor and Sunnyside (home to Washington Irving); and Hudson's Olana, estate home of Frederick Church, the renowned painter.

Long Island

Stretching into the Atlantic Ocean, New York's Long Island is more than an island—it is an integral part of, and gateway to, the metropolitan area of New York City and the rest of the Empire State. The island is alive with exciting attractions and activity, rich in history, yet it's an area where groups can be at ease with ocean breezes and beaches. Jones Beach State Park offers miles of Atlantic shoreline and broad white sandy beaches, as well as theater under the stars at the Jones Beach Marine Theater. New York's ocean oasis extends nearly 120 miles east from New York City to the easternmost tip of the island, Montauk Point, site of the Montauk Lighthouse. Join the whale-watch denizens off Montauk Point, fish the blue waters from a charter or party boat, or surf cast for bluefish. Ambitious anglers can try for bluefin tuna, plentiful every summer. The north and south fork award-winning wineries are a popular stop; they provide well-respected whites and reds every season. The southern shoreline toward the east includes the Hamptons, charming towns and villages world-renowned as summer homes to artists, writers, billionaire businessmen, people on the way up, has-beens, and ordinary folks who just want to smell the salt air and stroll through the three-century-old Main Streets.

From New England one can cross Long Island Sound to Orient Point or Port Jefferson by ferry. View historic homes and the Great Gatsby "Gold Coast" mansions of the North Shore. See the famed Old Westbury House and Gardens—a majestic vestige of a bygone era. Step back in time to the nineteenth century with a visit to Old Bethpage Village Restoration. Stop at Cold Spring Harbor's Whaling Museum or fish hatchery. Enjoy art and antiques at the Museums of Stony Brook. Shop smart boutiques and nationally known stores. Sample local cuisine at the many celebrated seafood restaurants and enjoy Long Island's hospitality at bed-and-breakfasts, inns, and hotels throughout the island.

Niagara Frontier

When the Ecumenical Patriarch Dimitrios I of Constantinople, spiritual leader of more than 250 million Eastern Orthodox Christians, visited the United States for the first time, he noted there was one place he particularly wanted to see—Niagara Falls.

Thundering Niagara Falls, one of the great accessible tourist attractions on the planet, plus the urban vitality of Buffalo, New York's second largest city, distinguishes the northwestern corner of the state. The Niagara River descends 325 feet on its passage from Lake Erie to Lake Ontario, plunging two hundred thousand cubic feet of water per second over a crest 3,172 feet wide—Niagara Falls. View this incredible spectacle from overlooks and observation towers or closer, by boat or catwalk, to feel the cool spray of the falls.

The city of Niagara Falls has many other attractions and events: an aquarium; the Wintergarden and the Festival of Lights, an annual winter holiday event from November to January that draws hundreds of motor coach tours each year. The Rainbow Center, Niagara Splash Water Park, and "the Turtle," dedicated to Native American history and culture, are other must-see attractions. Visit the million-dollar Niagara Power Vista power project. Explore Artpark in nearby Lewiston, with its 2,400-seat theater hosting top performers in music and dance, artists on-site, and nature trails. Old Fort Niagara at Youngstown delights history buffs; and at nearby Lockport, visitors can still see five original working locks on the Erie Canal.

Buffalo, known worldwide for its "Buffalo Chicken Wings," is one of the world's great inland ports. In a more stately vein, it is the home of the Albright-Knox Gallery, the nation's first modern art museum. It has all of the advantages of a metropolitan center—theater, symphony, art galleries, the zoo, major league professional sports, unusual attractions like the Naval and Servicemen's Park and a deserved reputation for excellent restaurants. In nearby Cheektowaga, tourists can shop at the newly opened Walden Galleria Mall or a variety of area outlet malls. Fantasy Island and Darien Lake Theme Park are major gathering places for many group tours, as is the steam train ride on the Arcade and Attica Railroad.

In Castile, discover the wonder of Letchworth State Park, with its seventeen-mile, six-hundred-foot-deep, spectacular Genesee River Gorge, often called the "Grand Canyon of the East."

New York City

Every year, millions of global travelers agree: New York City is the place at the top of their list for a vacation. New York City, known internationally as "the Big Apple," is the world's most visited destination. The term *Big Apple*, first used in the 1920s and 1930s by entertainers—particularly jazz musicians—was used to deliver a simple message: "There are many apples on the tree, but when you play New York City, you've played the Big Apple."

In New York City, there's more to see and do than in any other city in the world: theater, concerts to fit everyone's taste and budget, 150 museums and 400 art galleries, sight-seeing to enchant first-time and repeat visitors, exciting sporting events, nightlife that never stops, and thousands of stores catering to a wide variety of shopping clientele. Visitors have the pick of over seventy thousand rooms at a range of hotels that create special incentives for vacationers. From gourmet dining to pub fare, tours can enjoy cuisines from all over the world at more than seventeen thousand eating establishments. It may be the only place in the world where you can eat a terrific meal for $5 as well as $200. New York, with its city lights and exciting nights, dazzles tourists and brings them back again and again, wanting more and more of "the Big Apple."

Thousand Islands–Seaway

The Thousand Islands–Seaway region, bordered by the Finger Lakes and Adirondack region, offers a wide range of vacation and touring opportunities. More than 1,800 islands dot the St. Lawrence River in this region of northern New York State. Alexandria Bay, one of the main towns, is lively in the summer and fall, offering a variety of boating and other activities. The sport-fishing opportunities in this region are endless: rainbow, brook, and lake trout, coho and chinook salmon, and muskies. Tour groups can enjoy air-conditioned seaway cruises that include a visit to Boldt Castle and views of summer cottages and historic stately homes along the shore.

In Ogdensburg, one can explore the Frederic Remington Museum, which houses the world's largest collection of paintings and bronzes of Ogdensburg's most famous son. Tourists often marvel at the synthetic wonders created in water at the locks in Massena as oceangoing ships pass through and experience "power" at the Moses Saunders Power Dam. Visit the Antique Boat Museum and charming waterfront shops in Clayton. In Watertown, original home of F. W. Woolworth's five-and-dime stores, visit the Black River Valley Craft Store. Travel to Cape Vincent to see its stone houses and quaint main street. Tour Sackets Harbor and villages alive with the War of 1812. Travel along Lake Ontario to Oswego to visit Fort Ontario and the H. Lee White Marine Museum, which features artifacts dredged from the Great Lakes, with a small room behind the stairway where slaves hid on their escape route along the Underground Railroad.

The Thousand Islands International Bridge brings visitors to Alexandria Bay from Canada and gives an international flavor to the area. Two other bridges connecting Canada to New York, at Massena and Ogdensburg, allow group tours easy access to New York's Thousand Islands–Seaway region.

NATIONAL FIRSTS, 1983–JULY 1993

Agriculture and Rural Affairs

- Office of Rural Affairs
- Rural Assistance Information Network (RAIN)

Criminal Justice

- HUB System of Correctional Services
- New York State Law Enforcement Accreditation Program
- Drug Treatment Annexes at Prisons with Follow-up Services
- Statewide Automated Fingerprint Identification System (SAFIS)
- Community Narcotics Enforcement Teams (C-NET)
- Interstate Gun Trafficking Agreements

Disabled

- New York State Games for the Physically Challenged

Economic Development

- Centers for Advanced Technology (CATs)
- Global New York Export-Bound Program
- New York State Ceramic Corridor
- NYSERNET Digital "Thruways"

Education

-New York State Mentoring Program
-Community Schools
-Liberty Scholarships
-Summer Institutes for Mathematics and Science
-Magnet Schools
-Athletes Against Drunk Driving

Energy and Environment

-U.S. Department of Energy Awards (most in nation)
-Acid Deposition Control Act
-Shoreham Settlement
-New York State Energy Plan
-R134a Refrigerant
-Six-Phase Power Transmission
-Official Recycling Emblem

Fiscal Reform

-Generally Accepted Accounting Principles (GAAP)

Health Care

-State Certificate of Need System
-Life and the Law Commission
-Surrogate Decision-Making Committee Program
-Long-Term Care Insurance Demonstration
-Child Health Plus Insurance Program
-Single-Payer Demonstration Program
-Bad Debt and Charity Care (BDCC) Pools
-Community Rating System

-Health Care Worker Infection Control Law
-Diagnosis Related Group (DRG) Reimbursement System

Housing

-Homeless Housing and Assistance Program (HHAP)
-HELP Program
-Building Material Toxicity Testing

Human Rights

-Martin Luther King, Jr., Institute for Nonviolence
-Martin Luther King, Jr., Commission

Management and Productivity

-Excelsior Award Program

Social Services

-Alternate Avenues to Dignity
-Decade of the Child
-Comprehensive Employment Opportunity Support Centers (CEOSC)
-Child Assistance Program (CAP)
-Neighborhood Based Initiative (NBI)

Transportation

-Seat Belt Law
-DMV Digitized Imaging System

NEW YORK ALL-TIME FIRSTS

- First school in America (NYC, est. 1663)
- First uniformed police force (NYC, 1693)
- First algebra book (NYC, 1730)
- First state constitution (April 20, 1777)
- First commercial manufacture of ice cream (NYC, 1786)
- First dental drill invented (1790)
- First turnpike (between Albany and Schenectady, 1797)
- First insurance company (NYC, 1804)
- First steamboat (Robert Fulton, NYC–Albany, 1807)
- First commercial manufacture of gloves (1809) and origination of leather tanning (Johnstown, 1810)
- First circular saw manufactured (c. 1814)
- First savings bank (NYC, 1816)
- Natural gas first used as an illuminant (Freedonia, 1824)
- First engineering college (Troy, 1824)
- First opening to the Great Lakes (Erie Canal, 1825)
- First electric magnet, invented by Joseph Henry (Albany, June 1828)
- First railroad (between Albany and Schenectady, 1831)
- First telegraph (1831)
- First streetcar (NYC, 1832)
- First powered knitting machine operated (Cohoes, 1832)
- First lock-stitch sewing machine invented (NYC, 1832–34)
- First patent on rubber (NYC, 1837) and vulcanized rubber (NYC, 1844)
- First photograph taken in U.S. (NYC, 1839)
- First grain elevator (Buffalo, 1840)
- First cast-iron girder bridge (Frankfort, 1840)
- Birthplace of baseball (game created, 1842; rules adopted, 1845)
- Birthplace of Frederick Douglass's *North Star* (1847)
- First "authentically American literature"—James Fenimore Cooper

- Birthplace of the American women's rights (suffrage) movement (Seneca Falls, 1848)
- First cheese factory (Rome, 1851)
- First artificial insemination (NYC, 1866)
- First veterinary school (Cornell University, Ithaca, 1868)
- First advertising agency (N. W. Ayer and Son, 1869)
- Celluloid patented (June 15, 1869)
- First subway (NYC, invented, 1870, operated, 1904)
- Oleomargarine patented (by H. W. Bradley, Binghamton, January 3, 1871)
- Corrugated paper patented (NYC, 1871)
- Birthplace of tennis in U.S. (Staten Island, 1874)
- First practical typewriter manufactured (by Remington, 1874)
- First carpet power loom (Yonkers, 1876)
- First mass-circulation magazine in the U.S. (*McClure's*, 1881)
- First electric power company/plant (1881)
- First (electrical) engineering college (Cornell University, Ithaca, 1883)
- First tuxedo coat (Tuxedo Park, 1886)
- First chartered golf course in U.S. (Shinnecock Hills Country Club, 1891)
- First shredded-wheat breakfast cereal (Watertown, 1893)
- First hydroelectric power plant (1894)
- First commercial pasteurization of milk (Bloomville, 1895)
- Birthplace of legalized boxing (1896)
- First motion picture (April 23, 1896)
- First ice-cream sundae (Ithaca, 1897)
- First cancer laboratory (Buffalo, 1898)
- First escalator manufactured (NYC, 1900)
- First motorcycle (Buffalo, 1900)
- First billion-dollar corporation (U.S. Steel, organized by J. P. Morgan, 1901)
- First film-pack camera (Rochester, 1903)
- First airplane sold commercially (Hammondsport, 1909)
- First photographic copying machine (Rochester, 1910)
- Birthplace of the NAACP (1910)
- First Boy Scouts of America troop (Troy, 1911)
- First airmail service (NYC, 1918)
- First radio station (WABC-AM, October 7, 1921)

-First manufacture of cellophane (by DuPont Cellophane Co., Buffalo, 1924)
-First reformatory in U.S.
-First potato chips (1925)
-First Buffalo wings (1925)
-First national weekly newsmagazine (*Time,* first published by Briton Hadden and Henry R. Luce, NYC, 1925)
-First coast-to-coast radio network (RCA formed National Broadcasting Co.—NBC—1926)
-Development of tuberculosis vaccine (NYC, 1928)
-First artificial heart invented (NYC, 1935)
-First television network (NYC and Schenectady, 1940)
-First television broadcast/station (WNBC, July 1, 1941)
-First jet-powered plane built (the P-59 Airacomet, built by Bell Aerospace Textron, c. 1944)
-First atomic reactor in medical therapy (Brookhaven, 1951)
-First sugar-free soft drink (College Point, 1952)
-First bank credit card issued (1952)
-First transistorized hearing aid offered for sale (Elmsford, December 29, 1952)
-First solar-powered battery (NYC, 1954)
-World's first nuclear plant to produce electricity (GE, near Schenectady, 1955)
-First solid-state electronic computer (Ilion, 1958)
-First pole vault higher than sixteen feet (John Uelses, NYC, February 2, 1962) and higher than eighteen feet (Steve Smith, NYC, January 26, 1973)
-First television receiver and transmitter operated by laser beam—demonstrated (Bayside, February 20, 1963)
-First laser light beam program telecast on a network ("I've Got a Secret," NYC, May 14, 1963)
-First master skyscraper antenna (Empire State Building, NYC, erected 1965)
-First school for unmarried, pregnant, teenage girls (NYC, opened June 23, 1967)
-First wine museum (Finger Lakes Wine Museum, Hammondsport, opened July 1967)

-First book set into type completely by electronic composition (*The Long Short Cut,* by Andrew Garve, NYC, published 1968)
-First mobile coronary-care ambulance (St. Vincent's Hospital, NYC, October 1968)
-First bank automatic teller (NYC, 1969)
-First snowmobile to exceed 125 mph (Yvon Duhamel, Boonville, February 11, 1972)
-First acupuncture treatment center (NYC, July 12, 1972)
-First corporation to have more than three million stockholders (American Telegraph and Telephone Company, NYC, October 17, 1972)
-First pressure-sensitized adhesive postage stamp (Dove of Peace, NYC, issued November 14, 1974)

Selected New York Governmental Firsts in U.S. History

-First state bank legislation (enacted April 2, 1829)
-First state to require by law fire escapes for tenements (April 17, 1860)
-First state outdoor advertising legislation (March 28, 1865) and first state advertising legislation (April 30, 1898)
-First state-designated forest preserve (May 15, 1885)
-First state Board of Mediation and Arbitration (organized June 1, 1886)
-First state-authorized crematory (May 21, 1888)
-First state corrupt election practices law (enacted April 4, 1890)
-First state dog license law (enacted March 8, 1894)
-First state accountancy law (April 17, 1896)
-First license plates required by law (April 25, 1901)
-First modern state arbitration law (April 29, 1920)
-First state to offer aid to localities (1930)
-First program designed to supervise the distribution of state aid (Temporary Emergency Relief Administration, TERA), formed by Governor Roosevelt through the Wicks Act, 1930)
-First state-assisted housing project (Fort Greene, Brooklyn, 1940)
-First Council of the Arts (created by Governor Rockefeller, 1960)

-First statewide minimum-wage law (1960)
-First liberal arts college for police and corrections officers, established by a city (College of Police Science, NYC, opened September 20, 1965; first graduation, June 13, 1966)
-First public school built in conjunction with an apartment house (Bronx, opened September 13, 1971)

SELECTED BIBLIOGRAPHY

A People's History of the United States, Howard Zinn (New York: Harper and Row, 1980).

Agents of Influence, Pat Choate (New York: Knopf, 1990).

America: What Went Wrong?, Donald L. Bartlett and James B. Steele (Kansas City, Mo.: Andrews and McMeel, 1992).

America's Agenda: Rebuilding Economic Strength, Cuomo Commission on Competitiveness, edited by Lee Smith (Armonk, N.Y.: M. E. Sharpe, 1992).

America as a Civilization: Life and Thoughts in the United State Today, Max Lerner (New York: Henry Holt and Company, 1987).

America's Choice: High Skills or Low Wages! (Rochester, N.Y.: National Center on Education and the Economy, 1990).

Bankruptcy 1995: The Coming Collapse of America and How to Stop It, Harry E. Figgie, Jr., with Gerald J. Swanson (New York: Little, Brown, 1992).

The Book of America: Inside Fifty States Today, Neal R. Pierce and Jerry Hagstrom (New York: Norton, 1983).

Burning Money: The Waste of Your Tax Dollars, J. Peter Grace (New York: Macmillan, 1984).

Citizens and Politics: A View From Main Street America, (Dayton, Ohio: Kettering Foundation, 1991).

Congregation of the Condemned: Voices Against the Death Penalty, edited by Shirley Dicks (Buffalo, N.Y.: Prometheus Books, 1991).

Crisis in the Making: The Political Economy of New York State Since 1945, Peter McClelland (New York: Cambridge University Press, 1981).

Day of Reckoning: The Consequences of American Economic Policy, Benjamin M. Friedman (New York: Vintage, 1988).

Democratic Blueprints, Robert Levin (New York: Hippocrene Books, 1988).

The Disuniting of America: Reflections on a Multicultural Society, Arthur M. Schlesinger, Jr. (New York: W.W. Norton & Co., 1992).

Economic Competitiveness: The States Take the Lead, David Osborne (Washington, D.C.: Economic Policy Institute, 1987).

The End of Laissez-Faire: National Purpose and the Global Economy After the Cold War, Robert Kuttner (New York: Knopf/Random House, 1991).

Final Report of the XIII Winter Olympic Games, Lake Placid, 1980.

From Niagara to Montauk: The Scenic Pleasures of New York State, C. R. Roseberry (Albany, N.Y.: SUNY Press, 1982).

Governor Alfred E. Smith, Paula Dldot (New York: Garland Publishing, 1983).

Growing Together: An Alternative Economic Strategy for the 1990s, Alan Blinder (Knoxville, Tenn.: Whittle Direct Books, 1991).

Head to Head: The Coming Economic Battle Among Japan, Europe, and America, Lester Thurow (New York: William Morrow and Co., 1992).

The Health Care Crisis: Containing Costs, Expanding Coverage, prepared by the Public Agenda Foundation (New York: McGraw-Hill, 1992).

The History of New York City, Bill Harris (New York: Portland House/Crown, 1989).

History of New York State, edited by Ellis, Frost, Cyra, and Carmen (Ithaca, N.Y.: Cornell University Press, 1967).

History of the State of New York, edited by A. C. Flick et al., vol. 9 (Ira J. Freedman, Inc., 1962).

Hostages of Fortune: Child Labor Reform in New York State, Jeremy P. Felt (Syracuse, N.Y.: Syracuse University Press, 1965).

Ideals and Politics, Edward K. Spann (Albany, N.Y.: State University of New York Press, 1972).

Imminent Peril: Public Health and Declining Economy, edited by Kevin M. Cahill, M.D. (New York: The Twentieth Century Fund, 1991).

Imperial Rockefeller, Joseph E. Persico, (New York: Simon and Schuster, 1981).

"I Never Wanted to Be Vice-President of Anything!" An Investigative Biography of Nelson Rockefeller, Michael Kramer and Sam Roberts (New York: Basic Books, 1976).

The Italian-Americans Through the Generations, Rocco Caporale (Staten Island, N.Y.: American Italian Historical Association, 1986).

Lincoln on Democracy, edited by Mario M. Cuomo and Harold Holzer (New York: HarperCollins, 1990).

Listen for a Lonesome Drum, Carl Carmer (New York: Farrar & Rhinehart, Inc., 1936).

The Mohawk, Codman Hislop (Syracuse, N.Y.: Syracuse University Press, 1989).

A New Agenda For Cities, Richard P. Nathan (Columbus, Ohio: Ohio Municipal League Educational and Research Fund, 1992).

New York: A Collection from Harper's *Magazine* (New York: Gallery Books, 1991).

New Immigrants in New York, Nancy Foner, ed. (New York: Columbia University Press, 1987).

New York: Culture Capital of the World 1940–1965, Leonard Wallace, ed. (New York: Rizzoli International Publications, 1988).

New York: The Empire State, David M. Ellis, James A. Frost, and William B. Fink (New York: Prentice-Hall, 1964).

New York: A Physical History, Norval White (New York: Atheneum-Macmillan, 1987).

New York State: Folktales, Legends, and Ballads, Harold W. Thompson (Lake Ronkonkoma, N.Y.: Dover Publications, Inc., 1967).

New York State: Gateway to America, David M. Ellis (Northridge, Calif.: Windsor Publications, 1988).

New York and the Mid-Atlantic States, Dana Facaros and Michael Pauls (Washington, D.C.: Regnery Gateway, Inc., 1982).

New York City Draft Riots, Iver Bernstein (New York: Oxford University Press, 1990).

New York Intellect, Thomas Bender (New York: Knopf, 1987).

New York Observed, Barbara Cohen, ed. (New York: Abrams, 1987).

New York Past and Present (New York: New-York Historical Society/I. N. Phelps, 1939).

New York State and City, David M. Ellis (Ithaca, N.Y.: Cornell University Press, 1979).

New York State Insight Guides (New York: Simon and Schuster, 1985).

New York State Science & Technology Foundation (Albany, N.Y.: The Foundation, Directory of Projects, Fiscal Years 1980–1989).

On the Mountain, In the Valley (Hobart, N.Y.: Catskill Center for Conservation and Development, 1977).

Politics in the Empire State, Warren Moscow (New York: Knopf, 1948).

Politics in New York State, 1800–1830, Alvin Kass (Syracuse, N.Y.: Syracuse University Press, 1965).

The Politics of Rich and Poor, Kevin Phillips (New York: Random House, 1990).

The Politics of Social Policy in the U.S., Martha Weir et al. (Princeton, N.J.: Princeton University Press, 1988).

Poor Support: Poverty in the American Family, Daniel T. Ellwood (New York: Basic Books, 1988).

The Promised Land: The Great Black Migration and How It Changed America, Nicholas Lemann (New York: Knopf, 1991).

The Public Papers of Governor Mario M. Cuomo, (Albany, N.Y., 1983–1988) (Also see the *Public Papers* of previous New York State Governors: Lehman, Dewey, Harriman, Rockefeller, Wilson, and Carey).

Race: How Blacks and Whites Think and Feel About the American Obsession, Studs Terkel (New York: The New Press, 1992).

Reindustrializing New York State: Strategies, Implications, Challenges, edited by Morton Schoolman and Alvin Magid (Albany, N.Y.: SUNY Press, 1986).

Reinventing Government, David Osborne and Ted Gaebler (Reading, Mass.: Addison-Wesley, 1991).

Rockefeller of New York: Executive Power in the State House, Robert H. Connery and Gerald Benjamin (Ithaca, N.Y.: Cornell University Press, 1979).

Running on Empty: Bush, Congress, and the Politics of a Bankrupt Government, Lawrence Haas (Homewood, Ill.: Business One Irwin, 1990).

Savage Inequalities, Jonathan Kozol (New York: Crown, 1991).

Shadow Government, Donald Axelrod (New York: John Wiley and Sons, 1992).

The State of the States, edited by Carl E. Van Horn (Washington, D.C.: Congressional Quarterly Press, 1993).

The Statistical Abstract of the United States: The National Data Book, U.S. Department of Commerce, Economics, and Statistics Administration (Washington, D.C.: Bureau of the Census. 111th edition, 1991)

The Story of New York, Suzanne E. Lyman (New York: Crown, 1964).

Sustain Our Schools, Patricia Graham (New York: Hill and Wang, 1992).

Taking the University to the People, Wayne D. Rasmussen (Ames, Iowa: Iowa State University Press, 1989).

The Truly Disadvantaged: The Inner City, the Underclass, and Public Policy, William Julius Wilson (Chicago: University of Chicago Press, 1987).

The Underclass Question, Bill Lawson, ed. (Philadelphia: Temple University Press, 1992).

Upstate, Edmund Wilson (Syracuse, N.Y.: Syracuse University Press, 1971).

The Urban Underclass, Christopher Jencks and Paul E. Peterson (Washington, D.C.: Brookings Institute, 1991).

Way Home: A New Direction in Social Policy, Report of the New York City Commission on the Homeless, Andrew Cuomo (New York: Mayor's Office, February 1992).

Which Side Are You On? Trying to Be For Labor When It's Flat on Its Back, Thomas Geoghegan (New York: Farrar, Straus, & Giroux, 1991).

Who Built America? Working People and the Nation's Economy, Politics, Culture, and Society, volume II, From the Guilded Age to the Present, American Social History Project (New York: Pantheon, 1992).

Why Americans Hate Politics, E. J. Dionne (New York: Simon & Schuster, 1991).

Without Shelter: Homelessness in the 1980s, Peter Rossi (New York: Priority Press Publications, 1989).

Work of Nations: Preparing Ourselves for Twenty-first Century Capitalism, Robert Reich (New York: Knopf, 1991).

INDEX

ABB Traction, Inc., 242
Accountability, Audit and Internal Control
    Act (N.Y.S., 1987), 191
Acid rain law, 214, 247, 260
Adirondack and Catskill Forest Preserve,
    202, 203, 206–8
Adirondack region, 128, 203, 206–7, 258
Adoption Option, 166
Advertising, 89–90
AFDC. *See* Aid to Families with Dependent
    Children
Affordable Housing Corporation (AHC),
    142, 143, 144*n.29*
African-Americans, 18, 19, 27–28, 163, 247
A. G. Electronics, 242
Agriculture, 66, 98–103, 247, 259
AIDS, 139, 154–58, 163
Aid to Families with Dependent Children
    (AFDC), 171, 175
Airports, 53, 128, 229
Air quality, 107, 208, 212, 214, 228
Albright-Knox Gallery, 90, 91*n.47*, 257
Alcohol abuse, 148, 183–84, 260
Alexandria Bay, 258
Alfred University, 70, 70*n.25*
Alitalia Airlines, 242
Alternative Avenues to Dignity, 166, 261
Alternative-Fuel Vehicle Fleet
    Demonstration Program, 59*n.12*
Alzheimer's disease, 68, 68*n.22*, 136
American Dream, 1, 7, 8, 21, 245
American Party. *See* Know-Nothings
America Works, 173
Amgen, 68
Amtrak, 241*n.16*
Anatomy of Hate conferences, 32
Anheuser-Busch, 53
Ansaldo Industries of America, 242–43
Anti-Drug Abuse Council, 186–87
APM (automated people mover), 229
Apprenticeship programs, 84
Architecture Planning and Design, 93
Artificial intelligence, 66
Arts and culture, 90–93, 132; by regions,
    251, 253, 254, 255, 257
Assault weapons, 180–81
Athletes Against Drunk Driving,
    148*n.33*, 260
Attica uprising, 176
Austin, Joe, 168

Automobiles. *See* Cars
Auto racing, 96
Axelrod, David, 156

Babbitt, Bruce, 220
Babies. *See* Children
Baird, Zoe, 21
Ballard, Allen, 28
B. Altman's building, 236
Banca Di Roma, 242
Bane, Mary Jo, 170
Bar code scanning, 65
Baseball, 94, 96, 252
Baseball Hall of Fame, 94, 252
Basketball, 96
Battery Park City, 143–44*n.29*, 206,
    231, 233
Beaches, 204–5, 255
Bear Mountain State Park, 105–6
Bell, Alexander Graham, 63
Ben & Jerry's, 43–44
Betting, 97–98
Bias crimes, xiii, 28–29, 35–36
Big Apple (term), 257
Bill of Rights, 121–22
Biotechnology, 65, 67–69, 102–3, 136
Blackout (1977), 55
Bonds, 115, 116, 144*n.29*, 226–27
Borrowing policies, 114–16, 225–27. *See
    also* Capital investment
Bottle Bill, 194, 216
Brady Bill, 179–80
Bridgehampton, 96
Brighton Beach, 86
Broadcasting industry, 46
Bronx, The, x. *See also* New York City;
    specific institutions and sections
Bronx High School of Science, 82
Bronx-Lebanon Hospital, 149–50
Bronx River Corridor Preservation and
    Development Plan, 93
Bronx River Parkway, 51
Brookhaven National Laboratory, 235
Brooklyn, x. *See also* New York City;
    specific institutions and sections
Brooklyn Tech, 82
Brown, Lee, 185*n.75*
Brown v. *Board of Education*, 37
Brundtland, Gro Harlem, 60
Buchanan, Pat, 21

Budget, N.Y.S., 117, 197; debt, 3, 114–16, 226; local assistance aid, 112–13; reserve funds, 226. *See also* Fiscal responsibility
Budget deficit, U.S., 5, 115, 243
Budget deficits, U.S states, 3–4
Buffalo, 256, 257; arts, 90, 91n.48, 92; magnet schools, 77; as major port, 50, 51; sports, 96; waterfront revitalization, 233
Buffalo Bills, 95, 96
Building contracts, 113n.69. *See also* Infrastructure program
Bureaucracy: ethics, 190–91, 193; health care, 150–51; local government, 112–13; state government, 103–7
Bush, George. *See* Reagan-Bush administrations
Bus Industries of America, 230n.5, 241, 241n.16
Businesses: capital investment. *See* Capital investment; corporate management, 63–64; foreign investments, 239–43; government relationship with, 10–11, 41–48, 52, 247; high-tech, 62–74; immigrant-owned, 24, 25; incubator programs, 67–68; management-labor relations, 129–30n.12, 130n.13, 261; relocations, 46–47, 239–43; state-based, 237; state bid for, 239–43; tax incentives for, 46; tax rates, 109. *See also* Job training/retraining; Research and development; Workforce; specific businesses and industries

Calí cartel, 178
California, 2, 3–4, 21, 23n.8, 74, 212, 237
Campaign finance laws, 193
CAP. *See* Child Assistance Program
Capital investment, 6, 225–44; in biotechnology, 67, 68–69, 70; centralized planning process, 227; in energy, 54–62; financing of, 225–27; in infrastructure, 42, 48–53, 115–16; public-private partnership, 10–11, 41–48, 68–69, 70, 72–73, 105–6, 173
Capital-Saratoga region, 251
Career Pathways, 84
Carey, Hugh, 108, 131, 132, 133, 134, 208
Cargo. *See* Freight traffic; Shipping
Carleton Park, 142
Carlson, Chester F., 63
Carrier Corporation, 63
Cars: DMV reforms, 105; energy/environment measures, 59, 60, 211–12; safety, 148, 247, 260, 261; "smart" signage, 230
Carson, Rachel, 203
Casino gambling, 98n.56
Cathedral of St. John the Divine, 45
Cathedral Stoneworks, 45
Cato, Gavin, 28
CATO Institute, 108–9

CATs. *See* Centers for Advanced Technology
Catskills, 252. *See also* Adirondack and Catskill Forest Preserve
CBS headquarters, 46
Celeste, Richard, 214
Center for Integrated Manufacturing Studies (CIMS), 235
Centers for Advanced Technology (CATs), xiii, 65–67, 70, 234, 246, 259
Central-Leatherstocking region, 252–53
CEOSCs. *See* Comprehensive Employment Opportunity Support Centers
Ceramics Corridor, 69–70
Chautauqua-Allegheny, 253–54
Checks and balances, 122
Cheektowaga, 45, 257
Child Assistance Program (CAP), 171–72, 247, 261
Child Care Coordinating Council, 164–65
Child Health Insurance Program (CHIP), 166
Child Health Plus, 149, 152, 166, 260
Children: abuse, 159, 165; adoption, 166; as crime perpetrators/victims, 182; day care, 14, 131, 164–65; health care, 144, 146, 147, 149, 150, 152, 162–64, 166; HIV-infected, 155, 163; homeless, 138, 139–40; labor law, 126n.6; societal problems and, 160, 162–70; state programs for, 163–67, 169–70, 246, 247; support, 172–73; welfare reform, 171–76. *See also* Education
Chinese Exclusion Act (U.S., 1882), 19n.4, 27
CIMS. *See* Center for Integrated Manufacturing Studies
Cipriani, Harry, 242n.18
Cities. *See* Urban areas
City University of New York (CUNY), 66n.18, 85–86, 87–88, 117
Civilian Conservation Corps, 128, 208
Civil rights, 131, 133–34, 157. *See also* Discrimination
Clean Air Act (U.S., 1990), 107, 212, 214
Clean Water Act (U.S., 1972), 208n.9
Clestra Cleanroom Technology, 69
Climate Change agreement, 218n.20
Clinton, Bill, 74, 77, 108, 243; anti-crime measures, 179, 180n.66; environmental programs, 219–20; health-care plan, 151, 152, 154
Clinton, De Witt, 49, 50, 52, 123
Cocaine. *See* Crack cocaine
Coffee, Sugar, and Cocoa Exchange, 46n.4
Cohen, Ben, 44
Cold Spring Harbor Laboratory, 68, 235
Cold War end, 1–2, 70–72, 74, 236–37
Colgate University, 85
Collective generosity, 7–8
Colleges. *See* Universities and colleges
College Woods, 142, 142n.28
Columbia University, 85
Commerce, U.S. Department of, 74n.28
Commodities exchanges, 46

Community, sense of, 168, 249–50
Community-based programs, 135–38, 169–70
Community colleges, 86, 131
Community policing, 178, 179
Commuters: car pooling, 59; ferries, 230; trains, 52, 56–57, 229–30
Comprehensive Employment Opportunity Support Centers, 173, 261
Computers. *See* High technology
Con Edison, 209
Confindustria, 238
Connecticut, 47, 109, 181
Conservation. *See* Environment
Consolidated Westway Group, 241
Constitution, N.Y.S., 121, 122*nn.2, 3*, 128–29, 132, 195–96, 196*n.89*
Constitution, U.S., 15–16, 34, 109, 180, 188–98; safeguards in, 121–23
Constitutional convention, proposed N.Y.S., 196–98, 248
Consumer Protection Board, 132
Cooper, James Fenimore, 50, 252
Cooperative Extension Service, 100
Cooperstown, 94, 252, 253
Cooper Union, 91
Cornell, Ezra, 99–100
Cornell University, 66, 85, 99–100, 102
Corning Bypass, 228
Corning Glass, 63, 70, 76, 254
Corporations. *See* Businesses
Coughlin, Tom, 176, 177
Council of Great Lakes Governors, 215–16
Courts. *See* Criminal justice system; Judgeships
Crack cocaine, 159–60, 162, 177, 227
Credit. *See* Borrowing policies
Crime: bias-related, xiii, 28–29, 35–36; drug-related, 160–61, 177, 178–79, 182–87, 227; gun ownership and, 179–81; subway, 178
Criminal justice system, 35–36, 176–87, 247, 259
Cross Creek Townhouses, 143
Crown Heights, 28
CRS Computers, 53
Cultural events. *See* Arts and culture
CUNY. *See* City University of New York
Cuomo, Andrew, 139, 181
Cuomo, Matilda, 165, 167, 181, 239
Cuomo family background, xi–xii, 21–22, 29–30, 98, 168–69
Curative Technologies, 68*n.21*

Dairy industry, 99, 100, 102
Dairylea, 102
Dayton T. Brown, Inc., 72
Debt. *See* Borrowing policies; Budget, N.Y.S., debt; Budget deficit, U.S.
Decade of the Child, 163–67, 246, 261
Declaration of Independence, 34, 188
Defense Diversification Program (DDP), 72–73, 74

Defense industry, 1–2, 70–74
Deficit budget. *See* Budget, N.Y.S., debt; Budget deficit, U.S.
Delsener, Ron, 205*n.5*
Democracy, definition of, 188
Department of . . . *See* New York State Department of . . .
Depression, economic. *See* Great Depression; Recession impact
Dewey, Thomas, 51, 52, 131
Dinkins, David, 28, 94, 95, 206
Disabilities, 133–38, 166, 259
Discrimination, 27, 37, 77, 131, 157
DMV. *See* New York State Department of Motor Vehicles
DNA fingerprinting, 178*n.63*
DNA research, 68
Dominicans, 19, 23*n.8*
Doubleday, Abner, 252
Downey, Tom, 170*n.57*
Drug abuse and traffic, 159–60, 162, 168, 177, 178–79, 182–87, 247
Dunlop Tire, 45

Earth Summit, 218–19
Eastman, George, 63
Eastman Kodak, 63, 76
Eastman School of Music, 91
East River Drive, 128
Economic development offices abroad, 238
Economic development zones, 45, 142*n.28*, 169, 247
Economic growth, 41–53; fiscal responsibility, 108–17, 247; foreign investment, 239–43; global marketplace, 236–43; high technology, 62–74, 233–39; immigrants' role, 23–25; ingredients for, 42, 248; national stimulation measures, 243–44. *See also* Capital investment; Infrastructure program
Economic history, N.Y.S., 49–51, 62–63, 99–100, 108–9, 123–30. *See also* Economic growth; Great Depression; Recession impact; Taxes
Edison, Thomas Alva, 63
Education: antidropout programs, 165, 169*n.55*; *Brown* v. *Board of Education* on, 37; as economic growth factor, 42, 75–88; energy-saving building measures, 58; environmental, 220; federal aid cutbacks, 3; foreign standards, 75, 76; of immigrants, 23–24, 25, 86; multicultural, 33–34; NYSERNET, 234–35, 259; school-choice proposals, 77–79; science prize winners, 64; state aid, 79–81, 79*n.31*, 86, 87–88, 112, 117, 126, 131, 132; state firsts in, 260; test scores/attendance, 27–28, 79. *See also* Job training/retraining; Universities and colleges
Elderly, 147–48, 149. *See also* Social Security

Elderly Pharmaceutical Insurance (EPIC), 147*n.31*
Electoral reform, 192–94
Electricity. *See* Energy; Utilities
Electronic information systems, 234–36
Electronics, 66, 69–70
Elliott, Delbert S., 182*n.70*
Ellis Island Immigration Museum, 17–18
Elmhurst (Queens), 24
Elmira, 254
Elmira Heights, 241
Empire State Games, 95
Empire State Plaza, 132, 251
Employment. *See* Workforce;
　Unemployment and layoffs
Endicott-Johnson, 63–64
Energy, 54–62; efficiency programs, 57–60;
　environmental impact, 57–60, 209,
　212, 214, 247; high-tech applications,
　66*n.20;* national policy problems, 3,
　60; renewable sources, 57, 59, 215;
　state firsts, 260; state integrated plan,
　57–58
Energy Aid for Public Schools, 58
Energy Policy Act (U.S., 1992), 60
Engineers, 64, 236
English, as second language, 25
Environment, 201–21, 243; energy policy
　and, 57–60, 209, 212, 214, 247;
　federal aid cutbacks, 3; interstate
　cooperation, 214–16;
　national/international challenge,
　217–21; neg-reg procedure, 107; state
　firsts, 260. *See also* Waste materials;
　other specific aspects
Environmental Policy Act (U.S.), 209
Environmental Protection Fund, 217
Environmental Quality Bond Act (N.Y.S.,
　1986), 217
Environmental Quality Bond Act (N.Y.S.,
　1990), 217, 225–27
Environmental Quality Review Act
　(N.Y.S.), 208
EPIC. *See* Elderly Pharmaceutical
　Insurance
Erie Canal, 49–51, 52, 123, 233, 253, 257
Esopus Meadows Point, 211
Ethics in Government Act (N.Y.S.,
　1987), 191
Ethnic groups. *See* Immigrants
Excelsior Award, 130*n.13,* 261
Export Marketing Assistance, 238
Exports. *See under* Trade

Family, principle of, 11, 248
Family preservation measures, 164
Farmers' Market Coupon, 101–2
Farming. *See* Agriculture
Fashion Institute of Technology, 91
Federal aid: defense diversification, 73–74;
　drug war, 184; Great Depression, 128;
　Reagan/Bush cutbacks, 3, 116, 141;
　rural areas, 161
Federal Aid to Dependent Children, 127

Federal Express, 53
Federal government. *See* Government;
　specific presidents
Federalist Papers, 16
Ferguson, Colin, 179
Ferries, 230
Fiber optics, 63, 69–70, 234
Finger Lakes, 254, 258
Fingerprint identification system, 178, 247,
　259
Firsts, N.Y.S., 259–67
Fiscal responsibility, 108–17, 226–27, 247, 260
Florida, 74
Flushing (Queens), 24
Football, 96
Fordham University, 85
Foreign investment, in New York,
　239–43
Foreign trade. *See* Trade
Forests. *See* Wilderness preserves
Forfeiture law, 178–79
Frédéric Chopin Singing Society, 92
Free enterprise, 10, 123
Free Trade Agreement, U.S.-Canada
　(1988), 233
Freight Link America, 228
Freight traffic, 50–51, 228
Fresh Wetlands Act (N.Y.S.), 208
Fried-chicken franchises, 24
Fuel. *See* Energy; specific sources
Fulton County, 46, 161

Galeries Lafayette, 242
Gambling, 97–98
Garbage, 107*n.61,* 202, 212–14
Garment industry, 24
Gas, natural, 57
Gas stations, 24
GATEWAY training initiative, 169
Gay rights, 27, 28
GEMS. *See* Global Export Market Services
General Electric, 63, 64–65
General Fund, 79, 104
General Motors, 2
General Railway Signal, 239
Germany, 6, 58, 75, 76, 84
GI Bill of Rights, 84
Gideon Putnam Hotel, 105
Gifted students, 81
Glen Iris Inn, 106
Glimmerglass Opera, 253
Global Export Market Services (GEMS),
　238*n.12*
Global marketplace, 75–76, 237–39, 246
Global New York initiative, 238–39, 259
Goldberger, Paul, 231
Goodwill Games, 94, 95
Government: bureaucracy reforms, 103–7;
　Cuomo's philosophy and goals,
　245–50; defense industry
　diversification, 72–74; energy
　programs, 54–62; legitimate object of,
　8, 41–42, 48; misconduct/ethics issues,
　189–92, 194; political reform, 188–98;

private sector partnership. *See under* Capital investment; private sector stimulation by, 52; social welfare role, 7–9, 127–29, 247; state constitutional convention proposal, 196–98, 248; state constitutional provisions, 122*n.3;* state-federal partnership, 73–74, 128–29, 140; state firsts, 259–61, 266–67; state-local problems, 112–14; university partnership, 67–68. *See also* Constitution headings; Federal aid; Local government; Taxes; specific agencies and programs

Government employees. *See* Bureaucracy

Governor Malcolm Wilson Tappan Zee Bridge, 132*n.15,* 230

Governor's Arts Awards, 92*n.48*

Governor's Office of Management and Productivity (MAP), 103–4

Governor's powers, 122*n.3*

Grandma Moses, 251

Great Depression, 126–29, 171, 175, 208

Great Lakes Protection Fund, 215–16

Greenfield, Jerry, 44

Greengroceries, 24

Greenhouse gases, 60, 202, 218*n.20*

Griffith, Michael, 28

Grumman Aircraft, 1–2

Guilderland, 56

Gun control, 179–81, 259

Hamilton, Alexander, 16

Hamlets of the Adirondacks, 93

Handguns. *See* Gun control

Handlin, Oscar, 18

HARKhomes shelter, 43

Harlem: magnet schools, 77; public-private partnership, 43–44; Riverbank state park, 205–6

Harness racing, 97

Harriman, Averell, 131

Hart, Kitty Carlisle, 91

Hasidic Jews, 28

Hate crimes. *See* Bias crimes

Hawkins, Yusef, 28

Hayes, Kevin, 70*n.25*

Hazardous waste, 62*n.15,* 209–10, 215

Hazeltine Corporation, 72–73

Health care system, 144–58; AIDS problem, 154–58, 163; biotechnology, 67–69, 136; Carey reforms, 132; children, 144, 146, 147, 149, 150, 152, 162–64, 166; comprehensive reform proposal, 152–54, 247; drug treatment, 186–87; electronic information network, 234–35; federal cutbacks, 2; immigrant personnel, 23; managed programs, 150, 153; mental illness, 133, 135–38; prenatal, 149, 162*n.48,* 164; state aid, 117; state firsts, 260–61. *See also* Medicaid

HEAT. *See* Higher Education Applied Technology

HELP program, 139–40, 261

HHAP. *See* Homeless Housing Assistance Program

Higher education. *See* Universities and colleges

Higher Education Applied Technology (HEAT), 88, 236

High-speed transport, 229, 230

High technology, 42, 62–74, 233–39; agricultural, 247; defense industry diversification, 71–74; global marketplace, 238, 239, 240*n.14,* 242, 246; HEAT program, 88; incubator programs, 67–68, 70; inventors, 63, 64–65. *See also* Biotechnology

Highways and roads: construction projects, 51–52, 228; "smart" signage, 230; traffic congestion, 59

Hill, David, 203

HIV infection. *See* AIDS

Hockey, 96

Holland, Joe, 43–44

Holliswood (Queens), xii, 30

Homeless Housing Assistance Program (HHAP), 139, 143*n.29,* 247, 261

Homeless people, 43, 44, 136–41, 143*n.29,* 161, 247

Home Relief, 175

Homicide, 160, 179, 180, 182*n.72*

Horse racing, 96, 97, 251

Hospital Audiences, Inc., 92

Hospitals, 149–50, 151, 153

Housing: federal aid cutbacks, 3; homeless provisions, 137–41, 247; immigrant ownership, 24; property tax deductibility issue, 110; state firsts, 261; state programs, 128, 141–43, 143–44*n.29*

Housing Finance Agency, 144*n.29*

Housing Trust Fund Corporation, 143*n.29*

Howard Beach (Queens), 28

Howe Caverns, 252

HTFC. *See* Housing Trust Fund Corporation

Hudson River and Valley, 209, 211, 230, 255

Hudson River Fishermen's Association, 211*n.12*

Hudson River Greenway Council and Conservancy, 211

Hudson River Park, 206

Human needs. *See* Social issues

Hunter's Point, 231

Hyde Park, 255

Hydroelectric power, 56, 57, 215

IBM, 2, 63, 65, 70

IEP. *See* Industrial Effectiveness Program

IHAP. *See* Infant Health Assessment Program

Illegal aliens, 21, 25–26

Illiteracy, 6

Immigrants, xi–xii, 17–37; art grants, 93*n.49;* countries of origin, 23*n.8,* 24–25; Cuomo family, xi–xii, 21–22,

29–30; education and skills, 23–24, 25, 86; Endicott-Johnson employee policies, 64; and international business migration, 240, 243; and labor movement, 125; law revision (1990), 22, 23*n.9;* as mosaic, 34*n.21;* positive economic impact of, 23–25; resentment of, 20–22, 26–37; three waves of, 18–19
Income tax. *See* Taxes
Incubator programs, 67–68, 70
Index of Social Health, 159
Industrial Effectiveness Program, 73*n.27*
Industrial parks, 53
Industry. *See* Businesses; Economic growth; High technology
Infant Health Assessment Program, 164
Infant mortality, 144
Infrastructure program: borrowing for, 225–27; energy-saving measures, 59; Great Depression, 128; high-tech, 234–37; private/public investments in, 42, 48–53, 87, 115–16, 227–33, 246; under Rockefeller, 131–32. *See also* specific aspects
Initiative/referendum, 194–95
Inner Harbor Canal, 232
Inspector general, N.Y.S., 190–91
Integrated Pest Management, 102
Interest rates, 5–6, 243
International Boxing Hall of Fame, 253
International Partnership Program, 239, 243
Interstate highway system, 51–52
Inventors, 63, 64–65
Investment. *See* Capital investment
Investment-banking industry, 1
Israel, 239
Italian-Americans, xi–xii, 18, 240
Italian trade and investments, 238, 239, 240, 240*n.15,* 242
Ives-Quinn Act (N.Y.S., 1945), 131

Jacobs, Jane, 48
Jakko Poyry Consulting, 242*n.17*
Jamaica Hospital, 149–50
Jamestown, 253
Japan: biotechnology marketing, 69; educational rigor, 75, 76; energy efficiency, 58; manufacturing, 6; N.Y.S. trade/investments, 239, 239–40*n.14*
Japan Air Lines, 242
Jay, John, 16
Jefferson, Thomas, 50
Jeremiah, 348
Jews, 18, 28, 86
JFK International Airport, 53, 229
Job creation: defense industry, 72–74; foreign business, 241–43; Great Depression, 128; high-tech, 67–68, 69*n.23;* for homeless people, 43, 44; immigrant-owned businesses, 25; infrastructure, 228*n.3,* 232*nn.8, 9, 10;*

state economic development projects, 44–46; tourism, 89
Job Development Authority, 46, 69*n.23*
Jobs. *See* Workforce
Job training/retraining: as economic growth component, 42; federal cutbacks, 3; for global competitiveness, 75–76; school/workplace links, 83–84; state programs, 45, 73*n.27,* 74; welfare recipients, 173
Johnson, George F., 63–64
Johnson, Lyndon, 145, 161
Jones Beach Marine Theater, 205*n.5,* 255
Jones Beach State Park, 105, 204–5, 255
Judgeships, 177, 193–94, 197, 247
Juilliard School of Music, 91
Junior colleges. *See* Community colleges
Junk bonds, 1
Justice. *See* Criminal justice system; Law; Social issues
"Just in time" management, 73*n.27*

Kennedy International Airport, 53, 229
Kerner Commission, 28
Kinderhook, 255
King, Martin Luther, Jr., 32
Kingsborough Community College, 86
Know-Nothings, 20
Knox, Seymour, 91*n.47*
Kodak Corporation, 2, 105
Kopple, Barbara, 93
Kunin, Madeleine, 218*n.20*
Kyocera, 70

Labor movement, 124–26, 129–30
Ladbrokes, 97
LaGuardia Airport, 128, 229
LaGuardia Community College, 86
Lake Champlain, 214–15
Lake Erie, 50, 215, 233, 253
Lake Onondaga, 232
Lake Ontario, 215
Lake Placid, 95
Landfill, 107*n.61,* 213
Land grant universities, 99
Latinos, 27
Law: constitutional guarantees, 121–23; criminal justice system, 176–87, 247; social justice measures, 125–26
Lawrence High School, 28–29
Layoffs. *See* Unemployment and layoffs
Lead Screening Act (N.Y.S., 1992), 166
Lee, Spike, 93
Lehman, Herbert, 127–28, 131
Lehman, Orin, 205*n.5*
Letchworth State Park, 106, 254, 257
Lewis County, 98
Liberty Scholarships, 81, 260
"Library without walls," 236
Lighthouse for the Blind, 93*n.50*
LILCO. *See* Long Island Lighting Company
Lincoln, Abraham, 8, 20, 41, 48, 99, 188
Lincoln Tunnel, 128

Little New Deal, 128
Livingston County, 187
Lobbyists, 190n.81
Local government: Medicaid costs, 113,
    145; revenue sharing, 132; taxes and
    services, 111–16, 248
Local Government Assistance Corporation,
    115–16
Long Island, 255–56; defense industry, 72;
    housing, 142; local taxes, 111n.65,
    112; nuclear power plant, 61–62;
    research and development, 67, 68,
    235; sports, 96; transportation, 229,
    230; water quality, 210–11
Long Island City, 73n.27, 86
Long Island Expressway, 59, 228
Long Island High Technology Incubator,
    67
Long Island Lighting Company (LILCO),
    59, 61, 62
Long Island Pine Barrens, 211
Long Island Power Authority, 56
Long Island Rail Road, shooting on, 179,
    180
Long Island Research Institute, 235, 236
Long Island State Park, 204n.3
Los Angeles riots (1992), 36
Love Canal, 209
Low-birthweight babies, 162n.48
Lower East Side Tenement Museum, 124
Lower-income families: child health care,
    166; educational deficits, 27–28,
    76–77, 80; higher education
    opportunities, 86–87; housing, 141–43.
    See also Poverty
Low-Income Housing Trust Fund, 143
LUCK GmbH, 241
Lundine, Stan, 183, 229

MAC. *See* Municipal Assistance
    Corporation
Machine repair shops, 24
Madison, James, 16, 189
Madison Square Garden, 96
Maglev (magnetic levitation train), 229–30
Magnet schools, 77, 260
Managed health care, 150, 153
Management-labor relations, 129–30n.12,
    130n.13, 261
Mandatory Job Search Initiative, 175
Manhattan, ix. *See also* New York City;
    specific institutions and sections
Manhattan College, 85
Manufacturing, 6, 24, 73n.27, 84, 235–36.
    See also specific industries
MAP. *See* Governor's Office of
    Management and Productivity
Martinique welfare hotel, 139–40
Martin Luther King, Jr., Institute,
    32–33n.20
Mass transit: equipment manufacture, 241;
    federal aid cutbacks, 3; high-tech,
    228–30; New York City, 51, 52–53,
    56–57, 178, 228–29

McGill Commission, 47–48
Measles, 146
Medicaid, 2, 147n.32, 150, 151; coverage
    expansion, 148–49; HIV policy,
    156–57; local government costs, 113,
    145; matching formula, 154;
    misinformation on, 175n.61; public
    resentment of, 174, 175; state's costs,
    113, 132
Medicine. *See* Health care system
Melting pot concept, 34n.21
Melville, Herman, 50
Mental illness programs, 133, 135–38
Mental retardation, 133, 134
Merrill Lynch, 47
Metropolitan Transportation Authority
    (MTA), 52–53, 197n.91
Meucci, Antonio, 63
Military bases. *See* Defense industry
Milk Producers' Security Fund, 102
Milling, 51
Minolta, 242
Miringoff, Marc, 159
Mobro (garbage barge), 212–13
Montauk Downs, 106
Montauk Point, 255
Montgomery County, 45
Moody's Investor Services, 114
Moreland Act Commission, 81, 132
Morgan Stanley, 46
Morrill Land Grant Act (U.S., 1862), 99
Morris, Gouverneur, 122n.3
Morrison Knudsen Corporation,
    241n.16
Morse, Samuel F. B., 63
Mortgages, 114, 142, 226
Mosaic concept, 34n.21
Moses, Robert, 55, 204, 205
Moynihan, Pat, 108, 116, 170n.57, 214
MTA. *See* Metropolitan Transportation
    Authority
Multiculturalism, 33–34, 36
Municipal Assistance Corporation (MAC),
    83n.37

Nassau Coliseum, 96
Nassau County, 111n.65, 112
Nathan Kline Institute for Psychiatric
    Research, 136
National debt. *See* Budget deficit, U.S.
National Museum of Native American
    Culture, 92
National Safe Kids Campaign, 147
Native Americans, 92, 253, 256
Natural gas, 51
Natural resources. *See* Environment
Neg-reg procedure, 107
Nehemiah homes, 141–42
Neighborhood-Based Alliance, 169–70, 261
"New Compact for Learning, A," 79
New Deal, 127, 128, 129
New Federalism, 3, 4, 5, 108, 116–17
New Jersey, 47, 109, 181
Newsstands, 24

New York Agriculture 2000, 101
New York City, 257–58; arts and culture,
90–91; blackout, 55; boroughs, ix–x;
crime, 178, 179, 187; Erie Canal
boom, 51; foreign-based companies,
242; Great Depression projects, 128;
higher education, 85, 86; HIV-infected
people, 155*n.37;* homeless, 137;
hospitals, 149–50; housing, 141–42,
143–44*n.29;* immigrant contributions,
18–19, 22–25; parks, 205–6; political
term limits, 197*n.90;* population flux,
48; public power, 56–57; recycling,
213; schools, 80, 81–83, 113*n.69,*
220*n.22;* sports, 94–95, 96; tourism,
90, 95; transportation, 51, 52–53,
56–57, 178, 197*n.91,* 228–29. *See also*
specific institutions and sections
New York City Marathon, 96
New York City School Construction
Authority, 113*n.69*
New York Cotton Exchange, 46*n.4*
New York Futures Exchange, 46*n.4*
New-York Historical Society, 92*n.48*
New York Idea, defining principles of,
10–11
New York Institute of Technology, 142*n.28*
New York Islanders, 96
New York Knicks, 96
New York Mercantile Exchange, 46*n.4*
New York Mets, 96
New York/New York, 137–38, 227–33, 246
New York Philharmonic, 92
New York Power Authority, 57*n.9*
New York Power Pool, 56
New York Psychiatric Institute, 136
New York Public Library, 25, 82
New York Racing Association, 97
New York Rangers, 96
New York Sabres, 96
New York State. *See* Government; State
headings; specific agencies, locations,
organizations, and subjects
New York State Board of Regents, 79
New York State Citizens Task Force on
Child Abuse and Neglect, 165
New York State Constitution. *See*
Constitution, N.Y.S.
New York State Council of Parks, 204
New York State Council on Children and
Families, 166–67
New York State Council on the Arts,
91–92, 132
New York State Court of Appeals, 194*n.85*
New York State Department of Economic
Development, 46
New York State Department of
Environmental Conservation, 107, 209
New York State Department of Health,
151, 156, 157*nn.40, 41*
New York State Department of Motor
Vehicles (DMV), 105, 261
New York State Department of Social
Services, 173

New York State Education and Research
Network. *See* NYSERNET
New York State Energy Office, 58
New York State Energy Research and
Development, 59
New York State Ethics Commission, 191
New York State Forest Preserve, 204
New York State Games for the Physically
Challenged, 95, 259
New York State Human Rights Division,
32–33*n.20*
New York State Job Development
Authority, 45, 241
New York State Mentoring Program, 165, 260
New York State motto, 11
New York State Office for Regulatory and
Management Assistance, 106
New York State Office of Business Permits
and Regulatory Assistance (OBPRA),
106
New York State Office of Economic
Development, 44–46, 213
New York State Office of Management
and Productivity, 106
New York State Office of Mental Health,
135, 137*n.22,* 138
New York State Office of Mental
Retardation and Developmental
Disabilities, 134–35
New York State Office of Rural Affairs,
162*n.47*
New York State Pure Waters Program,
132, 208*n.9*
New York State Task Force on
Bias-Related Crime, 35
New York State Task Force on Poverty
and Welfare, 170–71
New York State Thruway, 51–52, 105, 131
New York State Weatherization Assistance
Program, 58
New York University, 85, 91
New York Yankees, 96
Niagara Falls, 55, 202, 256
Niagara Frontier, 256–57
Niagara Mohawk, 66*n.20*
92nd Street YMHA, 92
Nobel laureates, 64
Nonviolent conflict resolution, 32–33*n.20*
North Carolina, 91
North General Hospital, 149–50
Not-for-profit organizations, 58, 139
Nuclear power, 56, 60–62, 62*n.15,* 230
Nuclear Regulatory Commission, 61
Nursing homes, 132, 137, 147*n.32,* 148
Nutrition for Life, 165
Nutten Hook, 211
NYPA. *See* New York Power Authority
NYRA. *See* New York Racing Association
NYSERNET, 234–35, 259

Oak Point rail link, 228
OBPRA. *See* New York State Office of
Business Permits and Regulatory
Assistance

OED. *See* New York State Office of Economic Development
Office for/of. *See* New York State Office . . .
Off-Track Betting (OTB), 97
Ogdensburg, 258
Ohio, 214, 253
Oil, 59, 60
Olympia & York, 1
Olympic Games, 95
Olympus, 240n.14
Omnibus Drug Bill (U.S., 1986), 184
ONCenter, 48
Onondaga Convention Center, 48
Operation Firebreak, 185
Operation Gun Lock, 180n.67
"Opportunity" zones. *See* Economic development zones
Optics, 63, 66, 69–70, 234
Ossining Correctional Facility, 176–77
OTB. *See* Off-Track Betting

Paik, Nam June, 93
Palfinger, Inc., 242n.17
Pall Corporation, 65
Parks, 117, 202–7, 232
Parkways, 51, 205
People for Westpride, 93n.50
Petroleum, 50, 59
Pharmaceuticals, 68–69, 136, 147n.31
Phillips, Kevin, 6
Pocket Orchestra Program, 92
Police, 178, 179
Political reform, 188–98
Politics of Rich and Poor, The (Phillips), 6
Pollution. *See* Environment
Poly-Ceramics, 70n.25
Ports, 50–51
Poverty: community-based program, 169–70; educational failures and, 27–28, 76–77, 80; health care and, 147–49, 175n.61; minority, 7, 27; rural, 160–61; social ills and, 159, 161–62, 181–82. *See also* Welfare
Pregnancy: maternal/child health, 149, 162n.48, 164; teenage, 163, 165–66, 169n.55
Pre-Natal and Infant Care Act (N.Y.S.; 1989), 149, 164
Presidential election (1992), 1, 21, 31
Press freedom, 121n.1
Price, Richard, 168, 184n.74
Prisons and prisoners, 27, 115, 117, 176–78, 182–84, 227; drug treatment, 183–84, 259; nonviolent offenders, 181n.69, 185–86, 247
Private schools, 77–78, 79
Private utilities. *See* Utilities
Productivity Awards Program, 104
Profit-sharing, 64
Progressive movement, 129, 130–32
Property taxes, 110, 112, 248
Public Citizen, 58n.11
Public schools. *See* Education

Public sector. *See* Government; State headings; specific agencies
Public utilities. *See* Utilities
Public works, 50–53, 127, 128, 173, 208, 226

Quality Through Participation, 104–5
Queens, x. *See also* New York City; specific institutions and sections
Queens College, School of Law, 86n.42
Queens West, 231

R&D. *See* Research and development
Racetracks, 96, 97, 251
Racial tensions, xiii, 28, 36
Railroads, 51, 52, 56–57, 228–30; equipment manufacture, 241
RAIN. *See* Rural Assistance Information Network
Reagan-Bush administrations: anti-drug programs, 184; economic/social effects, 2–7, 110–11, 116–17, 143, 159; energy policy, 60, 61
Recession impact, 1–2, 21, 70–72, 88, 89, 92, 92n.48, 114–15
Recreation. *See* Arts and culture; Parks; Sports; Tourism
Recycling, 194, 213–14, 216
Referendum. *See* Initiative/referendum
Regan, Donald, 110
Regeneron Pharmaceutical, 68
Regents scholarships, 131
Regional Economic Development (REDS) Partnership Program, 45n.2
Regions, N.Y.S., 251–58
Regulatory reforms, 106–7
Reich, Robert, 74
Religious freedom, 121–22n.1
Rensselaer Polytechnic Institute, 66, 85
Republic Airport, 105
Republican National Convention, 31
Research and development: electronic information network, 234–35; facilities, 64–65, 67–68, 70, 72, 73n.26, 136, 236
Retraining programs. *See* Job training/retraining
Returnable Container Law (N.Y.S.), 208
Revenue sharing, 3, 132
Revolution of values, 32
Richmond County, x
Rio Summit (1992), 218
Riverbank, 205–6
Riverside South, 232
Roberts, Peter, 70n.25
Robert Wood Johnson Foundation, 151
Rochester, 254; arts, 90, 92; DMV redesign, 105n.59; Erie Canal boom, 51; health care, 153; magnet school, 77
Rochester Institute of Technology, 85, 235
Rockefeller, Nelson, 91, 108, 115, 131–32, 208
Rockland County, 24, 52, 143
Roosevelt, Franklin D., 54, 55, 56, 126–31passim, 204, 208, 245, 255

Roosevelt, Theodore, 54, 129, 208
Roosevelt Island, 52
Rosenbaum, Yankel, 28
Roswell Park Cancer Center, 45, 115
Rural areas: electric cooperatives, 56;
    farming, 98–103; firsts, 259; growth,
    98n.57; health care networks, 152;
    housing, 143; schools, 80; social
    problems, 160–61
Rural Assistance Information Network
    (RAIN), 161–62n.47, 259
Rural Rental Assistance Program, 143
Russian-Jewish immigrants, 86

Safe Streets, Safe City, 179
SAFIS system, 178
St. John's University, 85
St. Lawrence River, 54, 55, 258
St. Monica's Church, 29
Salamanca, 253–54
Salerno, Frederick V., 80
Salerno Commission, 80
Sales tax, 5, 47, 108, 111
Sandy Ground settlement, x
Sanitation. *See* Waste materials
Saratoga, 96, 97, 251
Saratoga State Park, 105
Scandanaving Profiling Systems, 242n.17
Scenic Hudson, 209
Schenectady, 251
Schleifer, Leonard, 68, 69
Scholarships, 87, 131
School Construction Authority, 83n.37
School desegregation, 37, 77
Schools. *See* Education
Science and Technology Foundation, 46,
    65, 240n.14
Scientists, 64, 75, 102–3, 217, 236. *See also*
    Biotechnology
Seat belt law, 148, 247, 261
Sewage treatment, 210–11
Shipping, 50–51, 228
Shock incarceration program, 185–86, 247
Shoe manufacture, 63–64
Shoreham nuclear power plant, 60–62,
    230, 260
Single-parent families, 163, 172, 173
Single Payer Demonstration Project,
    151, 260
Sithe Energies, 243
Smith, Al, 54, 125–26, 128, 131, 204, 205
Smith-Morris amendment (N.Y.S.), 122n.3
Smoking curbs, 166
Soccer Hall of Fame, 45, 252–53
Social Darwinism, 7, 8
Social issues, 121–98; child-related,
    162–70; constitutional guarantees,
    121–23; economic history, 123–30;
    governors' programs, 130–32, 247;
    intensification (1990s), 158–62; state
    firsts, 261; state leadership in, 7–9,
    15–16, 123–98; welfare, 2, 127–29,
    170–76, 247. *See also* specific issues
Social Security, 4, 129

Solar energy, 57, 59
Solid waste. *See* Waste materials
Solid Waste Management Act (N.Y.S.,
    1988), 213
SONYMA. *See* State of New York
    Mortgage Agency
Source Reduction Task Force (Coalition of
    Northeastern Governors), 213n.16
South Jamaica (Queens), xii, 21–22, 29,
    158–59, 168–69
Soviet Union, 19
Spalding Company, 46
Spinelli, Joseph, 191
Sports, 94–98, 252–53
Sports Facility Assistance, 96
Standard Motor Products, 73n.27
Staten Island, x. *See also* New York City;
    specific institutions and sections
State agencies. *See* Bureaucracy; specific
    names (under New York State . . .)
State and local taxes. *See* Taxes
State budget. *See* Budget, N.Y.S.
State employees, 104–5
State of New York Mortgage Agency, 142,
    144n.29
State parks. *See* Parks
State Parks Infrastructure Fund, 204
State police force, 178
State University of New York, 87–88, 117,
    132, 246
State University of New York (Albany), 27, 87
State University of New York
    (Binghamton), 87
State University of New York (Buffalo), 87
State University of New York
    (Farmingdale), 59
State University of New York (Geneseo), 87
State University of New York (Purchase), 91
State University of New York (Stony
    Brook), 67, 87, 235
Statewide Anti-Drug Abuse Council, 183
Steinmetz, Charles Proteus, 64
Sterling Winthrop Drug Co., 69
Stewart International Airport, 53, 105
Stockman, David, 3
Stoneworks, 45
Storm King Mountain, 209
Stuyvesant High School, 81–83
Substance abuse. *See* Drug abuse and traffic
Subways, 51, 52–53, 178, 229,
    241n.16
Suffolk County, 111n.65, 112
Sulfur dioxide emissions, 214
Sullivan, Barry, 94
Sumitomo Chemical Co., 68–69
SUNY. *See* State University of New York
Supercomputing Corridor, 235
Supplemental Nutrition Assistance
    Program, 149
Supply-side economics, 2–3, 4, 5
Symbol Technology, 65
Syphilis, 146
Syracuse, 254; clean room technology, 69;
    convention center, 48; Dairylea

cooperative, 102; Erie Canal boom, 51; homeless residence, 138; waterfront revitalization, 232
Syracuse University, 28, 66, 66*n.20*, 85

TAP. *See* Tuition Assistance Program
Tappan Zee Bridge: electronic toll collection, 230; renaming, 132*n.15*
Task forces. *See* New York State Task Force on . . .
Taughannock Falls, 254
Taxes, 108–13; business incentives, 46, 47; local, 111–16, 132*n.14,* 248; Reagan effects, 4–5, 110, 116, 244; revenue sharing, 3, 132; state and local deductibility, 109, 110–11; state bureaucratic savings, 103–4; state rate adjustments, 42–43, 108–9, 117; unemployment effects on, 1, 2
Technology. *See* High technology
Teenage pregnancy, 163, 165–66, 169*n.55*
Temporary Commission on Constitutional Revision, 132
Temporary Emergency Relief Administration (TERA), 127
Tennessee Valley Authority, 55, 129
Tennis, 96
Tese, Vincent, 94, 239
Theme schools, 77
Third World, 237
Thousand Islands–Seaway, 258
Thruway. *See* New York State Thruway
Toshiba, 45, 70, 242
Tourism, ix, 89–90, 95, 97, 128, 242, 247; New York State regions, 251–58
Toxic torts legislation, 210
Toxic waste. *See* Hazardous waste
Trade: as economic growth factor, 42; New York exports, 237, 238–39, 246; shipping, 50–51, 228; workforce skills, 75–76
Traffic. *See* Cars; Transportation
Training. *See* Job training/retraining
Trains. *See* Railroads
Transportation: equipment manufacture, 241; high-tech, 229–30; N.Y.C./suburbs, 50–53, 56–57, 178, 197*n.91*, 228–30; state pioneering concepts, 51–52. *See also* Mass transit; specific modes
Travel industry. *See* Tourism
Triangle Shirtwaist factory fire, 125
Triborough Bridge, 128
Tristate area, 47, 109, 181
Trusthouse Forte, 241
Tuberculosis, 146
Tuition Assistance Program (TAP), 87
Turner, Ted, 94–95
Twenty-first century, 75–88, 236–37, 246, 247

Unemployment and layoffs: African-American men, 27; defense industry, 1, 2, 71, 73–74; Great Depression, 126–27; homeless, 138;

job-saving strategies, 46–47, 73*n.27,* 74; mental illness link, 136*n.20;* state statistics, 41; tax effects, 1, 2; welfare caseloads, 173–74
Unions. *See* Labor movement
Universities and colleges: agricultural, 99–100; arts-focused, 91; scholarships, 87, 131; sports, 96; state programs, 84–88, 117, 131, 132; state research partnerships, 67–68, 70. *See also* specific names
University of Rochester, 66, 85
Upstate New York, ix, 251–58
Urban areas, 3, 47–48, 51, 158–59. *See also* Social issues; specific cities
Urban Development Corporation (UDC), 45*n.2*, 46, 69*n.23*, 115
U.S. Military Academy (West Point), 255
U.S. Open, 96
Utah, 91
Utica, 51, 232–33*n.10*, 253
Utilities: bill-saving measures, 58; environmental impact, 209; expansion of public, 56–57; high-tech applications, 66*n.20;* number of public, 56; private vs. public, 54–62

Vassar College, 85
Vermont, 214, 215
Violence. *See* Crime
Virginia, 91
Voter registration, 192–93, 197
Voucher system, 78

Wagering, 97–98
Wages, 6, 130*n.12*
Wagner Act (U.S., 1935), 129
Warehousing business, 51
Washington County, 251
Waste materials: garbage problem, 107*n.61*, 202, 212–14; toxic, 62*n.15*, 209–10, 215
Waterfalls, 254. *See also* Niagara Falls
Waterfront revitalization, 230–33
Waterpower, 54, 56, 57, 215
Water quality, 208, 210–11, 215–16, 247
Watkins Glen, 96, 254
Watson, James, 68
Watson, Thomas J., 63
Welfare: public criticism, 174; reform, 170–76, 247; spending, 2, 127–28, 129
Welfare capitalism, 64
Westchester County, 25, 51, 52, 57
West Indian–American Day Carnival, 23*n.8*
Westinghouse, 45, 70, 242
Westinghouse Science Talent Search winners, 64
White, E. B., 250
Whiteface Mountain Highway, 128
Whitestone Bridge, 128
Whitney, Willis R., 64–65
Wicks Law, 113
Wiesel, Elie, 32
Wilderness preserves, 202–4, 206–8, 211, 247

"Wilding," 182

Willowbrook Consent Decree, 133, 134

Wilson, Malcolm, 132

Wine and Grape Foundation, 101

Wine industry, 66, 101, 253, 254, 255, 256

Workforce: apprenticeship programs, 84; child-care facilities, 164–65; as economic growth factor, 41–43; employee benefits, 64; employee recognition, 130*n.13;* immigrant opportunities, 23–24; job-saving measures, 46–47, 73*n.27,* 74; labor movement history, 124–26, 129–30; skills for twenty-first century, 75–88, 246; as socioeconomic panacea, 41, 248; state employee productivity, 104–5; training. *See* Job training/retraining; welfare recipients, 172, 173, 175. *See also* Job creation; Unemployment and layoffs

Working Toward Independence (WTI), 173

Works Projects Administration, 127*n.9,* 128, 129

World markets. *See* Global marketplace

World Trade Center, 46, 106, 176; terrorist bombing, 21, 248–49

World University Games, 96

WPA. *See* Works Projects Administration

WTI. *See* Working Toward Independence

Xerox Corporation, 63, 65, 76

Yeshiva University, 85

Yiddish, 86

Youths. *See* Children; Teenage pregnancy

Zenger, John Peter, 121*n.1*

CANADA

Jeffer

Watertown

LAKE ONTARIO

Oswego

Oswego

Fulton

Oneida

Niagara

Orleans

ERIE   CANAL

Rochester

Wayne

Syracuse

Niagara
Falls

Lockport

Monroe

Onondaga

Tonawanda

Genesee

Ontario

Cayuga

Buffalo

Geneva

Seneca

Lackawanna

*Canandaigua
Lake*

Erie

Wyoming

Livingston

Yates

*Cayuga
Lake*

*LAKE
ERIE*

*Keuka
Lake*

Cortland

Dunkirk

*Seneca
Lake*

Ithaca

Chautauqua

Watkins
Glen

Tompkins

*Chautauqua
Lake*

Cattaraugus

Allegany

Steuben

Schuyler

Chemung

Tioga

Broc

Jamestown

Olean

Elmira

Binghamton

PENNSYLVANIA

New York State

0   25   50 Miles

0   25   50 Kilometers